how to build
Collectors' Display Cases
DOLLS, CHINA, OBJETS d'ART

DONALD R. BRANN

FIRST PRINTING — 1979

Published by

EASI-BILD DIRECTIONS SIMPLIFIED, INC.
BRIARCLIFF MANOR, NY 10510

Library of Congress Card No. 78-57773

Acknowledgement
The antique dolls are from
the Jean Van Cleef Collection

NOTE:
All metric dimensions shown are within 5/100 of a centimeter.

Due to the variance in quality and availability of many materials and products, always follow directions a manufacturer and/or retailer offers. Unless products are used exactly as the manufacturer specifies, its warranty can be voided. While the author mentions certain products by trade name, no endorsement or end use guarantee is implied. In every case the author suggests end uses as specified by the manufacturer prior to publication.

Since manufacturers frequently change ingredients or formula and/or introduce new and improved products, or fail to distribute in certain areas, trade names are mentioned to help the reader zero in on products of comparable quality and end use. The Publisher

BE AN EGO BUILDER

How we feel about that image we see in the mirror each morning helps us find, face and achieve our potential. When we like what we see, it boosts our ego and helps activate positive vibrations in others. Dislike what you see and you subconsciously generate negative vibrations. Good feelings are vital to your mental and physical health, marital and business success. Learning to continually rebuild an ego, yours, and those important to you, provides a key to the good life.

The magic and power of a positive vibration surfaces everytime we voice a sound opinion, make a repair, use time in a constructive manner, or economically solve an important problem at a cost we can afford. The thrill of being a winner is experienced by everyone who makes the clear acrylic projects offered in this book.

Regardless of age, income, business or social status, people collect what they prize, and pride of ownership helps shape the way they live. Those who have learned how collecting rebuilds an ego, while it provides a beneficial form of escape, are a special breed. Each has learned to refocus the mind's eye on an interest that generates peace of mind, companionship, a constructive use of spare time, plus hope in the future.

Create a showcase for a collection. Start a part or full time business building the many projects in this book and you discover how to be an Ego Builder.

Don R. Brann

TABLE OF CONTENTS

LEARNING TO COPE

At birth we receive a body, a brain and an inheritance of time. As we grow, we do what we feel capable of doing and this helps shape that image we face each morning. How we grow and how we live is determined by what we do and keep trying to do. The result of each effort, like sunshine on a growing plant, shapes our lives. Each physical and mental effort imprints an impression on our mind.

Positive and negative impressions influence every physical relationship. If we happened to be a star student or athlete during our school years, it's disappointing not to generate the same acclaim and success in our chosen field of employment. In the same vein, what we previously failed to achieve in our youth influences many adult efforts. Those destined for success rationalize these impressions. They continue to grow, to expand their sphere of activity by doing today something they couldn't succeed in doing earlier in life. Facing each problem as a mature adult, accepting each opportunity to enter and explore new areas, keeps them in the game called living. This helps groove new impressions while it confirms one fact of life: Only the players get a chance to score winning goals.

Today's way of life necessitates creating periods of relaxation, a chance to unwind, as readily as it requires developing sources for additional income. When you learn to economically solve a costly problem, you can earn money rendering the same service to others. A display case that complements your prized possessions appeals to all who take pride in theirs. Learning to save heat while you add protection against a break-in appeals to all who have the same needs. Learning to solve problems, finding a need and filling it, offers a business of your own without leaving home.

Solutions to both problems are offered in this book. Busy executives seeking relief from tension, retirees facing an abundance of free time, youth desperately searching for work they can enjoy and find profitable, to housewives climbing the walls with boredom, find stimulating answers working with acrylic. While considerable detail is focused on building display cases, readers can save and/or earn a bundle using acrylic as step by step directions suggest.

Every protective action you take to prevent a break-in is of prime interest to all who recognize the need. Protection is of special interest to the elderly who live alone. If you want to turn spare time into income, or just meet new people, do this. Print a small quantity of letters. Use a message similar to that offered on page 176, or revise same. Place a copy in each mailbox, in every neighborhood where a burglary has been reported.

Starting a part time business with no investment, other than for material and tools, doesn't require any special skill as a salesman. Most sales are consummated when one person shows or tells another something the latter needs, wants and can afford to buy. People BUY many, many more times than they are sold. When you find one customer, you can usually find many others. Show a neighbor how to cut fuel costs, or burglarproof his home and he'll tell others. You can then install the acrylic or sell precut panels to size job requires.

To fully appreciate the potential in making and selling the projects described in this book, read it through a second time. Consider how each piece will complement your home and/or those of your friends. Note how certain pieces fit into a doctor's, dentist's or realtor's office, a local jewelry, department or shoe store. Learning to create what others are willing to buy necessitates finding a need and filling it.

Opportunity is continually being created by many, seemingly unrelated economic trends. A case in point is the current cost of packing and shipping any large or fragile article. These costs add a substantial amount to the selling price of a display case. When an amount equal to shipping is used to purchase acrylic locally, and you deliver the finished article, the customer can buy for less, while you, the manufacturer, make a normal margin of profit. This simple example of today's economics provides an opportunity to start a profitable part or full time business without gambling.

To make a meaningful, time saving presentation of your craftsmanship, note the merchandise a retailer features in advertising. Show the store display manager a photo, a scale model or a finished sample of an acrylic fixture that complements the product. If he likes what he sees, the manager will probably recommend changes in overall size or shape. Encouraging a prospective client (the display manager) to suggest changes builds the ego, generates those positive vibrations essential to the success of every business transaction. Every retailer of gifts, china, jewelry, etc., can either use the display cases or sell same.

If your church, favorite charity, fraternal order or other fund raiser, needs a sound money making idea, recommend building all the projects offered in this book. When sold at an auction, each attracts prices that range from four, five to six times the cost of material. Place a card alongside each project stating name of builder-donor, with this message, "We will build to any size desired."

To fully appreciate the many ways acrylic can be fabricated and the success even a beginner can expect after the first read through, buy a scrap piece of ⅛" acrylic, 12 x 18" or 18 x 24", a scoring tool, Illus. 1, sandpaper, solvent and applicator. As your starting project, make a four sided box, as explained on page 40.

Creating with Acrylic

Directions for building a see through, sliding door display case, measuring 14½ x 44 x 75½", start on page 64.

Top cabinet can be built to size required. Directions starting on page 74 explain how to build a base cabinet measuring 15 x 17 x 36".

Individual showcases can be made from ⅛" acrylic to size required.

Museum quality ¼" acrylic cabinet fits into routed wood base. Base provides dust and tip proof security.

Directions on page 90 explain how to build a wall cabinet. Door optional.

Building a wall cabinet that complements your collection, or building for resale, generates positive and profitable vibrations. Each cabinet also broadens your choice of where prized possessions may be displayed. Since storage is vitally important to everyone who has anything to sell, directions explain how to build two wall cabinets, one with a decorative facing, the other with straight facing panels.

An interesting clothes and shelf storage cabinet is shown on page 116. This offers a highly decorative and convenient solution to the problem of clothes and shelf storage space in doctors', lawyers', dentists' and other professional and business offices. Since it requires no structural alterations, its design permits use in every rental area.

Construction of a locked roadside display enclosure is described on page 131.

Directions starting on page 164 explain how to vandalproof and burglarproof* windows and doors in homes, schools, and other commercial buildings.

Those seeking release from tension and/or an opportunity to start a business of their own will find directions on page 174 of special interest. It explains how to Etchacrylic, apply design to or in acrylic.

Since some projects can be built following an alternate method of construction, read directions through completely before purchasing any material.

Note the many different ways acrylic can be used and how each offers a fun and profitable way to invest free time.

*i.e., a deterrent

TOOLS

Handsome, easy to build, easy to sell acrylic projects can be fabricated with hand or power tools. Cutting, edge finishing, forming and assembly with solvent or thickened cement requires reading and following step by step directions. Acrylic can be cut to size desired with the scribing tool, or with a special saber, circular or table saw blade. It can be drilled with a hand drill using standard twist drills, or with an electric drill using special purpose high speed twist drills. All cutting, drilling and sanding of edges must be done with the masking paper protecting surface.

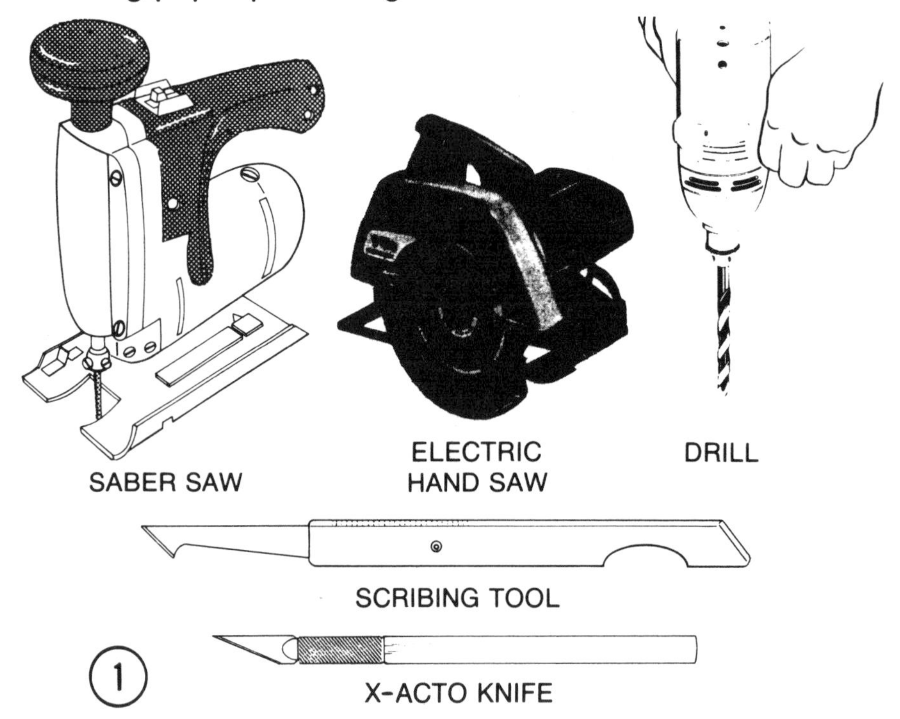

With masking paper intact, cut parts to size required. Sand or scrape edges to obtain finish specified. Drill all holes in position directions indicate. After all drilling and sanding is completed, remove masking paper.

The saw blades, special bits, edge and scribing tool, solvent, cement, polish, buffing wheel, etc., are available from acrylic distributors. Directions covering the use of each tool are printed on the mounting card. Tools designed for acrylic should only be used on acrylic, never on other material.

The parts can be bonded using thickened cement following directions on page 38, or parts can be taped together, Illus. 2.

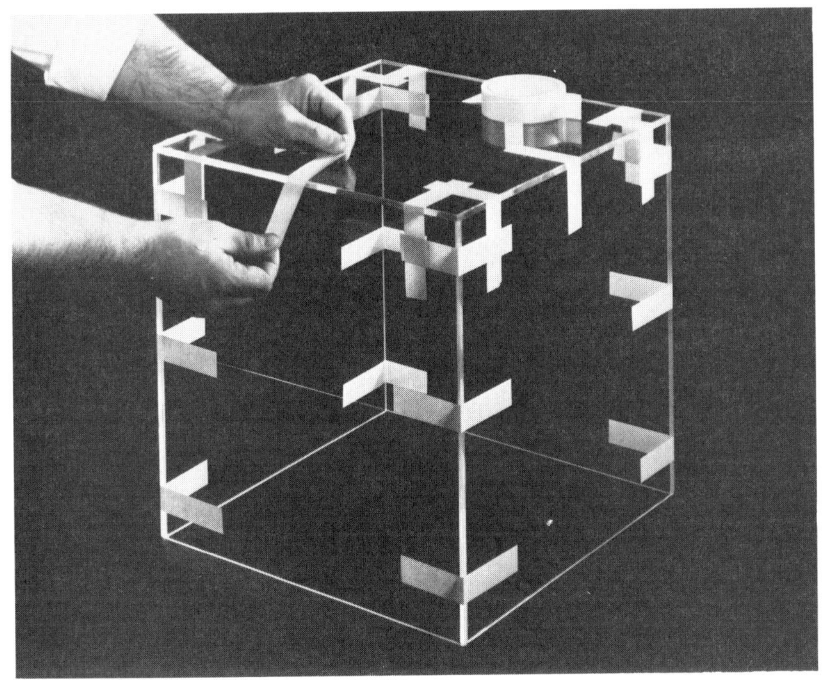

2

Using the needle nosed applicator, Illus. 3, each horizontal joint can be bonded with Weld-On #3 solvent. Or joints can be cemented with thickened cement, Illus. 33. Apply a fine bead to edge, Illus. 35.

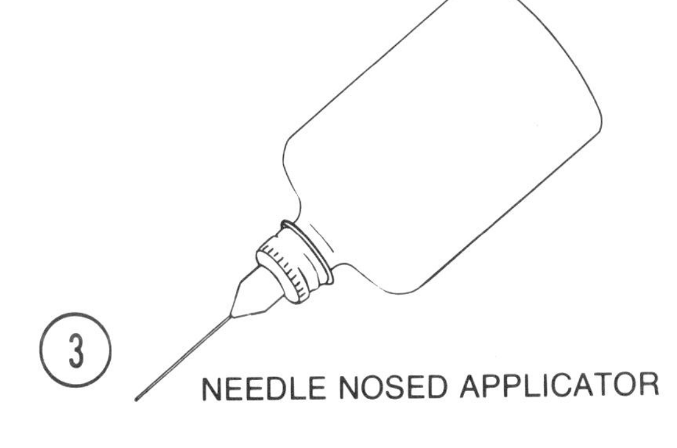

3 NEEDLE NOSED APPLICATOR

Interesting projects can be made by heat forming acrylic. This is done with the strip heater, Illus. 4. As directions on page 171 explain, the 36" heating unit is mounted on a plywood frame. Longer bends can be heated over two units, mounted end to end.

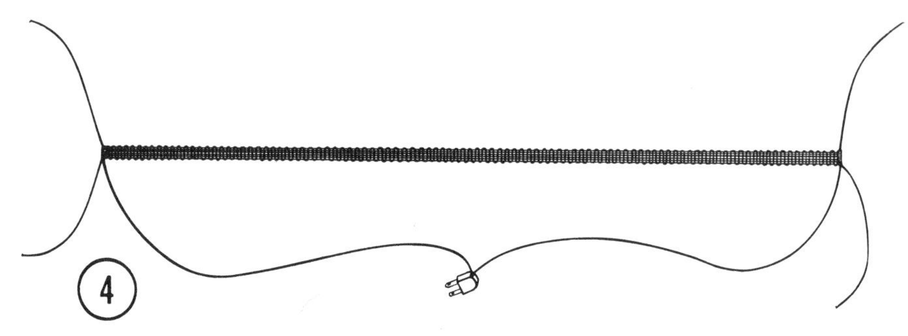

Handsome gift items, like the book holder, Illus. 5, are easy to shape with the heating unit.

Many saleable acrylic projects can be constructed following established methods. The outdoor display cabinet, Illus. 6, and the wall display, Illus. 7, are two typical easy to build projects. Merchandise displayed in the outdoor cabinet is protected by ¼" acrylic sandwiched between two ⅜" quarter round, Illus. 8, glued and nailed in place.

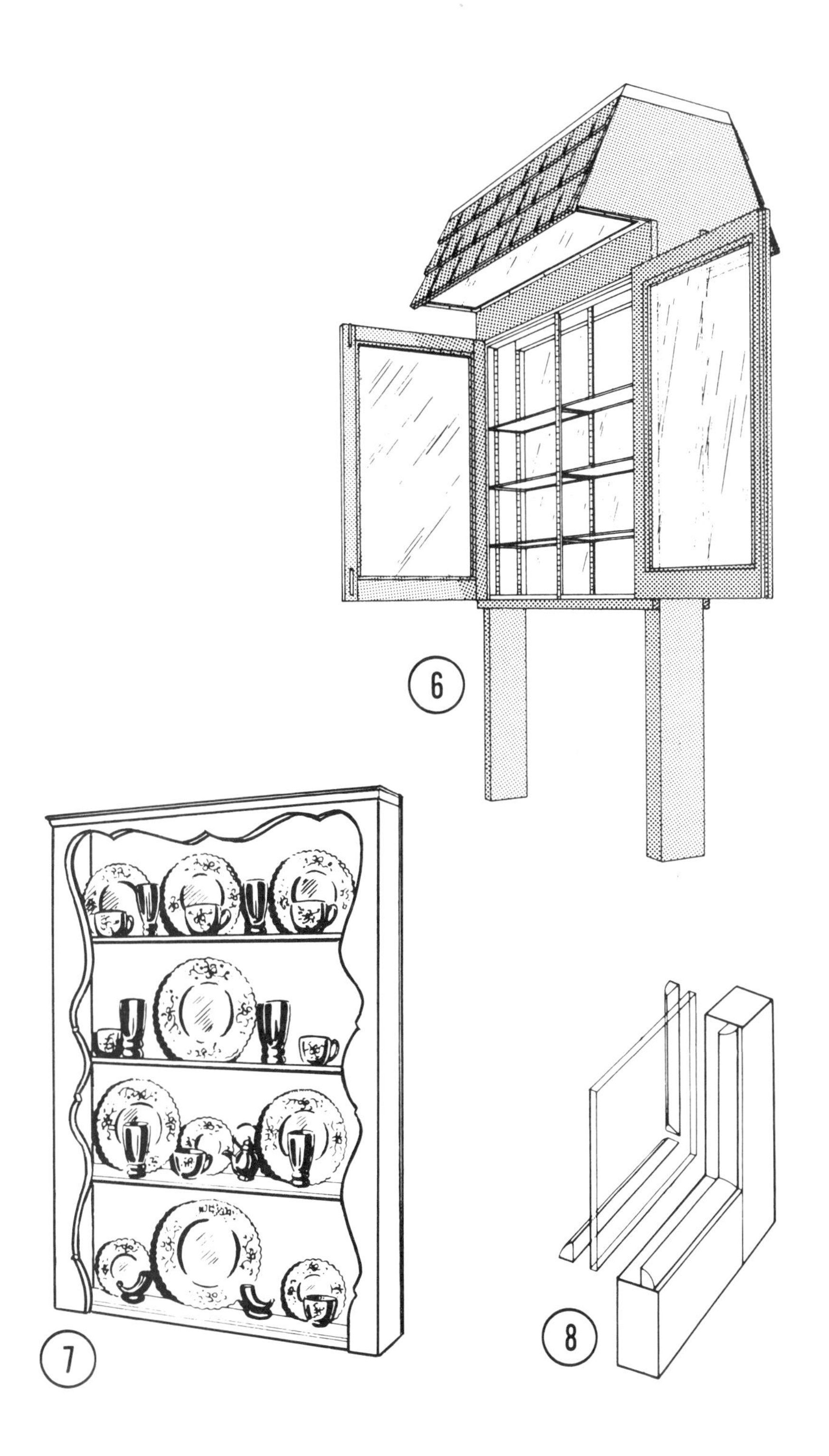
6
7
8

Acrylic is manufactured under the trade name Plexiglas and other brand names. Most distributors stock 4 x 6 and 4 x 8' sheets in the following thicknesses: 1/16, 1/8, 3/16, 1/4''. All will cut sheet to size required.

The projects offered in this book were built with Plexiglas G in ⅛, 3/16 and ¼'' thicknesses. The cutting tools, solvent, cement and assembly directions pertain to this material. As there are many different acrylics, the author suggests buying solvent and cement recommended by the acrylic distributor. Always ask to see the tools and accessories the distributor offers.

Only buy material for your first project. As you gain experience and confidence, considerable savings can be effected when you buy full sheets and do your own cutting.

NOTE: Plexiglas acrylic plastic is a combustible thermoplastic so it's important to use caution. To become thoroughly familiar, practice using scrap. Test sawing or scribing, sanding and cementing following directions provided. When you have gained confidence and satisfactory bonding results, build one of the smaller projects. Never cut parts for two or more of the same article until you have successfully completed one. Never remove protective masking paper until the part has been cut to exact size required, edges have been sanded or scraped, all holes drilled. Remove masking paper when you are ready to start final assembly.

Always drill holes 1/16'' larger than screw shank, Illus. 9.

A hand drill, Illus. 10, and standard twist drills, recommended for metal, can be used. Always use a sharp drill. Be sure Plexiglas is backed with wood so drill can go clear through. Drill slowly using minimum pressure.

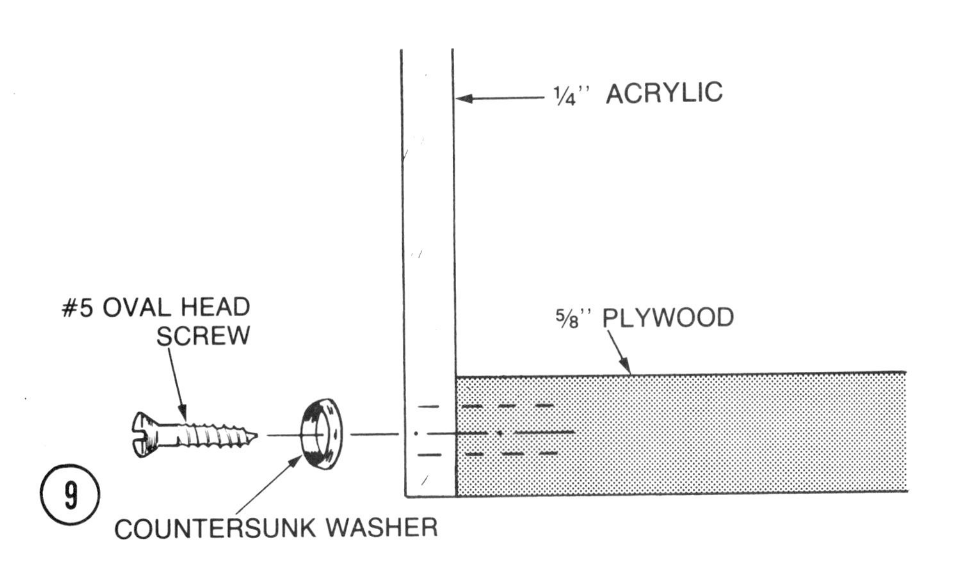
1/4'' ACRYLIC
#5 OVAL HEAD
SCREW
5/8'' PLYWOOD
9
COUNTERSUNK WASHER

PLEXIGLAS
ACRYLIC SHEET
10

Use special purpose, high speed, twist drills, recommended by acrylic distributor, when using an electric drill, Illus. 11. Be sure to tighten drill in chuck.

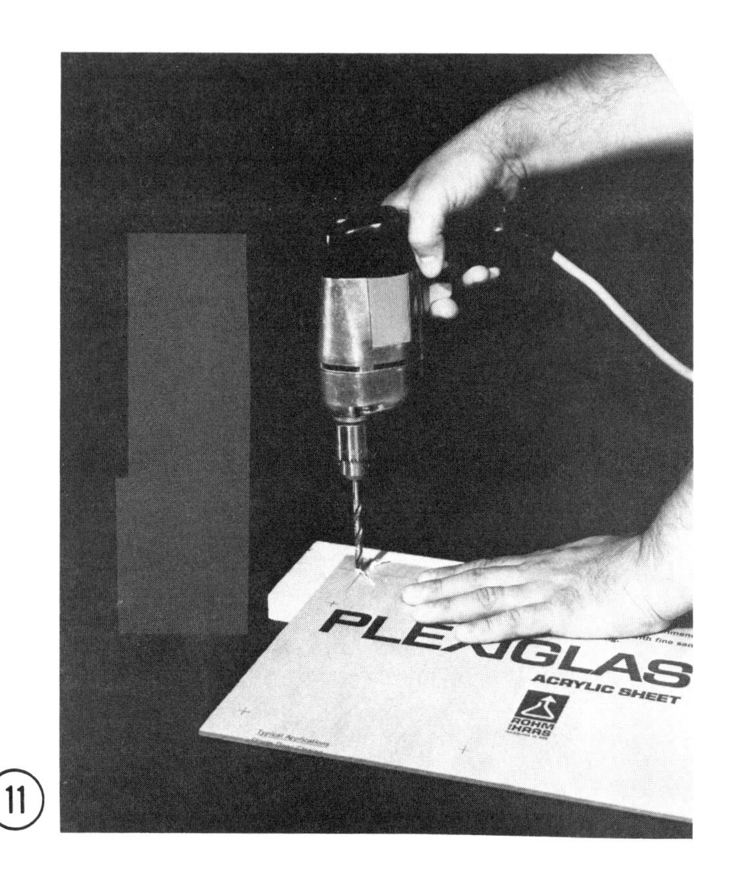

11

Holes are bored with a twist drill using only enough pressure to keep drill on target. The drills recommended for acrylic are available in the following sizes: ⅛, 5/32, 3/16, ¼, 5/16, ⅜, 7/16, ½'', Illus. 12.

Use a large square to draw all parts, Illus. 13. After all parts are cut to size required, edges sanded and holes drilled, remove masking paper. Tape parts in position and again check parts with a square.

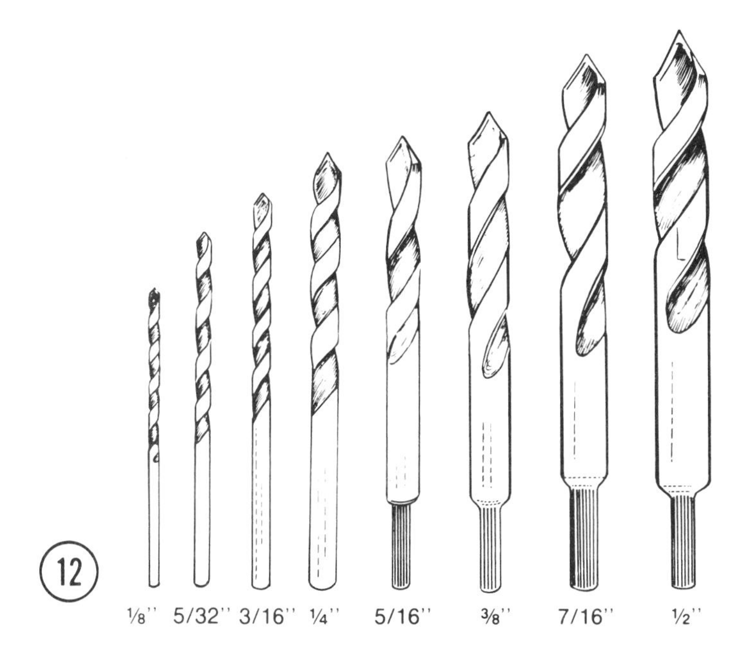
12
1/8''
5/32''
3/16''
1/4''
5/16''
3/8''
7/16''
1/2''

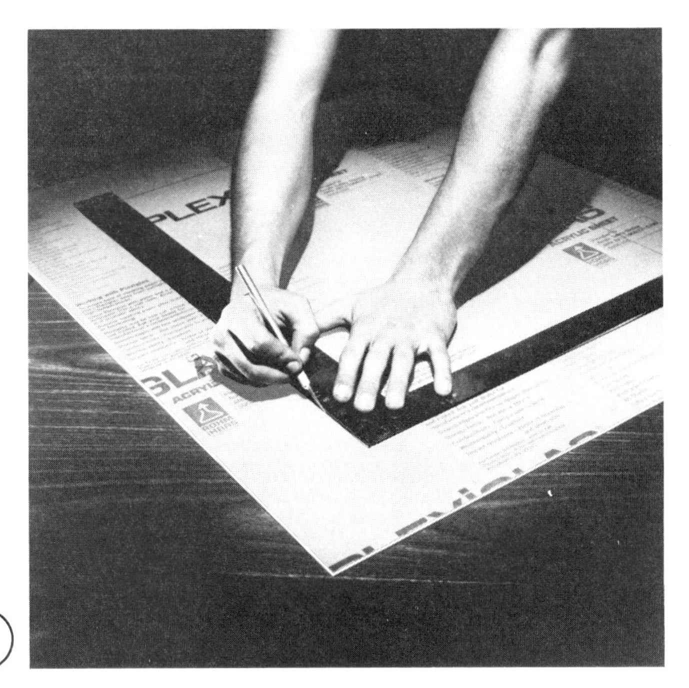
13

Learning to work with acrylic, like learning to cook or sew, requires following step by step direction and using the tools specified. You develop confidence with the first project, skill and experience with each succeeding one. The material requires a relaxed approach. Allow saw blade or scribing tool to follow a drawn line. Don't push acrylic through the special blade recommended for a saber, circular or table saw. It must be fed into the blade. Practice with a piece of scrap to get the feel. Always use these special blades for acrylic. Do not use with any other material.

A circular saw equipped with a saw blade having 7 teeth per inch, Illus. 14, or a saber saw with a blade having 14 teeth to the inch, Illus. 15, simplifies cutting a large sheet of acrylic. If you have a table saw, use a RH-800 blade. A coping or jeweler's saw, Illus. 15a, with a spiral saw blade, simplifies cutting curves.

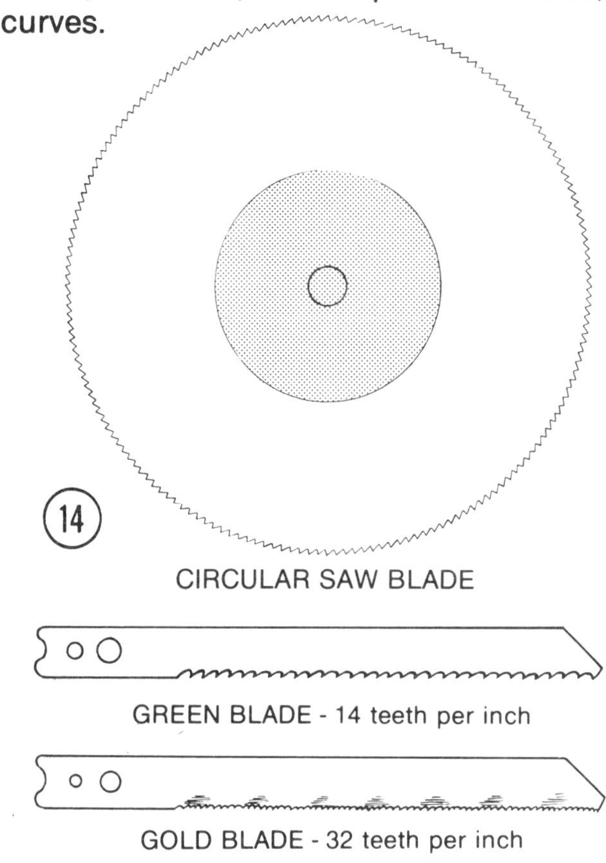

CIRCULAR SAW BLADE

GREEN BLADE - 14 teeth per inch

GOLD BLADE - 32 teeth per inch

Cutting acrylic with a saber saw requires using special blades. A gold blade, Illus. 15, cuts 1/8" or thinner sheet, a green blade cuts 3/16" and thicker sheet.

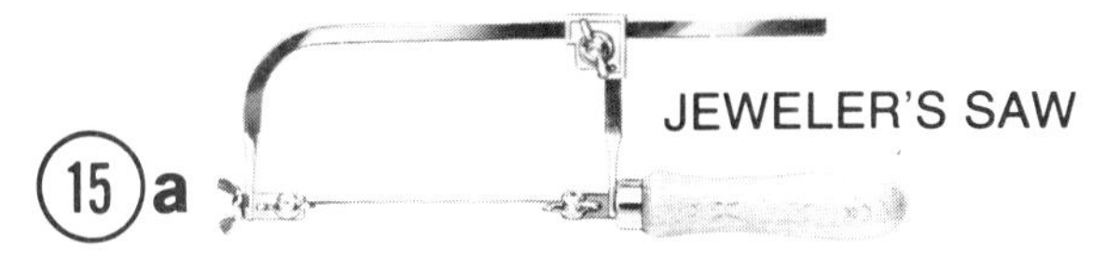

Since it's necessary to support a large sheet of acrylic at all times, use sawhorses and a 1/2, 5/8 or 3/4" x 4 x 8' plywood panel to make a level extension to a table saw. Place extension tables so the panel is supported while it enters and leaves the saw blade.

Raise table saw blade so it projects slightly above acrylic. Using extreme care, and concentrating on what you are doing, press acrylic against table top and edge of panel against a straight edge. Gently feed the blade, Illus. 16.

Always support acrylic by using a level work table. When using a circular, saber or table saw, apply necessary pressure to keep acrylic flat against work surface.

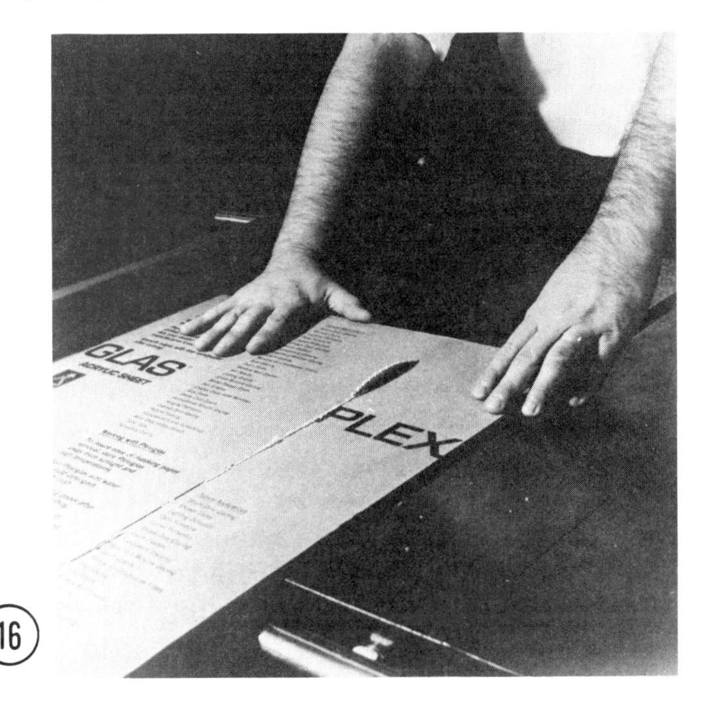

16

Always slow the feed as blade leaves material. This helps prevent chipping corners.

Always clamp a straight edge in position, Illus. 17, to keep a saber or circular saw blade on drawn line.

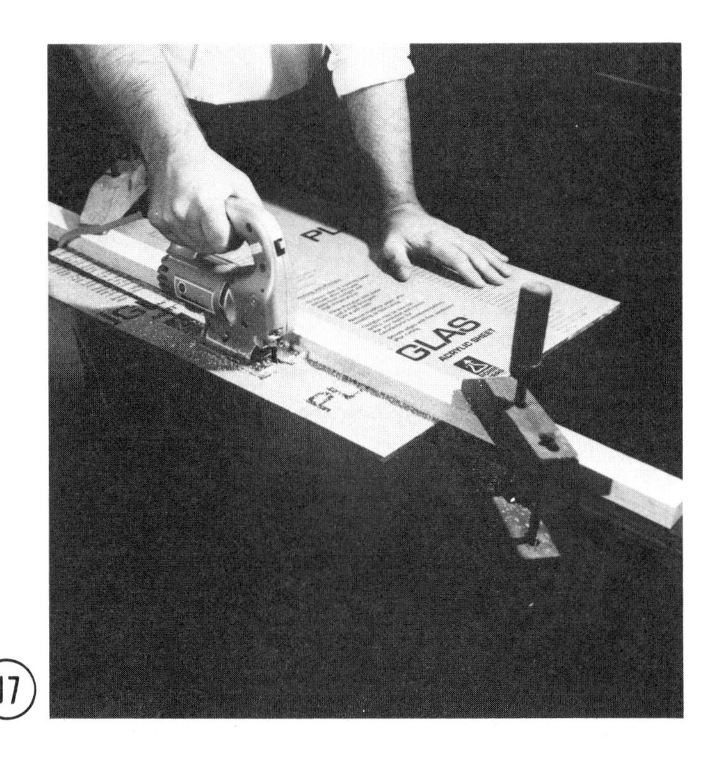

(17)

While the scribing tool, saber, circular and table saw blades insure making smooth, clean cuts, if it isn't clean and smooth, the edge can be scraped or sanded.

Those who have a circular or table saw can purchase the special 6, 8 and 10" blades from an acrylic distributor. These are available for a ½ or ⅝" arbor. The 8" blade will have 180 teeth, 7 per inch. It cuts acrylic like a sharp knife cuts bread. Only use these blades, and those specified for the saber saw, when cutting acrylic. If masking tape gums up the blade, apply a small amount of oil, grease or white soap to the blade.

A special 6" blade is available for a circular saw. 8 or 10" blades can be used in a table saw. Each of these special blades cuts through acrylic like a radar range cooks food. And just as you learn to push the right button when using a range, so must you learn to feed the material against the blade with a firm, yet surprisingly light touch.

Always draw a cutting line and location of each hole on the masking paper. When using the scribing tool, clamp a metal straight edge, Illus. 18, in position so scribing tool is positioned on cutting line.

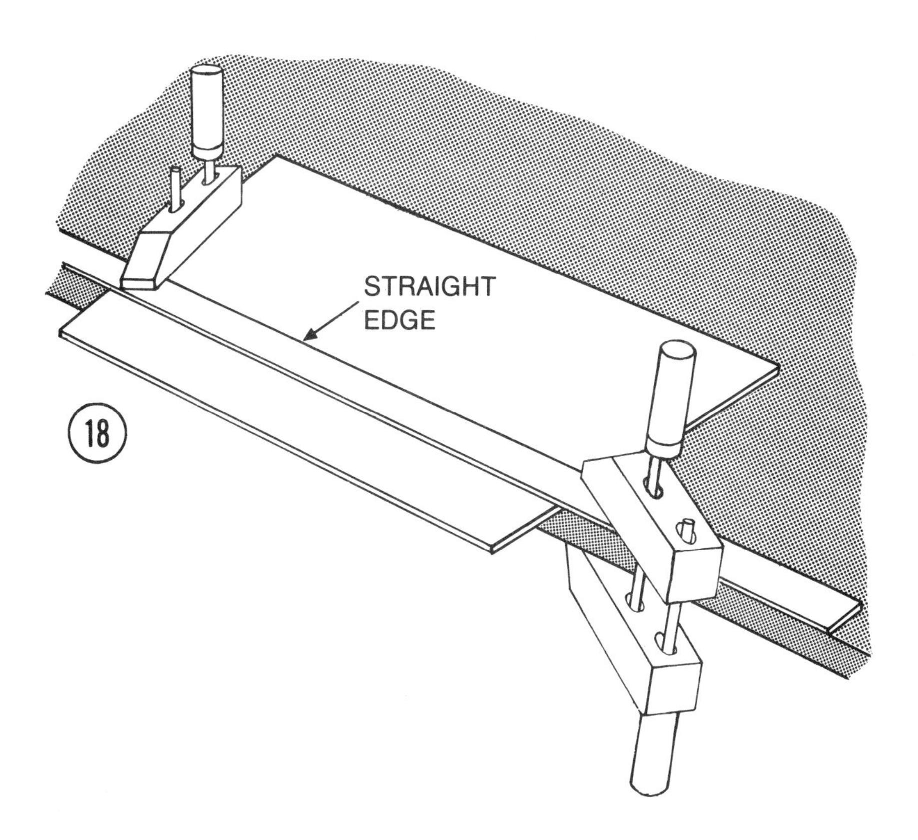

As previously mentioned, always saw, scribe, drill, sand or scrape edge of acrylic with masking paper on both faces. If you find it necessary to recut, drill or finish an edge by sanding or scraping, after masking paper has been removed, apply masking tape 2" over adjacent area, on both faces of cutting line.

The scribing tool, Illus. 19,20, is easy to use. It requires a straight edge and a little practice. For ⅛" thick acrylic, make 5 to 6 full passes. Apply equal pressure when making each pass. 3/16 and ¼" thickness requires 7 to 10 passes. You must make the necessary number of passes to successfully cut acrylic.

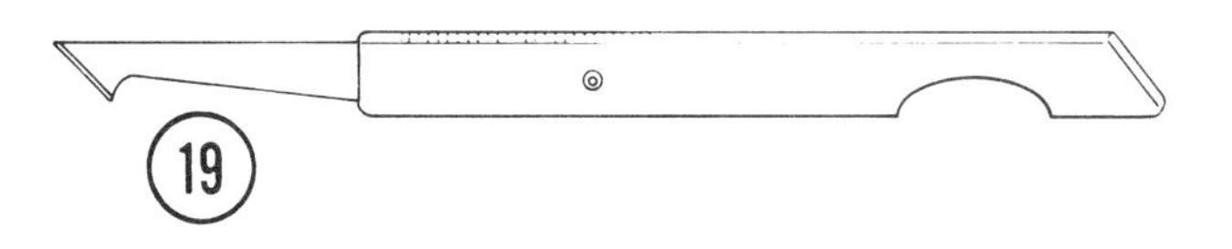

(19)

(20)

Never attempt to scribe a line less than 1½" from edge. 2" minimum is better. Always start to scribe at one edge and apply equal pressure all the way. After making the necessary number of passes, place the panel, scribed face up, over a ¾" diameter wood dowel, Illus. 21. The dowel should be equal in length or longer than the scribed line and be positioned directly under. Place hands opposite each other as shown and apply downward pressure progressively all along the scribed line. Sand or scrape edge to prepare for solvent or cement.

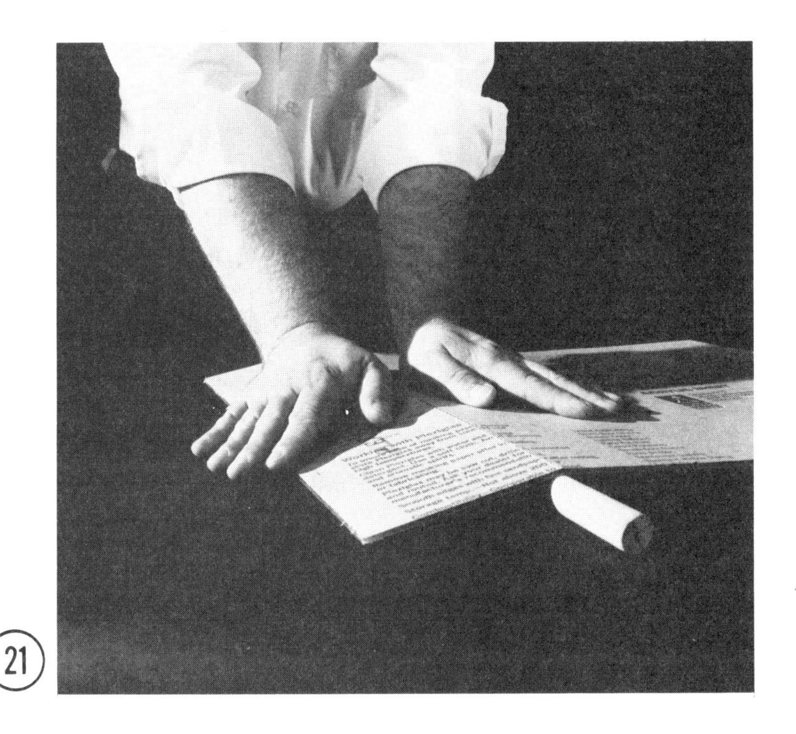

21

When cutting a full panel with a circular or saber saw, toenail four 2 x 6 or 2 x 8 across two sawhorses, Illus. 22. A flat, clean supporting surface is important.

Clamp a 1 x 2 or 1 x 4 straight edge where needed to position blade on cutting line, Illus. 17. Allow blade to ride between planks. Always wear safety goggles when using power tools.

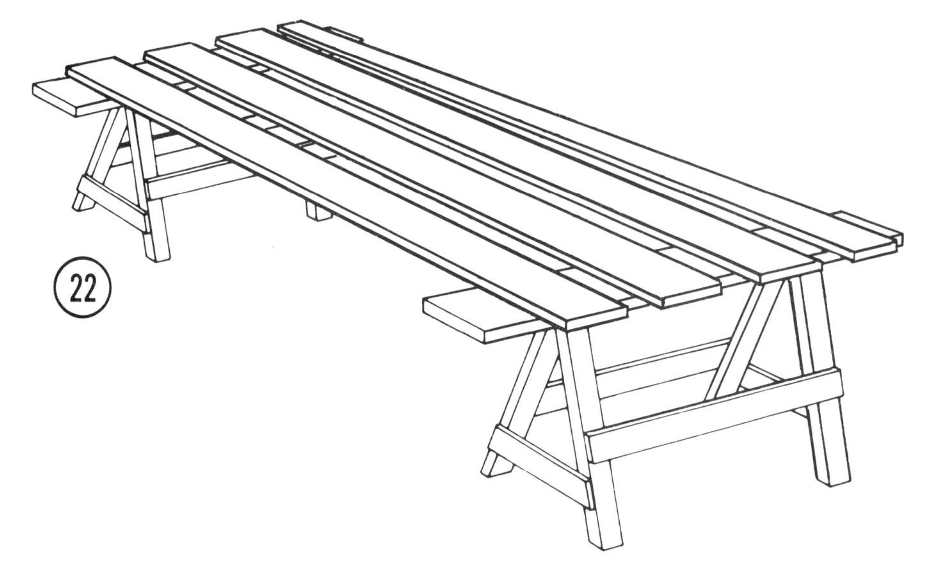

Those who go into production should position a 4 x 8 plywood table alongside the table saw. Build to exact height of table saw. This provides support when cutting 4 x 8 sheets.

Making square, smooth cuts is vital to every project. The R&H edging tool, Illus. 23, simplifies making a square edge. This can be used on material up to ½'' thick. It can also be used to bevel an edge when same is required to fit into a storm door frame, Illus. 24.

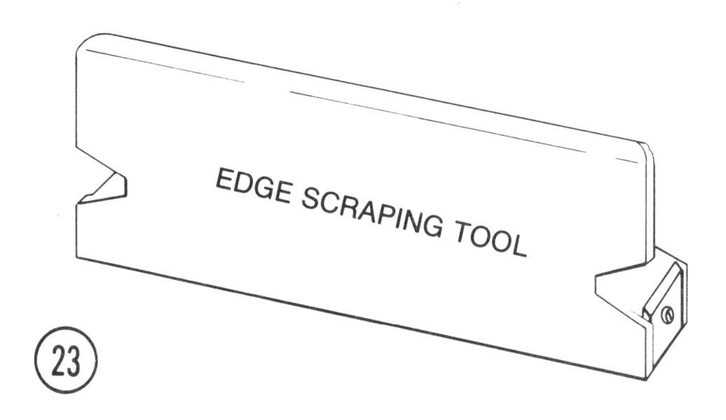

24

Always butt frame of tool against panel. This insures planing edge square. Always make a full length sweep of the edge. Remove all particles and dust prior to making successive passes. You can plane the edge of Plexiglas as easily as the edge of a 1 x 2 can be finished with a wood plane.

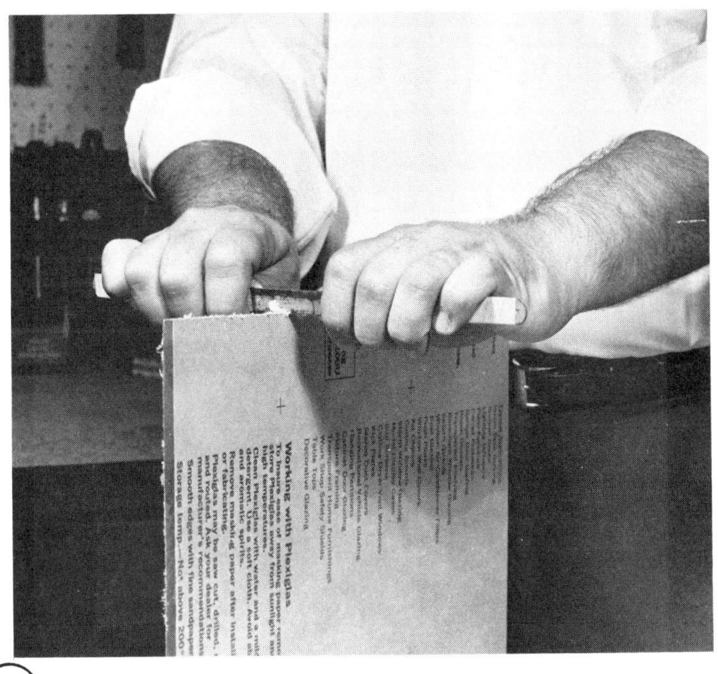

25

The back edge of a hacksaw blade, Illus. 25, also makes a good scraper. Wrap masking tape at ends of blade to make grippers. All edges must be square and finished according to its end use.

After sawing or scoring, an edge to be bonded can be prepared by first using a 60-80 grit sandpaper, then a 220-320 grit. In text we refer to this edge as a CE finish.

Scraping an edge smooth with the back edge of a hacksaw blade, Illus. 25, or the R&H edging tool, Illus. 23, helps eliminate rough edges, knicks, etc. If you then go over edge lightly with a 220-320 wet or dry sandpaper, it provides an excellent edge for bonding with solvent or thickened cement. Be sure to remove all shavings and dust before taping in position. It's vitally important to keep bonding edge square. If you have any doubt, place edge on a mirror or other flat surface.

To finish an exposed edge to a transparent finish, use the 60-80 grit, 220-320, then a 400-500 wet or dry paper. This edge is then finished with the Dico buffer and compound. In text we refer to a transparent finish as an EE edge.

To sand edge square, use a sanding block, Ilus. 26, made from 1 x 2 x 12" and ¼ x 2 x 12" plywood. Drill two holes through plywood so it, the sandpaper and 1 x 2 can be screwed together. Always keep sanding block squarely against edge while the plywood rides flat on the masking paper.

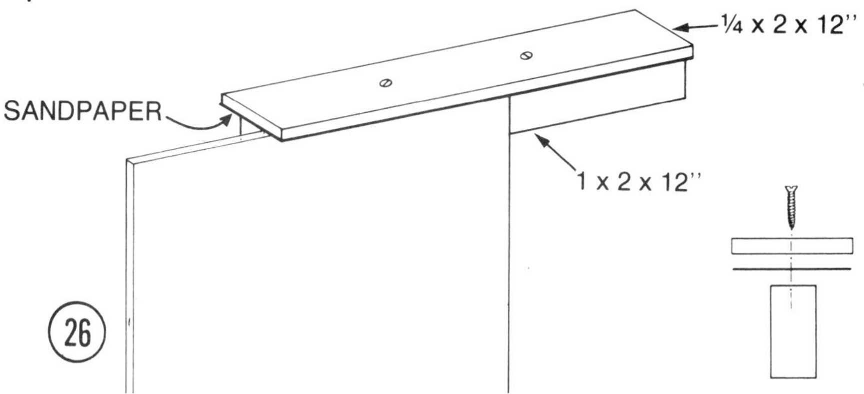

While horizontal joints can be taped and bonded with solvent, you will need support boxes, Illus. 36, when using thickened cement.

To achieve a transparent finish on an exposed edge, finish with the Dico muslin buffer, Illus. 27. Apply Tripoli buffing compound to buffer, Illus. 28. Using a ¼" drill, buff edge to a transparent finish. A highly polished transparent edge is designated an EE edge. Never use the 400-500 grade or buffer on an edge to be cemented.

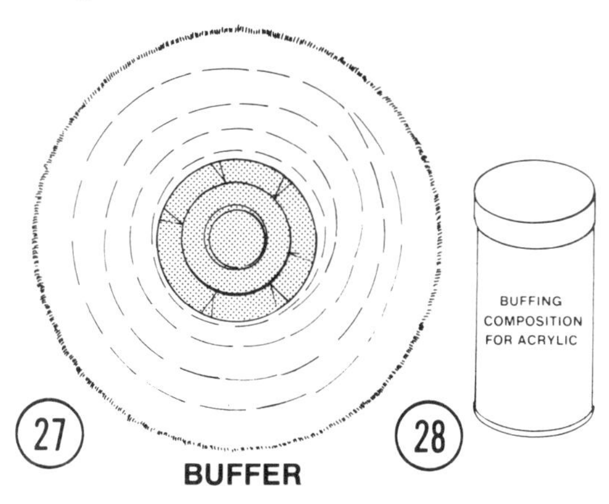

(27) BUFFER (28)

Those wishing to drill large holes, up to 6", should use a steel hole saw, Illus. 29. A new line permits drilling 9/16 to 6" holes.

(29)

Be sure acrylic is placed against a level, clean, firm surface. One that can take the marks of the saw as it leaves acrylic.

BONDING ACRYLIC

Working with acrylic generates considerable enthusiasm that frequently negates using the proper amount of caution. Always work in a well ventilated room. Never in a heated, closed area. Unless room is well ventilated, with a free flow of fresh air, DO NOT USE THE SOLVENT OR CEMENT.

Information recently published by the Federal Government regarding the carcinogenicity of Ethylene Dichloride (EDC) reveals that EDC is carcinogenic to rats and mice. EDC was, at one time, used to bond acrylics. Studies conducted by the National Cancer Institute have demonstrated that exposure of rats and mice to EDC produces malignant tumors in both species of animals. The National Institute for Occupational Safety and Health has recommended that EDC should be treated in the work place as though it were a human carcinogen. For this reason, we strongly recommend you do not use EDC for cementing Plexiglas or other plastics.

Methylene Chloride (MDC) - Methylene Chloride, also known as Dichloromethane, has not been evaluated for carcinogenic potential, but is scheduled for evaluation in the future. The manufacturer does not believe this solvent to be carcinogenic. It is known that, when inhaled, MDC metabolizes to carbon monoxide causing oxygen depletion in the bloodstream. For this reason, the Consumer Products Safety Commission has proposed that products containing MDC be labeled to warn of the toxic effect. Individuals with cardiovascular disease may be particularly susceptible to MDC. Methylene Chloride is used directly as a solvent cement for Plexiglas and other plastic sheets. Rohm and Haas Company, manufacturers of Plexiglas, recommend Methylene Chloride as a solvent for cementing Plexiglas. Their technical literature specifies this product be used with CAUTION in WELL VENTILATED areas exactly as their directions specify.

Since there are many solvents available, it's important to read and follow directions supplied with the solvent or thickened cement you purchase. Its use in a well ventilated area should present no problem. But care must be taken not to inhale fumes or allow the solvent to contact the skin, eyes, etc. Apply cement exactly as directions on container recommend. The bonding directions offered in this book provide an overview. Since solvent manufacturers frequently change formulae, always read and use each as their directions specify. Never allow a child to use or be in close proximity when these solvents are being used. As previously stated, never use in a heated, closed area. Use only where there is a free flow of fresh air.

Bonding acrylic to acrylic isn't difficult. It requires preparing the edge as previously described, taping parts square and plumb, and supporting same when necessary. Apply solvent as directions specify.

To gain experience and confidence at the lowest possible cost, don't start working with acrylic building a large project. Get dry behind the ears working with scrap. Saw, sand, drill, tape parts together and test use of applicator and solvent following directions outlined. Only consider starting your first project after you learn to finish a CE edge, tape it plumb and square in position, and have satisfactorily applied solvent to a number of joints. Then select a fairly small starting project. If you can't restrain from building a large and more exciting piece, build a scale model, following every step outlined for the project.

Always make certain each part is cut to exact size required, and each edge is square and smooth. If an edge needs touching up, now is the time to do it. An edge must butt squarely against contacting surface all the way. Always remove dust and shavings. Position and tape parts in position. Only apply solvent to level and horizontal joints. Never apply solvent to a vertical joint. Reposition assembled parts so joint to be bonded is level and horizontal, Illus. 30.

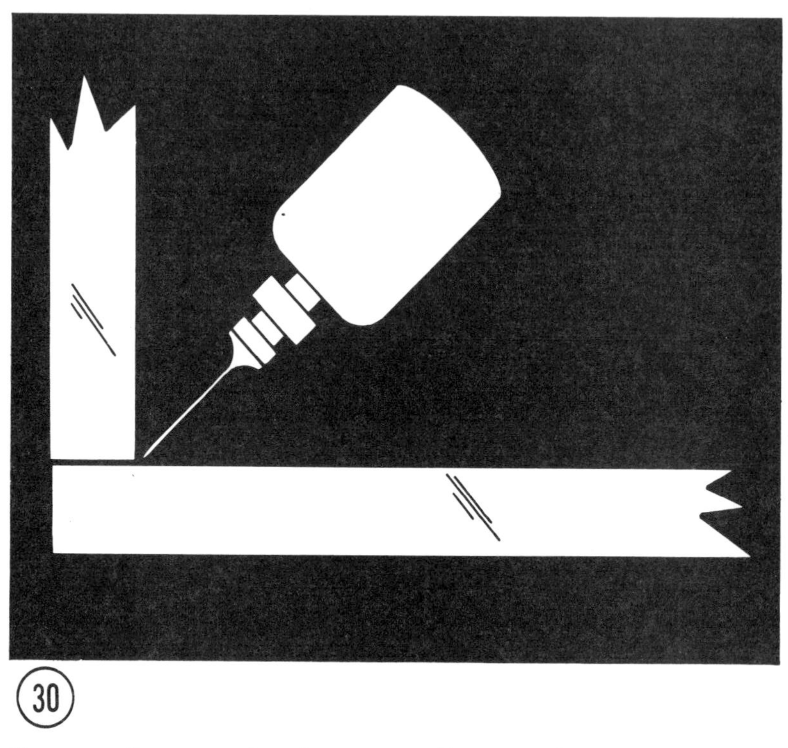

30

Fill the needle nosed solvent applicator, Illus. 3, with acrylic solvent such as Weld-On #3 or equivalent, Illus. 31.

31

SOLVENT FOR CEMENTING ACRYLIC

When using the solvent applicator, Illus. 32, start at far end. Allow needle to fill joint, and only the joint, the full length. Don't overload joint. Keep moving the needle along at whatever speed necessary so only the joint gets filled. If you didn't thoroughly clean away all dust, the applicator will pick it up and clog the point. Remove applicator from area of acrylic and attempt to shake the clogged needle open. Use extreme caution when shaking the applicator. Never allow solvent to get on your face, hands, body or clothes, or on any furniture or other useable article. Wear safety goggles. If solvent does make contact, wash immediately and thoroughly. Never use this solvent in a closed room. The fumes are not for inhaling. The manufacturer's directions spell out all the dangers. For survival and common sense, READ, LEARN and USE as directions specify and in a well ventilated area.

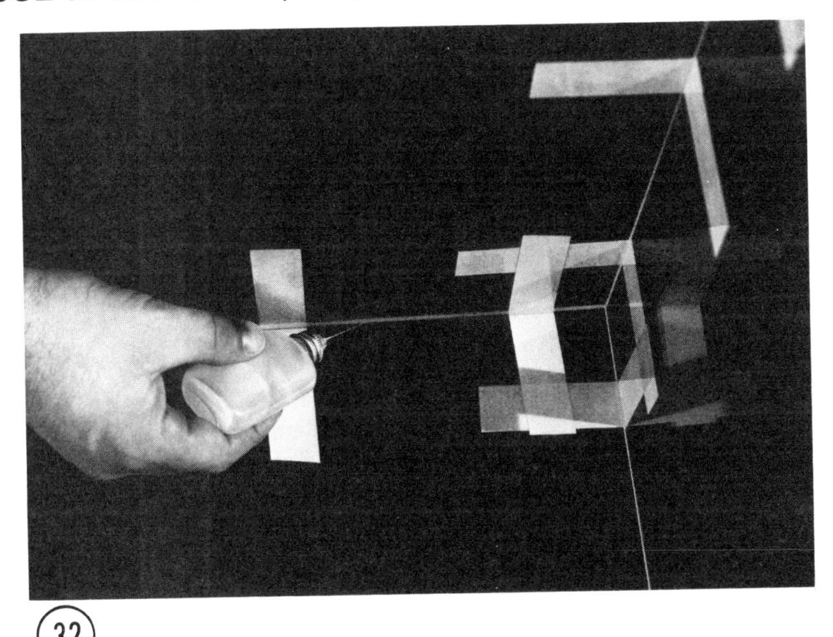

(32)

If the needle nosed applicator gets clogged and shaking doesn't free it, placing the nipple protector over the needle and standing applicator needle nose down frequently allows the solvent to loosen the crud. As a last resort, use a very fine wire to open needle.

The solvent is easy to apply, but does take practice to fill the joint and not the adjacent surface. As previously suggested, test using the applicator on scrap joints.

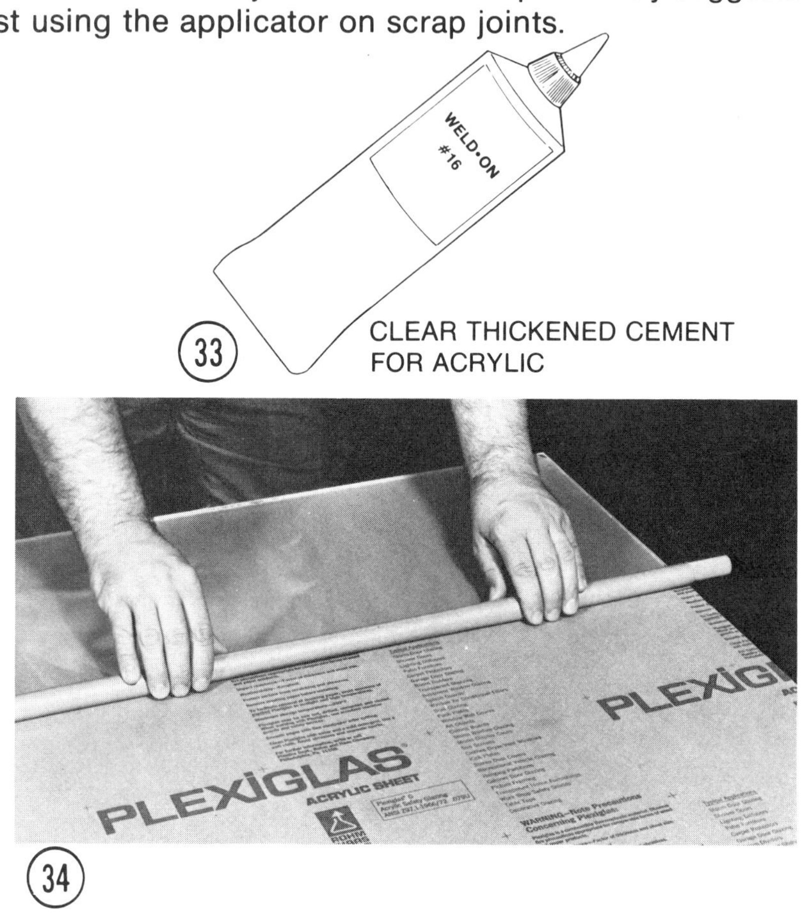

Contact cement, such as Weld-On 16 or equal, Illus. 33, is available in tubes. Edges to be cemented are given a CE finish. Check edge to make certain it's square. When parts have been test assembled and prove OK, use a length of broom handle or ¾'' dowel, Illus. 34, to remove masking paper.

Apply a small bead of cement along edge, Illus. 35. This can be spread with a spatula to evenly cover edge. Join pieces. Wipe away excess cement. Clamp a right angle or support box, made from ⅝ or ¾'' plywood, to height and length required, Illus. 36, to support joint until cement sets.

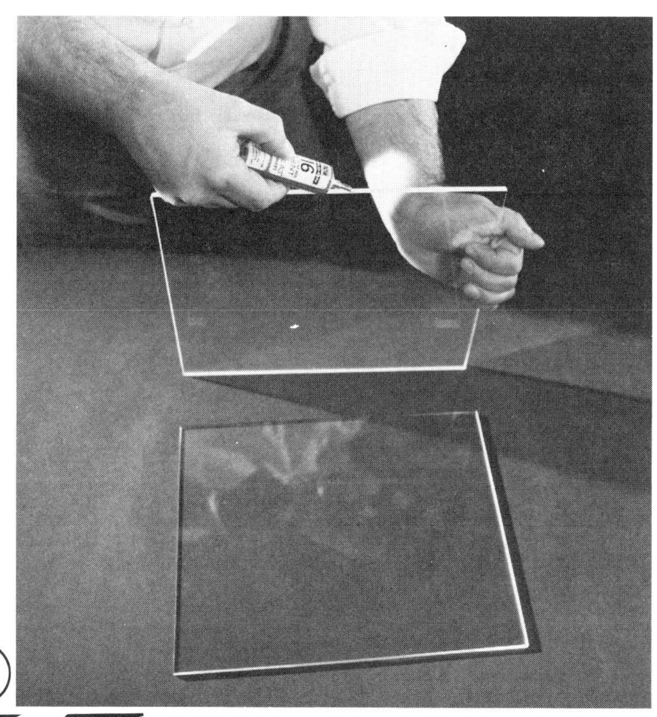

35

For a support box measuring 7 x 8⅝ x 12'' cut:
2 — ⅝ x 5¾ x 8'' end
2 — ⅝ x 8 x 12'' side
1 — ⅝ x 7 x 12'' top
Nail sides to ends, top to sides and ends.

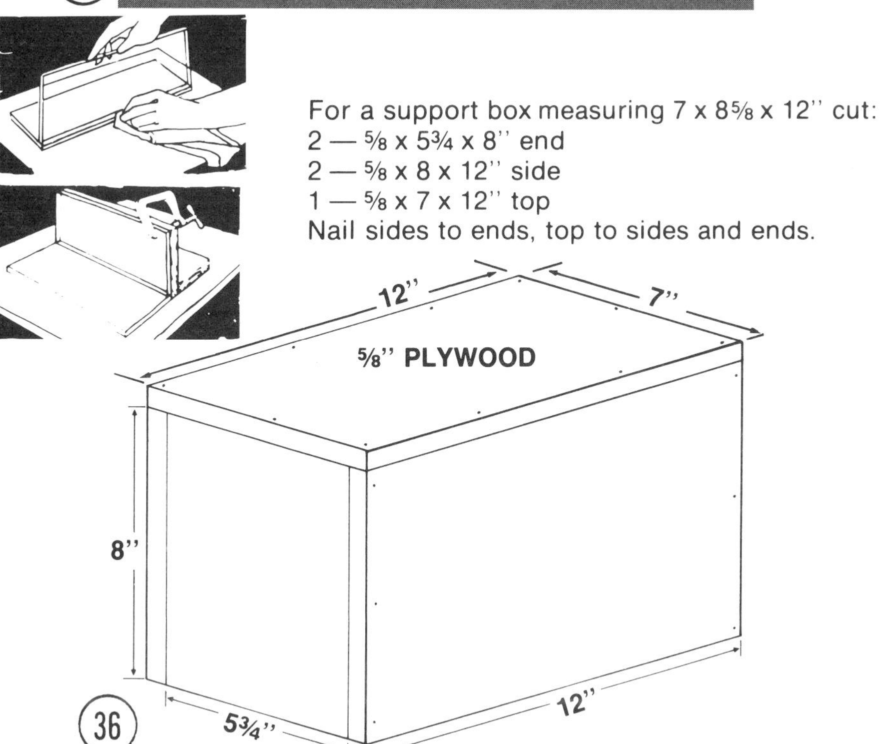

36

TO START

Buy a scrap piece of ⅛" Plexiglas, one of sufficient size that permits making a four sided box, Illus. 37. Cut two ends A, two sides B and one bottom C, Illus. 38.

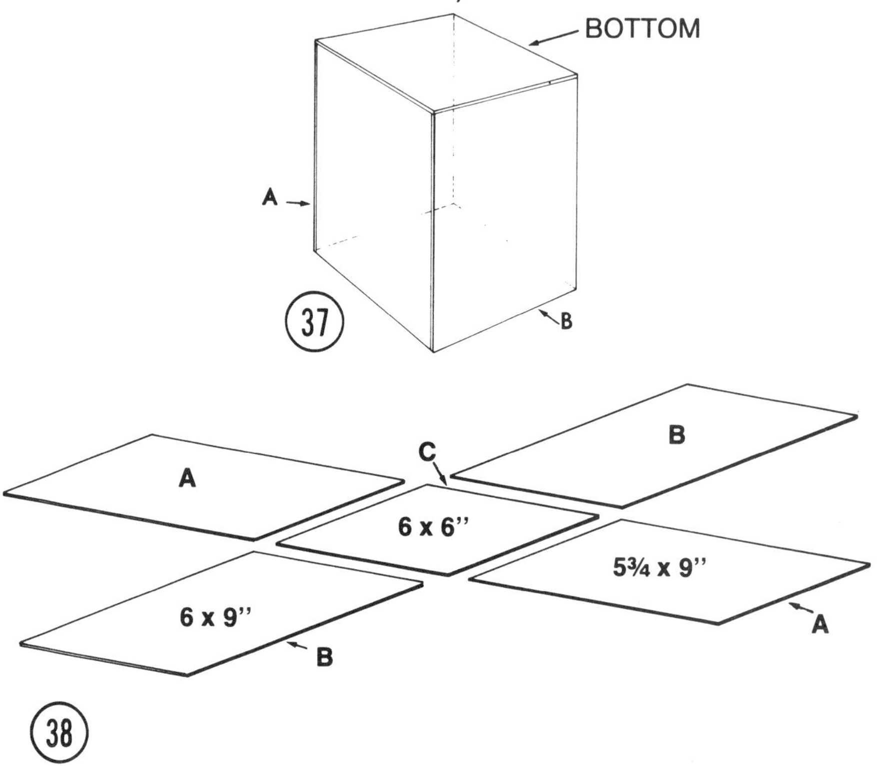

Apply a CE finish to 9" edge of A and to bottom 5¾" edge. Apply an EE finish to top 5¾ and 6" edges of AB.

Clean away all dust and tape CE edge of A to B, C to AB in position shown, Illus. 37.

Fill the needle nosed applicator (Hypo-RH200) with Weld-On #3 solvent. Apply solvent to each horizontal joint, Illus. 32.

Test your first read through by building this box. If you don't score all A's, make a second reading before starting construction of the handsome display cases, pedestal cabinet, wall cabinet, outdoor showcase, or other projects.

PLYWOOD BACKED DISPLAY CASE

A desire and drive to collect can take root at almost any age. Girls with dolls, boys with trains, coins, stamps; housewives with cups, plates, silver, cut glass, etc. Every kind of miniature, every type of article from ash trays to tin toys are but a few of the many collectors articles that offer constructive escape from today's pressurized society.

Creating a time consuming hobby expands your sphere of activity, helps insure mental survival. All too many of our peers take a powder, a sleeping pill, drug or drink when they should make a major effort to create a new and constructive use of spare time. Creating a collection and showing it at every opportunity enhances the ego of its owner. Encourage a youngster to invest earned money starting and expanding a collection, swapping unused toys, learning facts about the sale and manufacture of the article. Encouraging a time consuming interest can be far less expensive than a cure. An area of prime concern to every parent revolves around a seldom heard piece of advice. As a youngster always seeking part time work, I delivered special delivery letters, sorted mail, pumped gas, etc. Every job brought me in contact with adults. Having developed an interest in carpentry tools, I asked everyone I worked for whether they had any old tools they wanted to sell or have carted away. Those that didn't have any frequently talked to friends and early in life I became a collector. Adults like helping a child, and particularly children who are willing to pay for what they ask for.

Collecting is especially important to parents in today's drug oriented world. Collectors enjoy conversation, companionship and a cure for loneliness. Developing and discussing a collection can prove a time consuming, richly rewarding endeavor. Encouraging a girl to collect and play with dolls, furnish and decorate a dollhouse, accents the positive. Raising a girl to be feminine is no small task in today's mixed up world.

39

The plywood backed display case, Illus. 39, can be built to size specified, or to size desired. It's important to first select a location, then build to overall size the location permits. If necessary, make a cardboard template of the required floor area. Note whether it interferes with opening any door or window. Since this project has popular appeal, those who build for resale must first obtain exact overall dimensions the customer specifies (in writing) before starting construction.

Since collectors are birds that flock together, everyone interested in starting a part or full time business should show a photo, scale model or the full size cabinet to exhibitors at collectors shows. It sparks great enthusiasm. You quickly discover what one likes, others also want. Watch newspapers for any announcement concerning antique doll and other special interest shows. Visit exhibitors who display old china, tin toys, statues, cut glass, silver, objets d'art, etc. Call on every jewelry and gift shop owner, department store manager and buyer of special goods that can be effectively presented in these cabinets.

To estimate a selling price, keep an accurate record of the time needed to build, and cost of all material. Before fixing a selling price, make inquiry to ascertain what a store paid for a similar size glass display case. Since the retailer also paid for shipping, if you set a selling price four to six times cost of material, it could prove a low starting point. If you sell your first cabinet at too low a price, you can always raise the price before presenting it to the next customer.

Directions simplify construction of two different cabinets. One contains a plywood back, top and bottom; acrylic sides, doors and shelves, Illus. 39. The all clear model, Illus. 40, requires cutting back, top, bottom, sides, door and shelves from acrylic. Construction of the plywood cabinet begins on page 46; the all clear cabinet on page 64.

40

Collectors who place a free standing cabinet in a high ceilinged room, or position one or more end to end, as a room divider, find the all clear cabinet, Illus. 40, extremely attractive. These are in great demand by banks and retailers of gifts, jewelry, china, silverware, etc.

The potential sale within any area you want to serve is unlimited. Few out of town manufacturers can pack and ship a cabinet of this kind unless they add all packing and shipping costs to its selling price, or ask the retailer to assume same. If you build locally, you don't need more than a good sized blanket and a station wagon. Since you can carry the case into the store, then set doors and shelves in place, you deliver a competely acceptable product. To present this case to a prospective customer, build and photograph it. Show a color photo. Another smart way is to build a model using a scale of ¼" = 1". Use ⅛" Plexiglas for the model. Suggest use of model to display jewelry, cosmetics, etc.

Scale models are easy to handle. They also generate great interest. Whenever possible, invite the prospect to see a finished sample.

Owners and display managers of fine shops are prime customers for both of these cabinets. When a single cabinet is to be placed against a wall, both ends exposed, suggest they use a cabinet with a plywood back, top and bottom, acrylic on sides, doors and shelves. Paint or cover inside of back with fabric or prepasted wallpaper that matches room decor. Sandpaper edge of plywood using 60-80 grit, then a 220-320 grade. Sandpaper surface before applying first coat of paint. Prime coat edge and back. Sand again before applying second coat.

Use ¼" acrylic for both cabinets.

When cabinets are to be placed against a wall, use ⅝ or ¾'' plywood, good two sides, for top, back and bottom. Always select a location where the floor is level and solid, no spring, and where the cabinet is completely clear of a door and/or the mainstream of traffic. If you alter overall size of cabinet, revise cutting chart, Illus. 41,42,43. Always position shelves at a height that complements the articles displayed.

NOTE: A collectors' cabinet should be built to height room permits. While a 75'' cabinet standing on 6'' legs provides excellent display space in a room with an 8'0'' ceiling, a collection of small miniatures may show to better advantage in a smaller cabinet.

The antique doll collection, Illus. 39, required a 75'' cabinet to obtain space for three tiers. The same cabinet will accommodate five shelves of china or silverware, six shelves of books.

A 14½ x 44 x 75'' cabinet with a plywood back, top and bottom will require the following:

LIST OF MATERIAL

2 — ¼'' x 4 x 8' acrylic panels, C,D,E,F
1 — ⅝ or ¾'' x 4 x 8' plywood good two sides, A,B
1 — ⅝ x 16 x 48'' '' '' '' '' B
2 — 6' slotted wall standards
4 — 10'' matching shelf brackets
1 — pr. ¼'' x 4' sliding door track
4 — 6'' metal or wood legs and brackets
Weld-On #3 Solvent and Applicator
Sandpaper as specified
Buy legs that match or complement color used to paint or cover inside of A.

Use plywood good one side if cabinet is to be placed against a wall or two are placed back to back.

Cut back A — 43½ x 75'', top and bottom B - 13⅝ x 43½''.

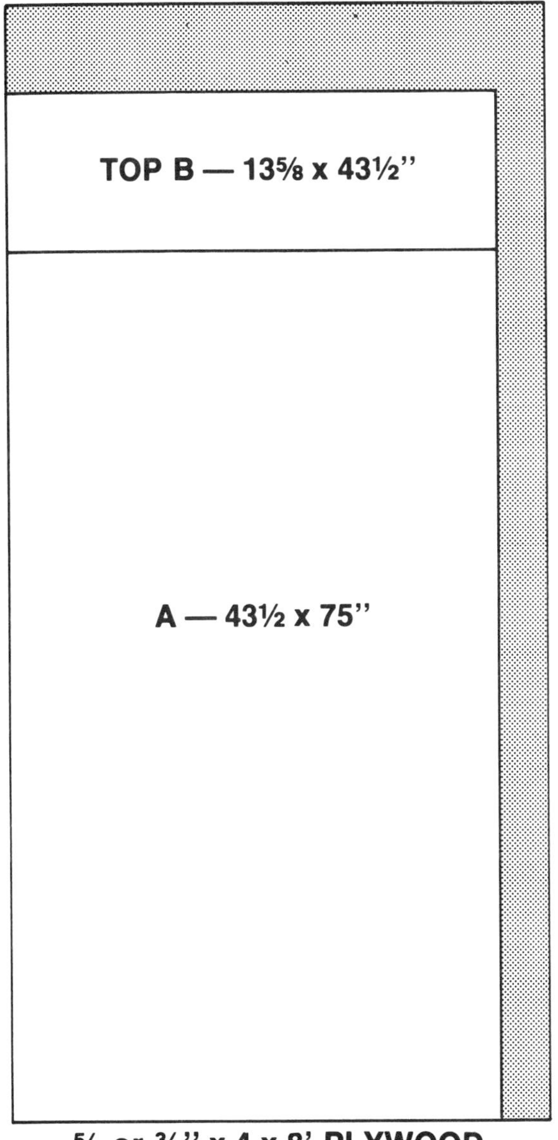

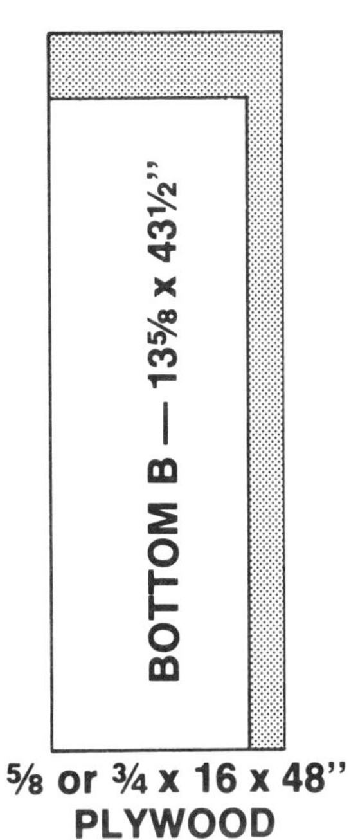

¼'' acrylic is used for sides C, front support D, shelves E, doors F, shelf stiffeners G, Illus. 42,43,44.

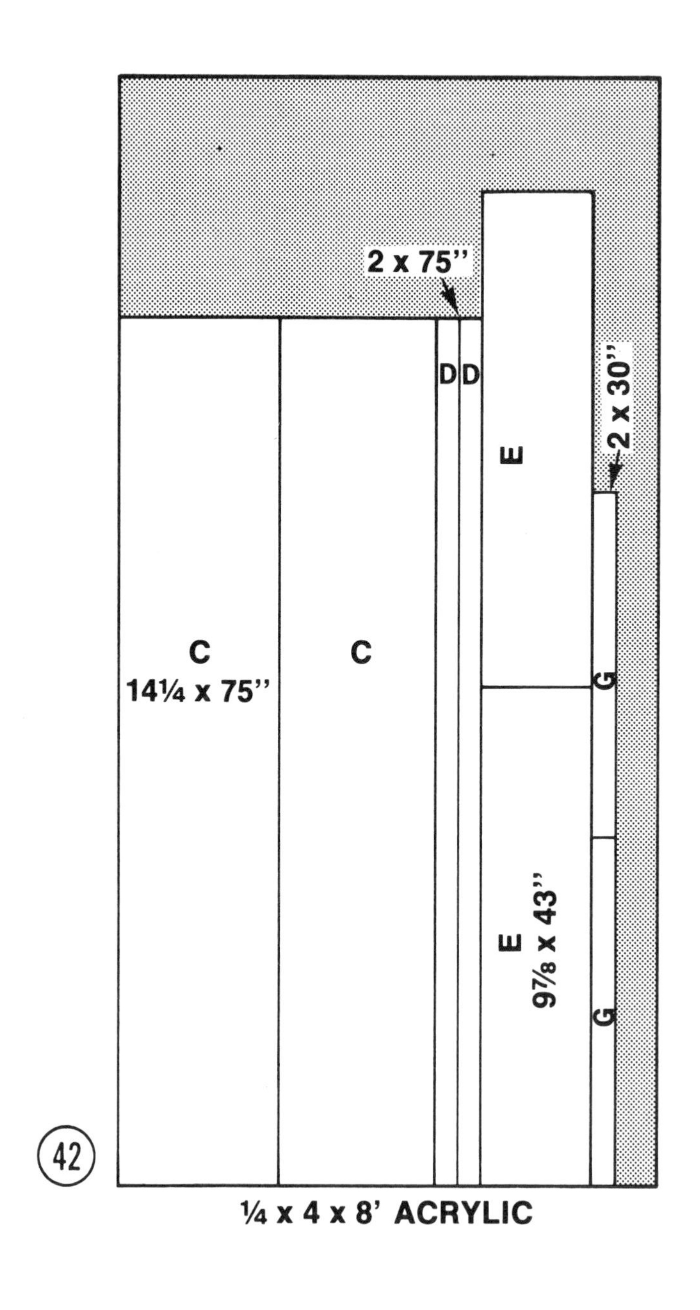

DO NOT CUT DOORS F until actual size is checked against installed track.

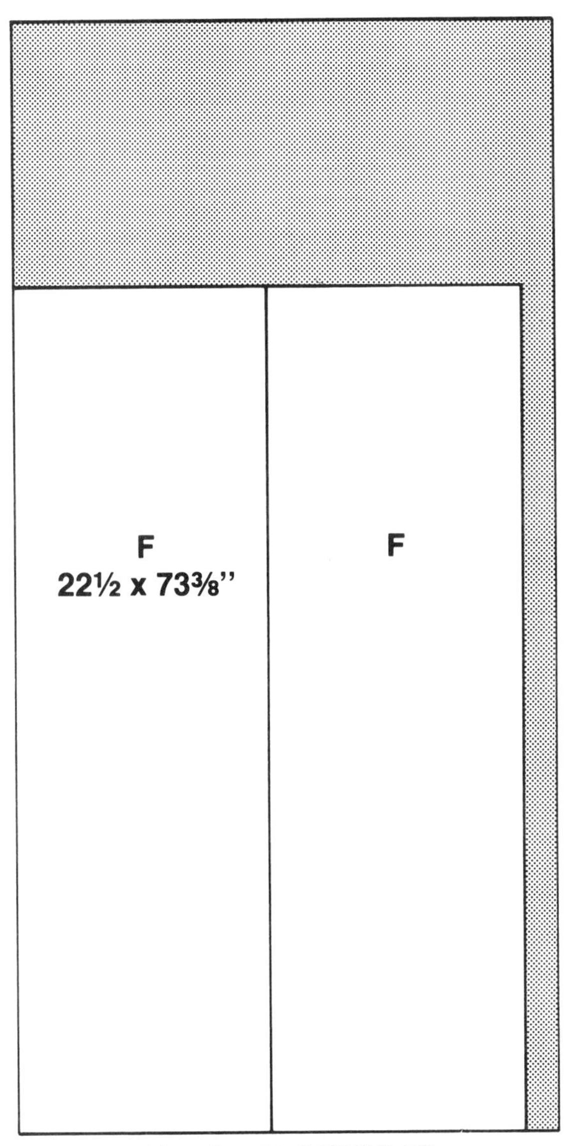

When directions specify, cut shelves to width shelf bracket requires. Some 10" brackets take a 9⅝", others a 9⅞" width shelf. Where heavy objects are to be displayed, i.e., books, cut glass, etc., stiffen shelves with a stiffener G, Illus. 44. Only cut shelves when cabinet is assembled, Illus. 60. Check actual size required for shelf and stiffener. The stiffener should be cut to length that fits between standards.

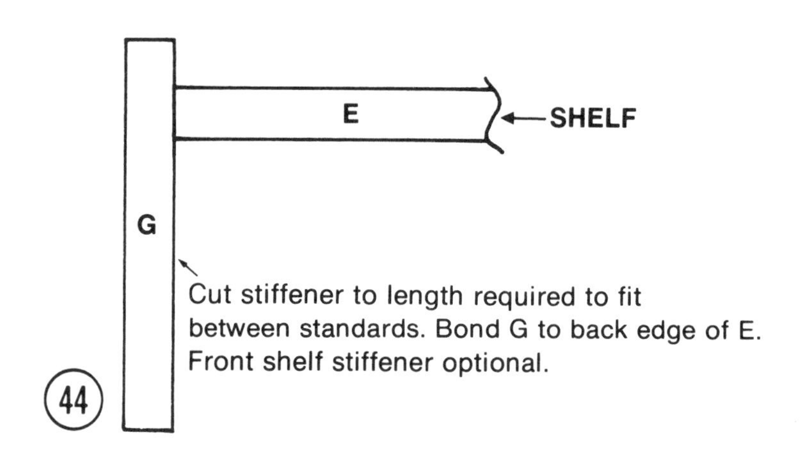

If you plan on loading cabinet with books, stacks of plates or other heavy objects, cut a 1 x 2 to overall length of base, less 4". Apply glue to edge of 1 x 2. Nail bottom to 1 x 2, Illus. 45.

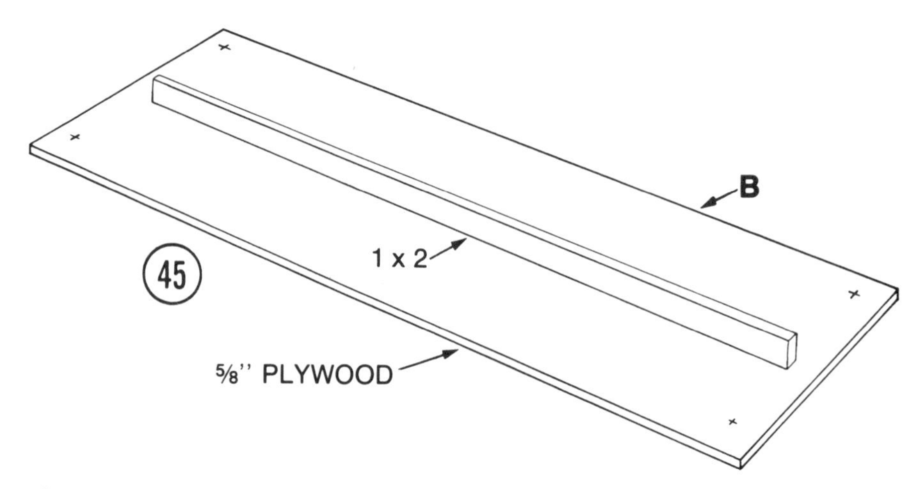

Paint or stain bottom. When dry, fasten four leg brackets to bottom, Illus. 46, in position shown. Use screws provided by manufacturer of brackets. If you build a wider than 44" cabinet, use six leg brackets.

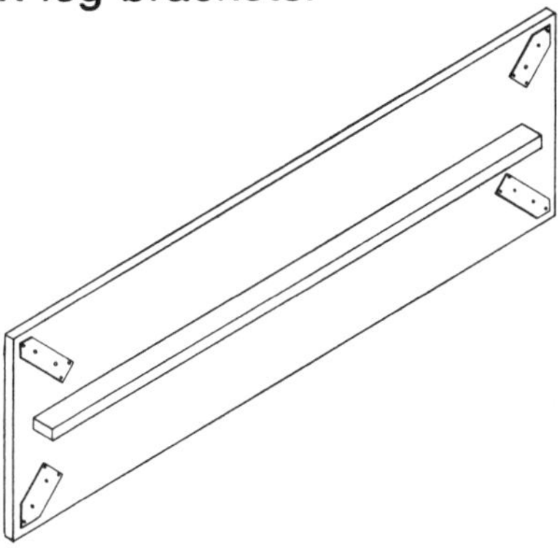

46

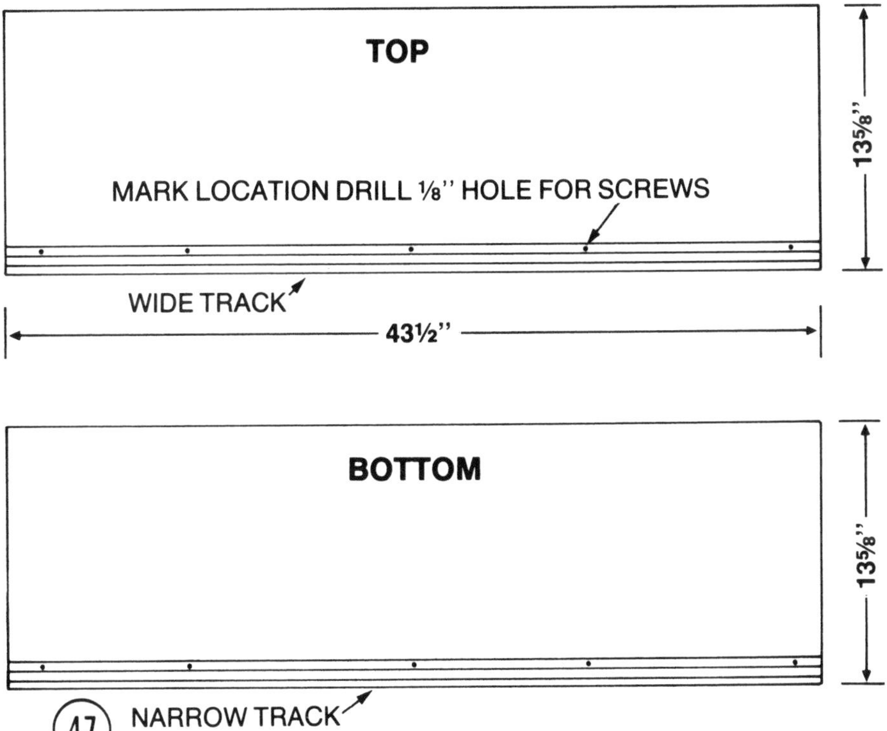

TOP

MARK LOCATION DRILL 1/8" HOLE FOR SCREWS

WIDE TRACK

43½"

13⅝"

BOTTOM

13⅝"

47 NARROW TRACK

Fasten sliding door track flush with front edge of B, Illus. 47. Install wide track at top, narrow track at bottom using screws provided by manufacturer, Illus. 48.

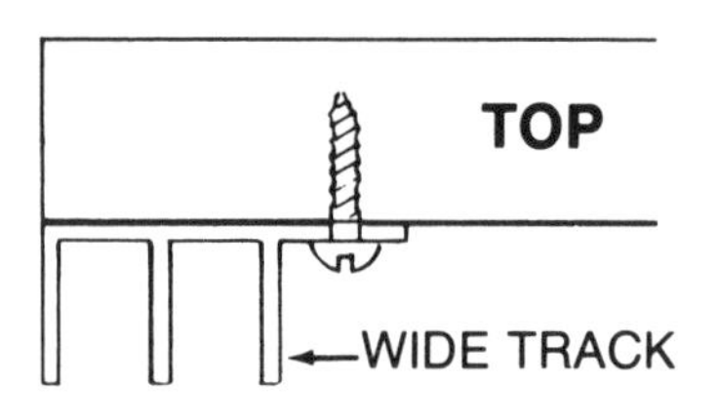

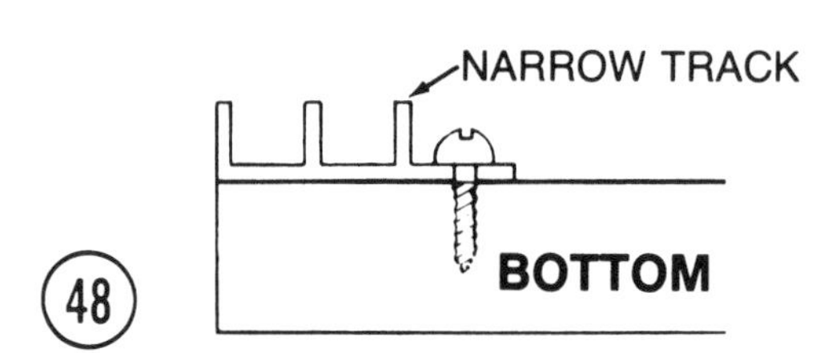

Cut two ¼" acrylic sides C, 14¼ x 75", Illus. 42. Apply a CE finish to one 75" edge of C where it butts against D. Finish exposed, back edge of C, top and bottom edges with an EE finish. Cut two ¼ x 2 x 75" strips for D. Apply an EE finish to four edges of D.

Do not cut shelves E, or doors F, Illus. 42,43, at this time. Only cut doors after cabinet has been assembled and an accurate distance between track can be checked.

Sandpaper edge of plywood. Fill all cracks with wood filler. Sandpaper before applying a primer. Sandpaper prime coat before applying first coat of paint. Sandpaper each coat lightly before applying another. If you are building a cabinet for resale, ask customer to supply paint to eliminate any question concerning color.

Apply glue to back edge of B. Nail A to B, Illus. 49, with 6 penny finishing nails. Countersink heads. Fill holes with wood filler. If your customer wants to cover the inside of back, floor and ceiling with fabric or prepasted wallpaper, do not paint. Cut fabric to size. Glue in position. Finish edge of plywood with a color that matches standards, Illus. 50.

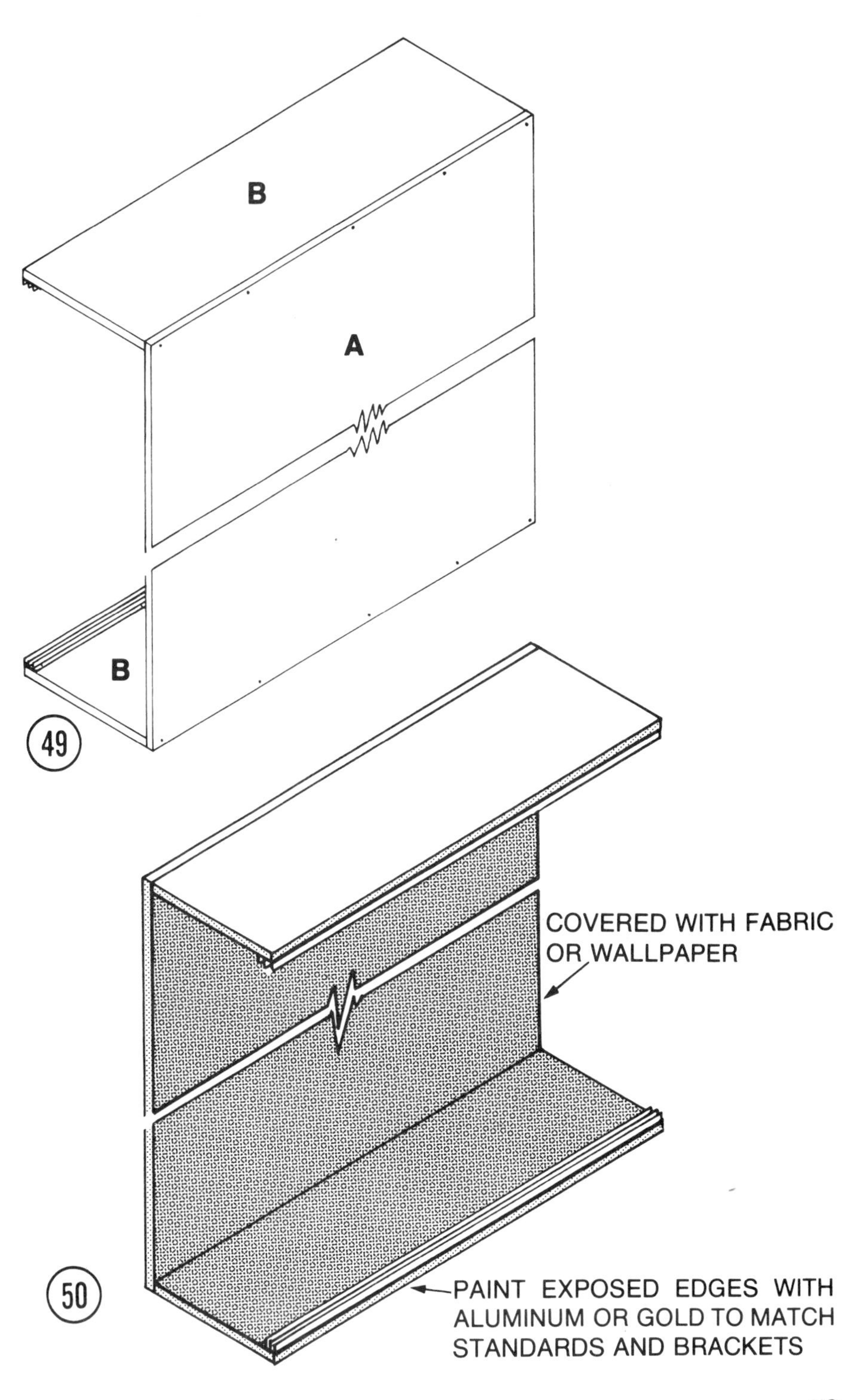
B
A
B
49
COVERED WITH FABRIC
OR WALLPAPER
50
PAINT EXPOSED EDGES WITH
ALUMINUM OR GOLD TO MATCH
STANDARDS AND BRACKETS

If you place a plywood panel or two 2 x 4's on sawhorses, it simplifies working on assembled AB, Illus. 51.

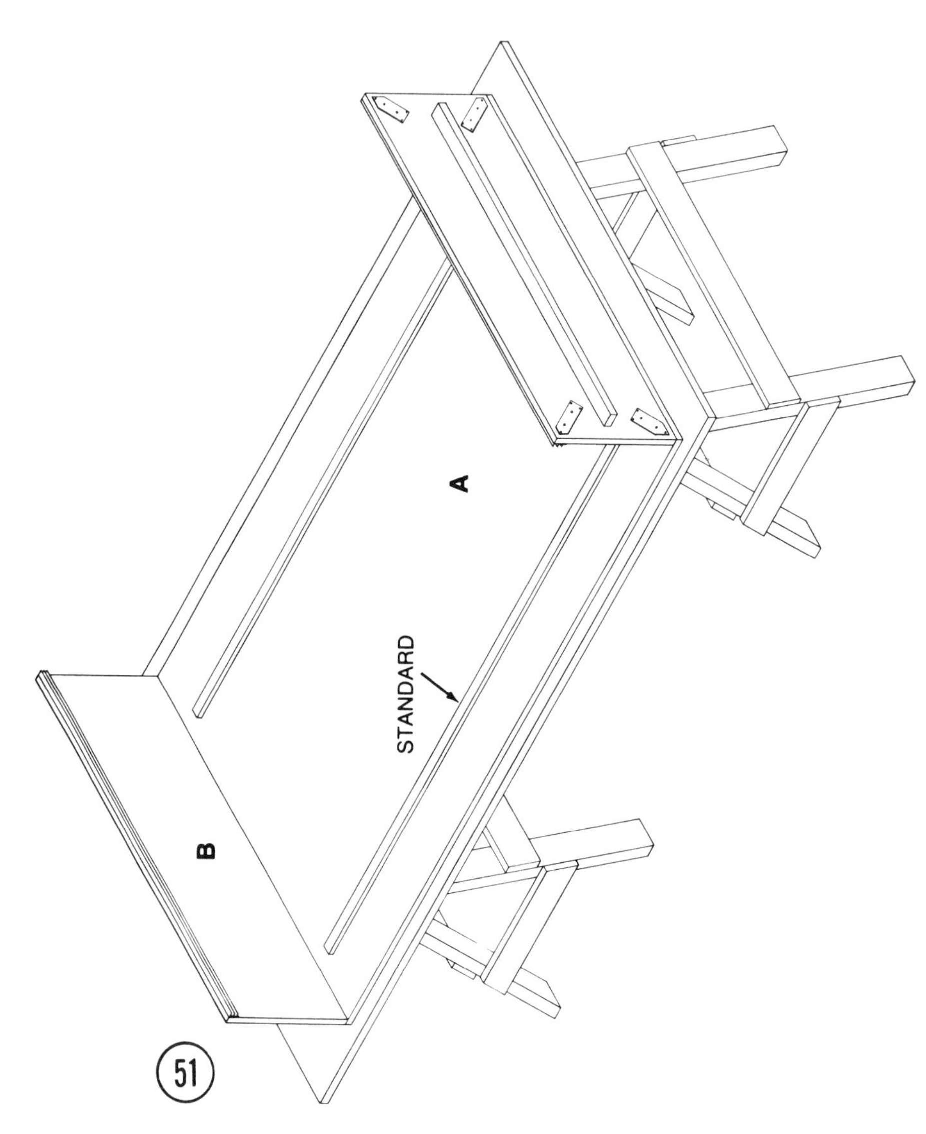

After inside of cabinet has been painted or covered with fabric, fasten two 6' shelf standards, 6'' from edge, ⅜'' from B, Illus. 52. Fasten standards with screws manufacturer specifies. Since slots in standards must be in line, after fastening one in place, use a square and straight edge to make certain slot in second standard is on line.

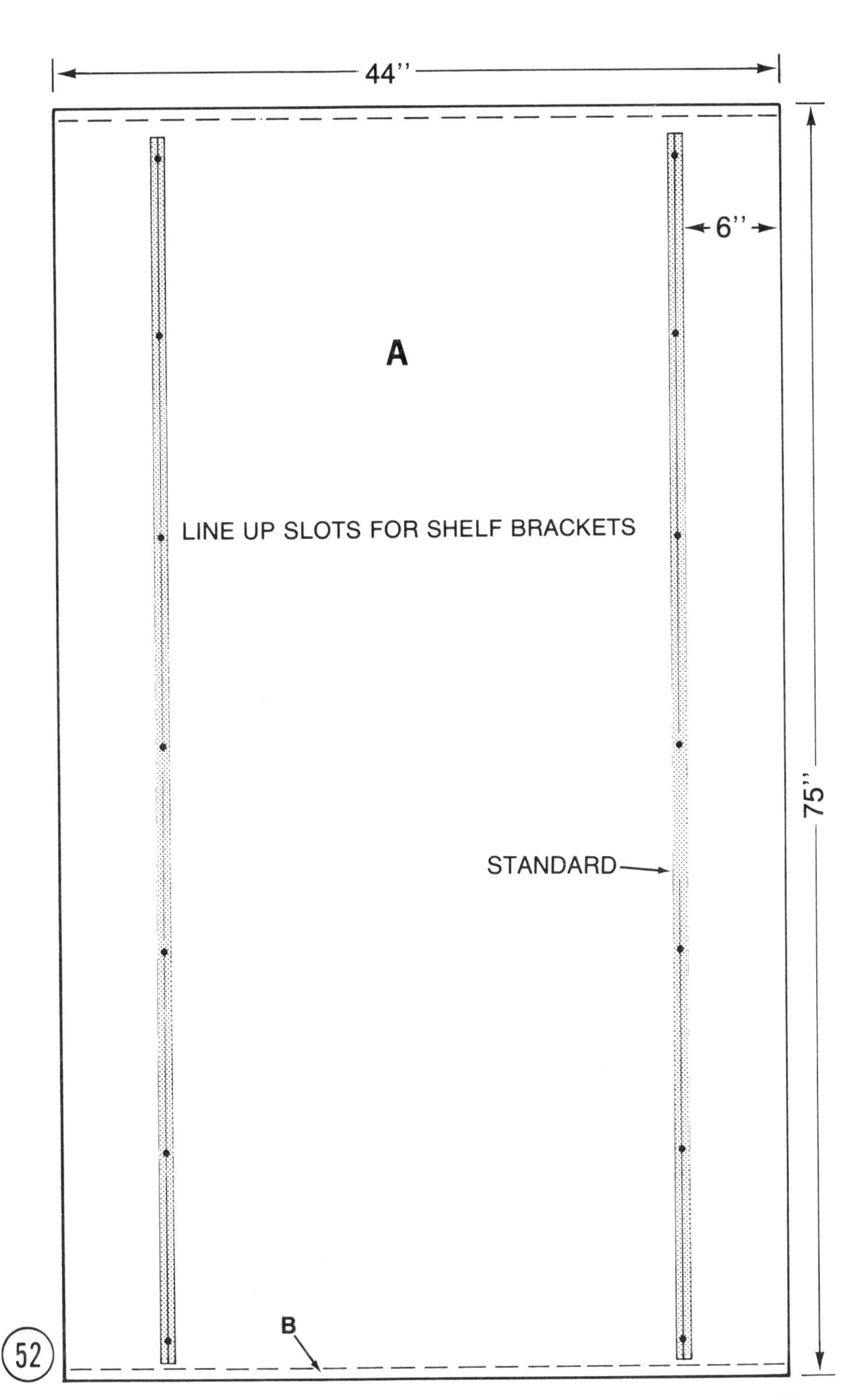
44''
6''
A
LINE UP SLOTS FOR SHELF BRACKETS
75''
STANDARD
B
52

Place C (1/4 x 14 1/4 x 75") against AB, Illus. 53. Draw a line 3/8" from edge as indicated. Drill 3/16" holes approximately 6" apart at ends, approximately 12" apart on 75" edge.

Place C on a 2 x 4 and drill 3/16" shank holes through C. Replace C on AB and drill 1/16" pilot holes 1/4 to 3/8" deep in edge of plywood.

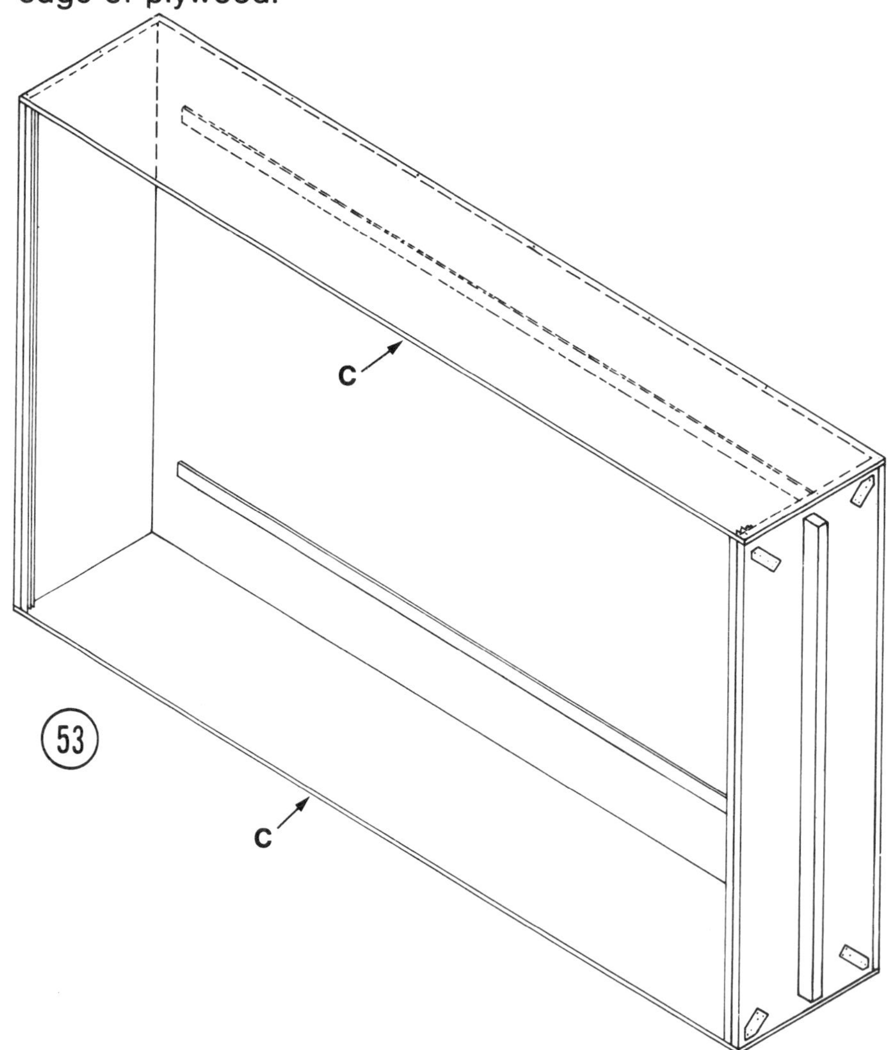

Apply a clear, silicone sealant to edge of A and B. Fasten C to BA with 3/4" No. 5 oval head chromium plated screws and countersunk washers, Illus. 9. Always fasten screws snug, never tight.

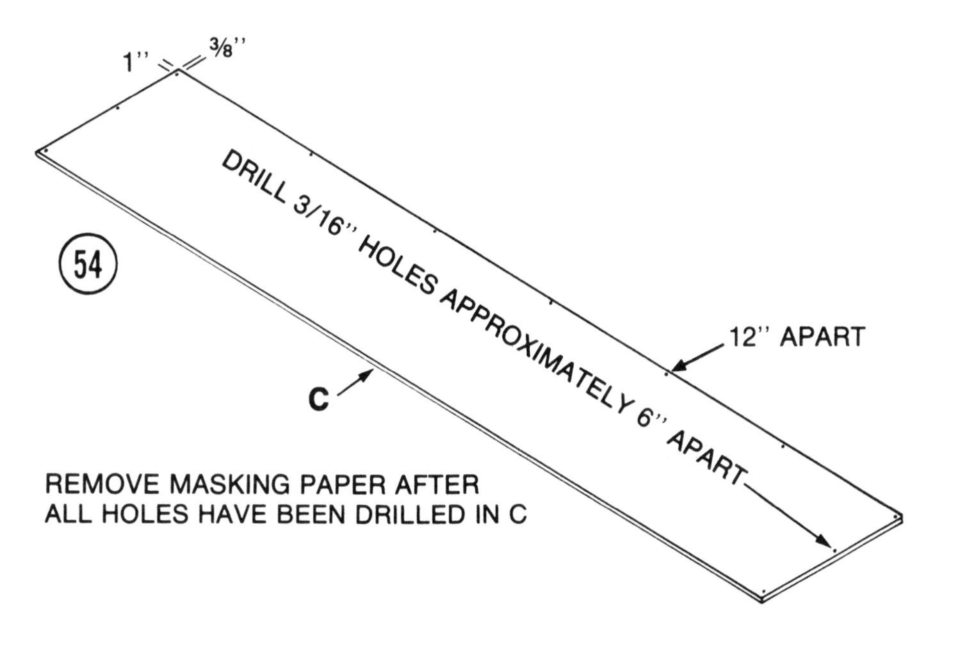

Using pattern, Illus. 55, drill two 3/16" holes at top and bottom of D. Place D in position, Illus. 56, and drill 1/16" pilot holes ¼" deep in B. Remove masking from D.

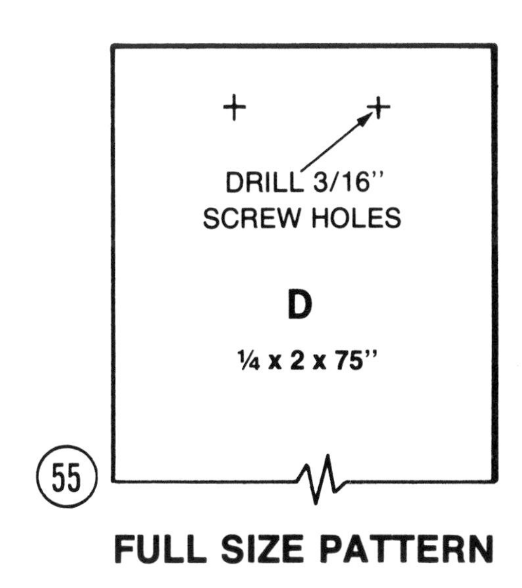

FULL SIZE PATTERN

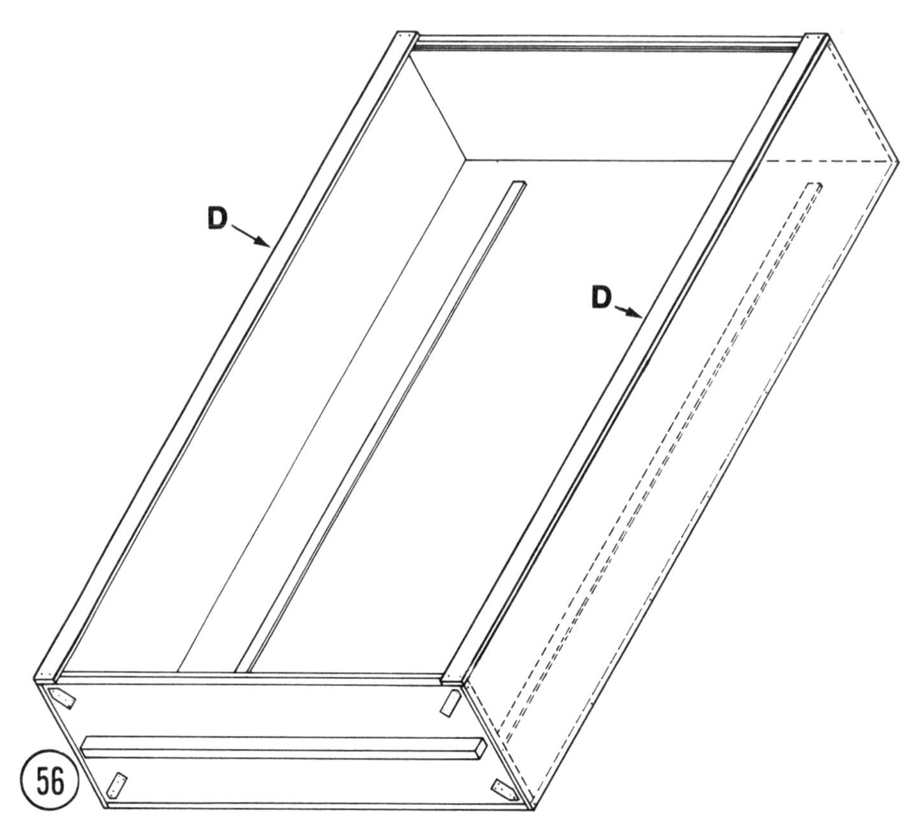

Apply clear silicone to edge of B where it contacts D; apply thickened cement to edge of C. Tape D to C, Illus. 58. Fasten D to B with ¾" No. 5 oval head screws and countersunk washers, Illus. 57.

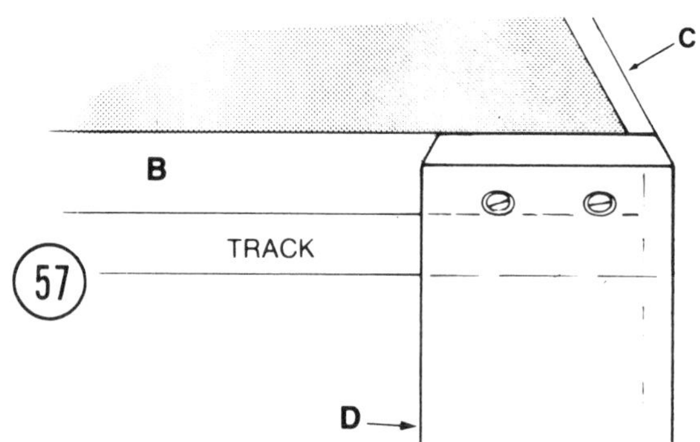

Allow cement to set time manufacturer specifies, then remove tape from DC.

Screw legs into brackets, Illus. 59.

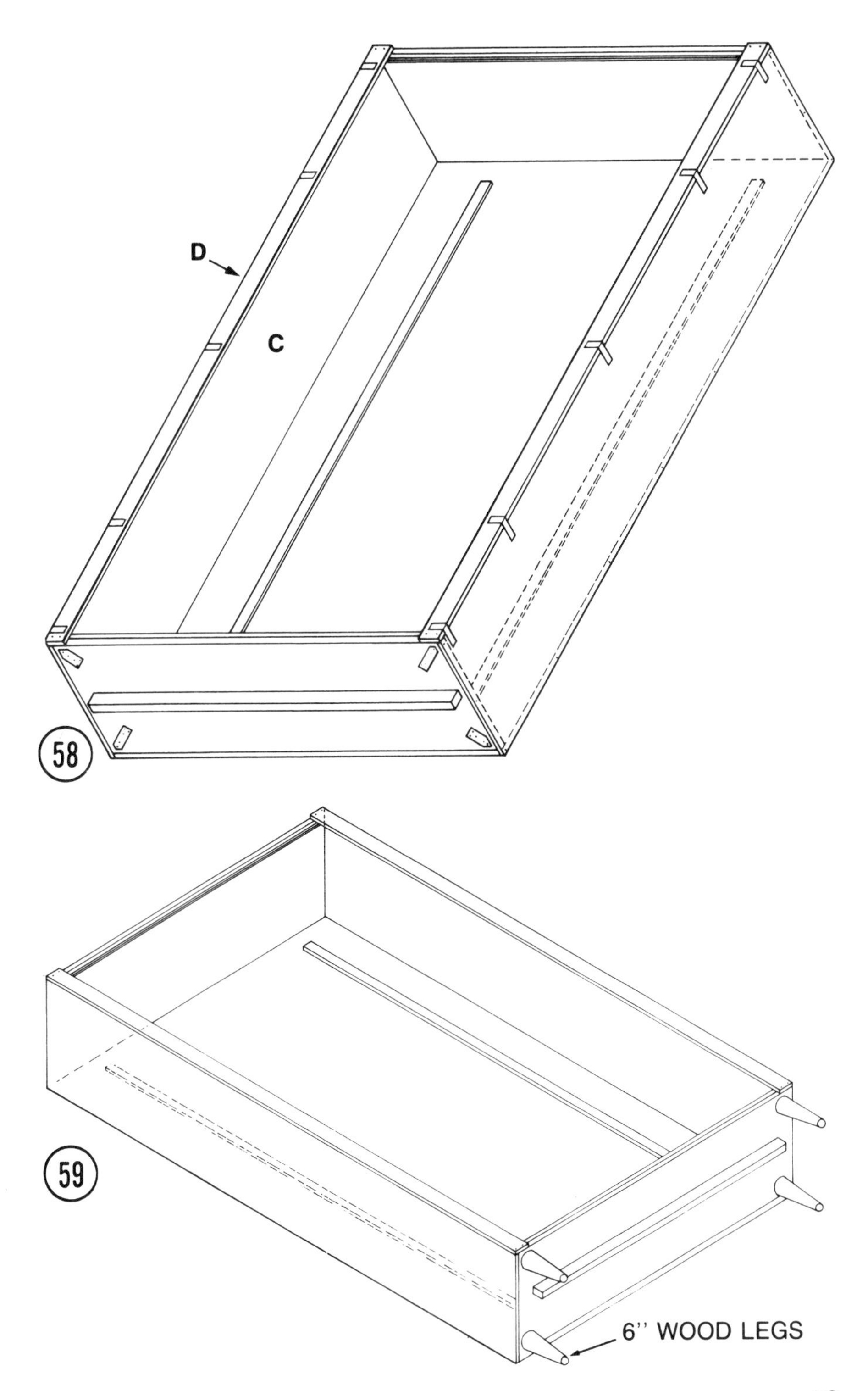
D
C
58
59
6'' WOOD LEGS

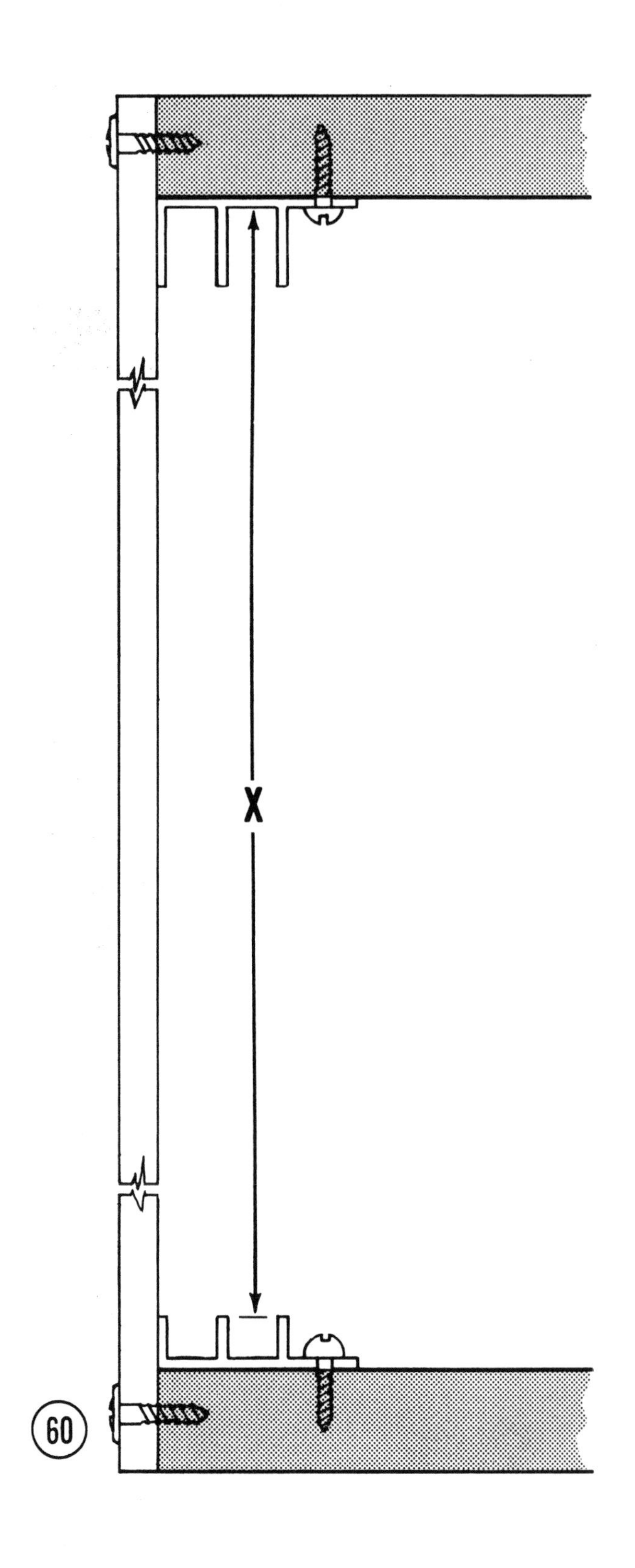
X
60

To estimate exact overall height of doors, insert end of yardstick fully into top track. Allow a second yardstick to touch top of bottom track. Double check spacing at both ends and again in middle. If you find any difference, it will be necessary to shim track level. Cut two 22½" wide doors to height yardstick indicates. Overall height of door is indicated by X, Illus. 60. Finish four edges with a transparent finish.

If in doubt, do this. Cut a ¼" fir plywood panel or corrugated board to overall height and width needed for a door. Nail panel to two 1 x 2 stiffeners. Position stiffener 1" up from bottom, 1" down from top, about 2½" in from edge. Insert and slide panel back and forth. If test door works well, cut acrylic same size.

While ¼" acrylic doors work well in a 75" cabinet, if a larger case is being constructed for store use, cut ¾" wide strips of ¼" acrylic, 2" less in overall length than height of door, Illus. 61. Apply CE finish to one edge of door stiffener, buff front edge and ends to a transparent finish. Since door stiffeners prevent doors from opening fully, we only recommend their use where required.

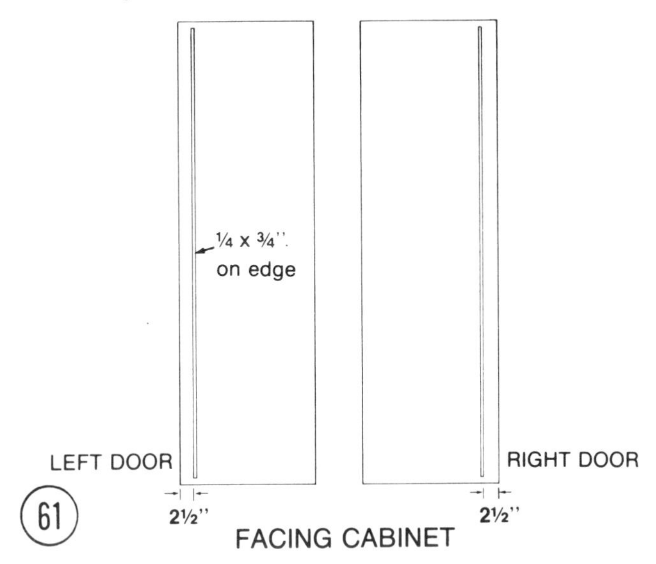

Lay door on work table. Bond stiffener to door, 2½" from C. Apply cement to CE edge.

Cut shelves, Illus. 62, to width bracket requires and to length that provides ½" clearance from C.

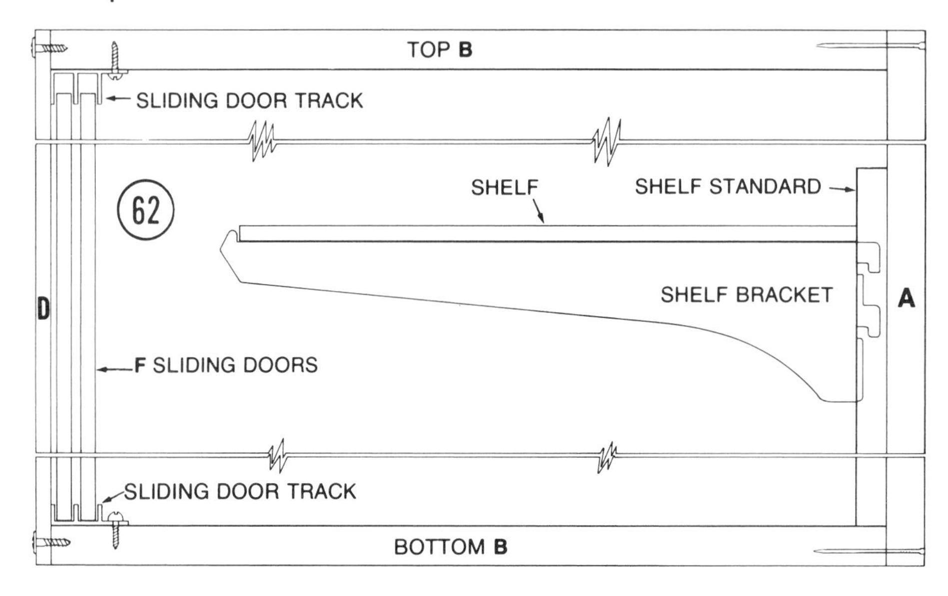

Cut a 2" strip of acrylic for a back stiffener to length that fits between standards, Illus. 63. Where needed, cut a front stiffener to fit between brackets. Apply an EE finish to all edges. Apply a CE finish to edge of shelf where stiffener is to be bonded. Bond stiffeners in place, Illus. 44. Install shelf brackets in position articles require.

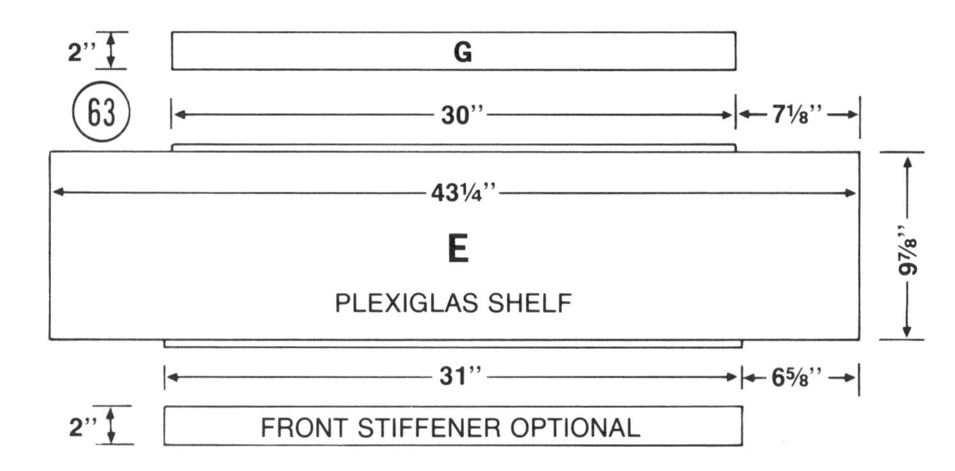

NOTE: Never position an acrylic cabinet close to a radiator or hot air register. Never move a loaded acrylic cabinet. Always remove contents, doors and shelves before moving. To avoid accidental tipping, note where cabinet butts against chair rail. Drill a 3/16" hole through each shelf standard and through back so cabinet can be screwed to chair rail. Use No. 8 roundhead screw of sufficient length to penetrate chair rail ¾".

If location selected has a baseboard, but no chair rail, use a furring strip equal in thickness to baseboard. Cut to length needed.

Drill holes through shelf standard and furring strip. Drill pilot hole in wall so shelf standard and furring strip can be fastened to a stud in wall. Use length screw required.

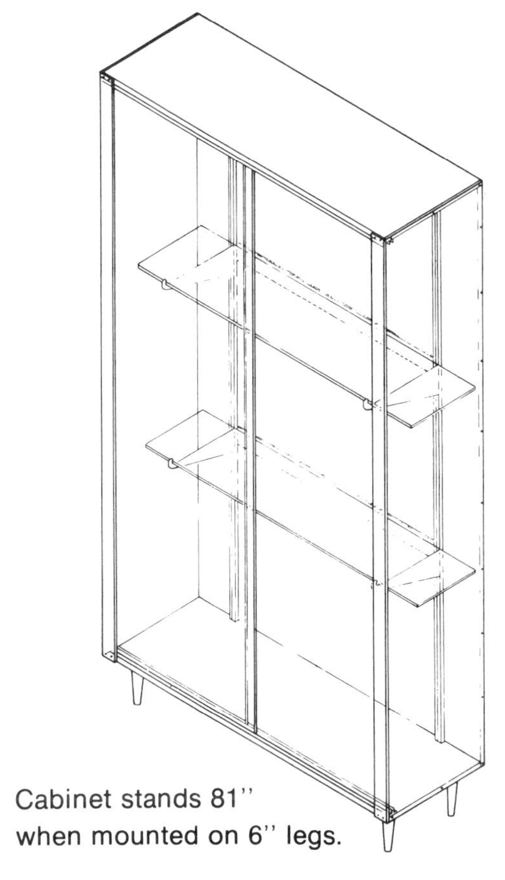

Cabinet stands 81"
when mounted on 6" legs.

TO BUILD AN ALL CLEAR CABINET

For a 14½ x 44 x 75½" cabinet,* Illus. 40, with an acrylic back, sides, top, bottom, doors and shelves, you will need:

LIST OF MATERIAL

3 — ¼" x 4 x 8' Acrylic, A,B,C,D,E,F.
1 — ⅝ x 14½ x 44" plywood good one side, G
1 — 1 x 2 x 44" (optional)
2 — 6' slotted shelf standards
4 — 10 or 12" shelf brackets
4 — 6" metal or wood legs and mounting brackets
1 pr. ¼" x 4' sliding door track
Weld-On #3 Solvent
Bolts to fasten shelf standards to back A

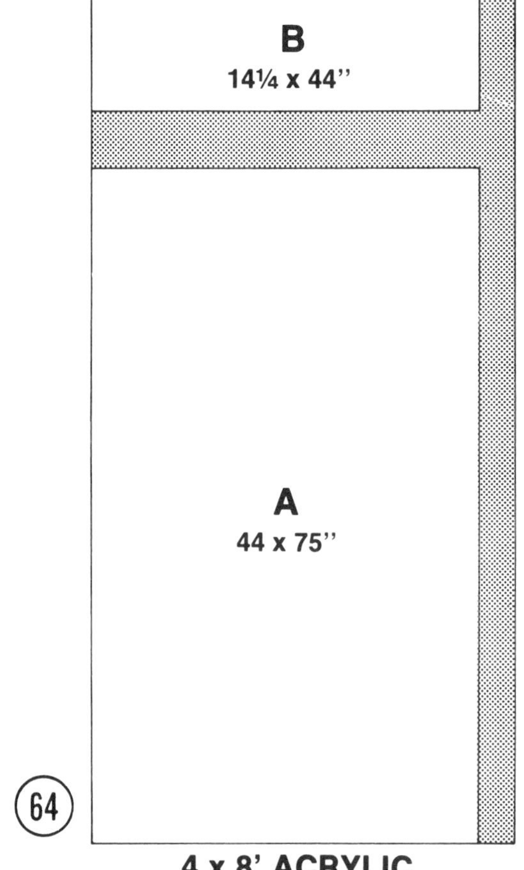

4 x 8' ACRYLIC

*Overall height will be 80⅛" on 4" legs; 82⅛" on 6" legs.

Cut back A, 44 x 75", Illus. 64. Cut two B, 14¼ x 44", Illus. 64,65,77. Cut two C, 14 x 75"; Illus. 66. Apply an EE finish to 75" edge of A; a CE finish to 44" edge. Cut two D, 2 x 75½". Apply an EE finish to four edges.

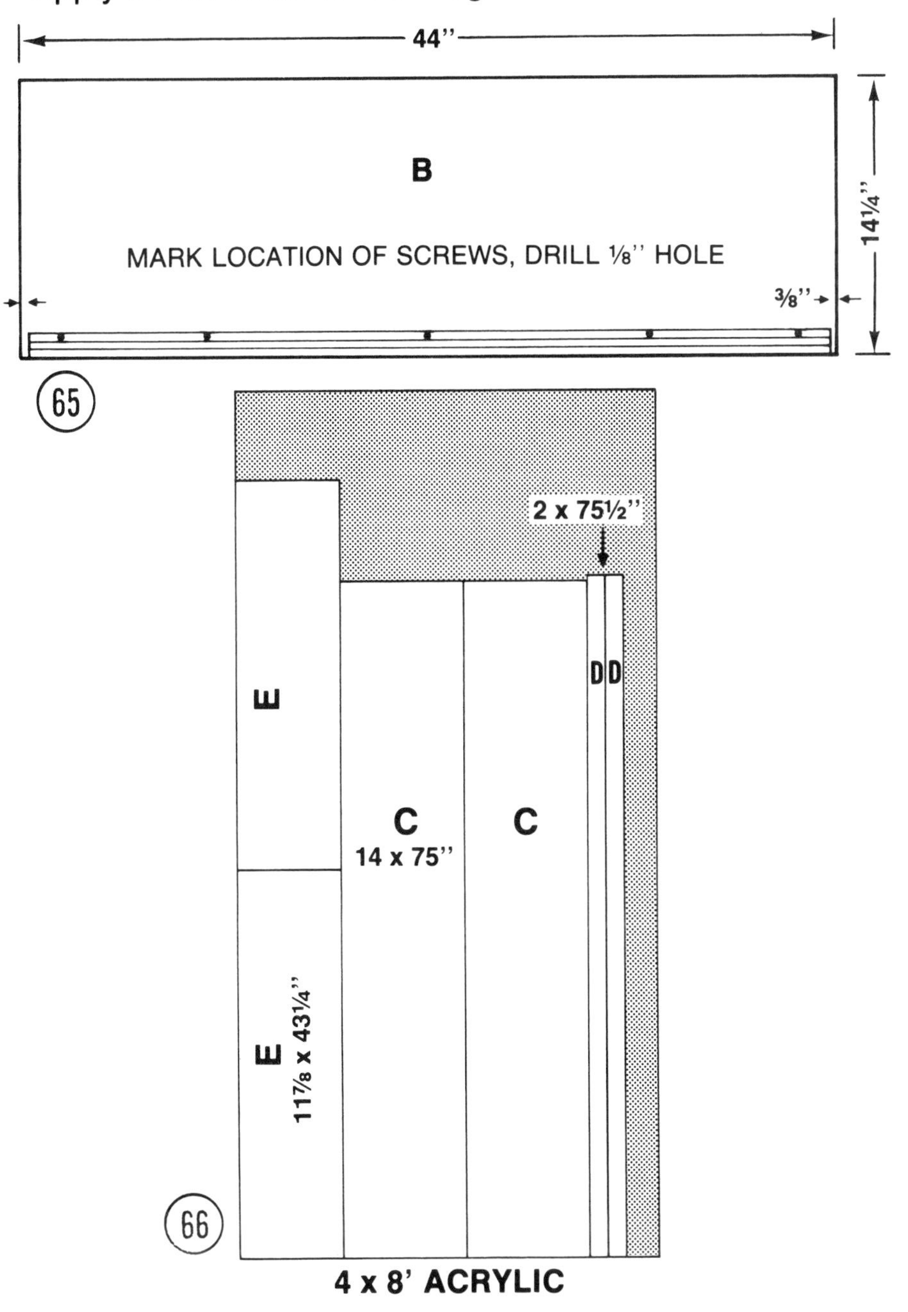

Place two 2 x 4 x 6' on plywood work table, Illus. 67.

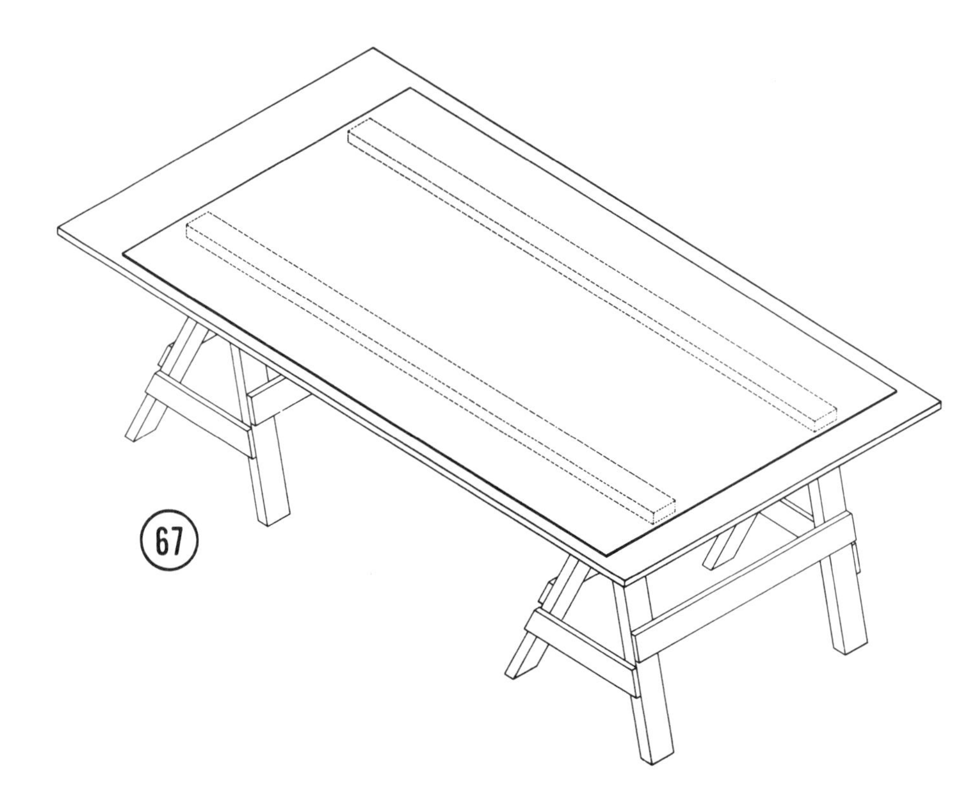

Apply a CE finish to four edges of C. Apply an EE finish to edge of B, except the 2" end butting against D. Apply a CE finish to permit bonding D to B.

After finishing edge of A, position two 6' shelf standards, 6" from edge, 3/8" up from bottom, Illus. 68. Using a square, check to make certain slots in standard are on line. Locate bolt holes in standard and mark same on masking paper. Remove standard. Drill bolt holes through A. Drill these holes 1/16" larger than shank on bolts standard manufacturer supplies.

Cut sliding door track 43½". Fasten wide track to top B flush with front edge, narrow track to bottom, Illus. 65, 69. Use ¼" No. 8-32 bolts. Drill ⅛" hole. Tap hole using 8NC32 tap.

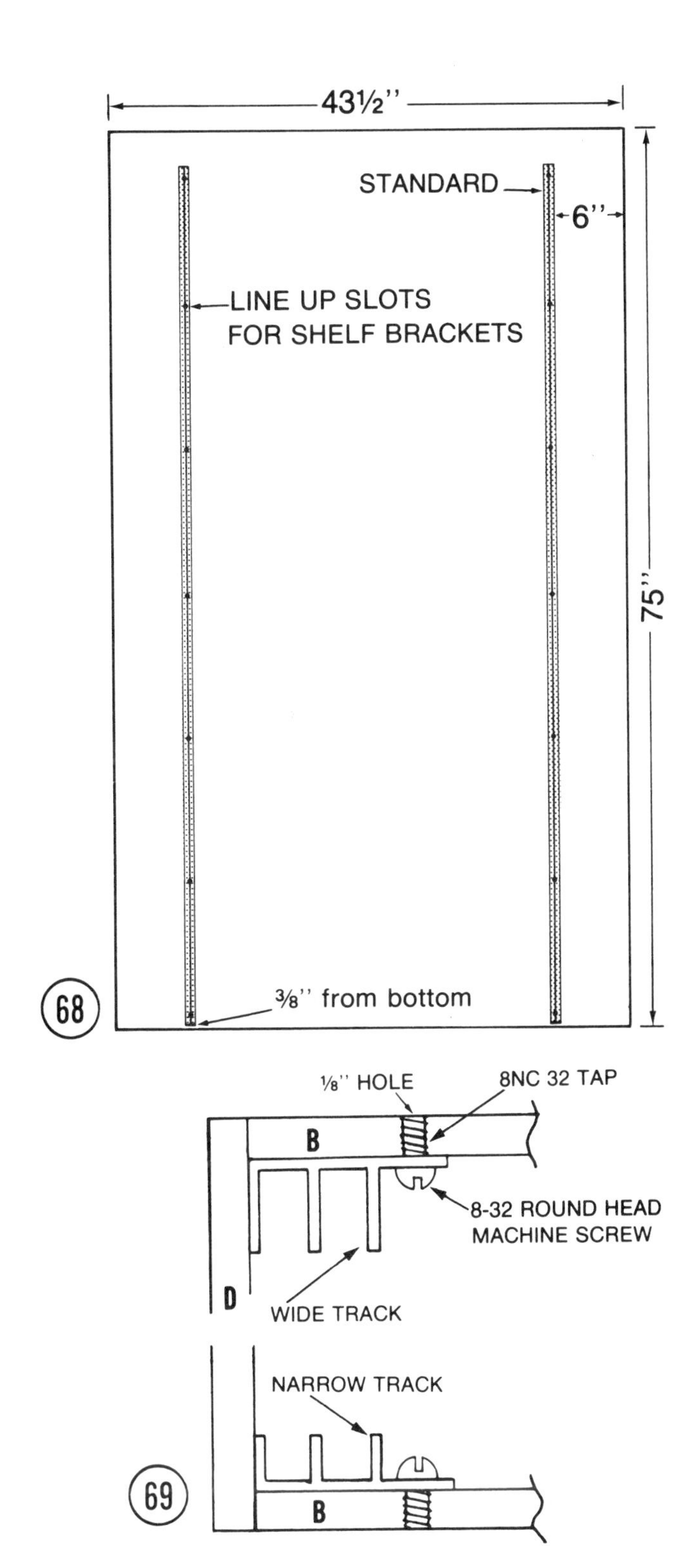
43½"
STANDARD
6"
LINE UP SLOTS
FOR SHELF BRACKETS
75"
68
⅜" from bottom
⅛" HOLE
8NC 32 TAP
B
8-32 ROUND HEAD
MACHINE SCREW
D
WIDE TRACK
NARROW TRACK
69
B

Remove masking from AC, Illus. 34. With 75" edge of A projecting over 2 x 4, and with help holding C on A, tape C to A. Then tape box supports to outside face of C. Check CA with a square, then apply solvent using needle nosed applicator, Illus. 70.

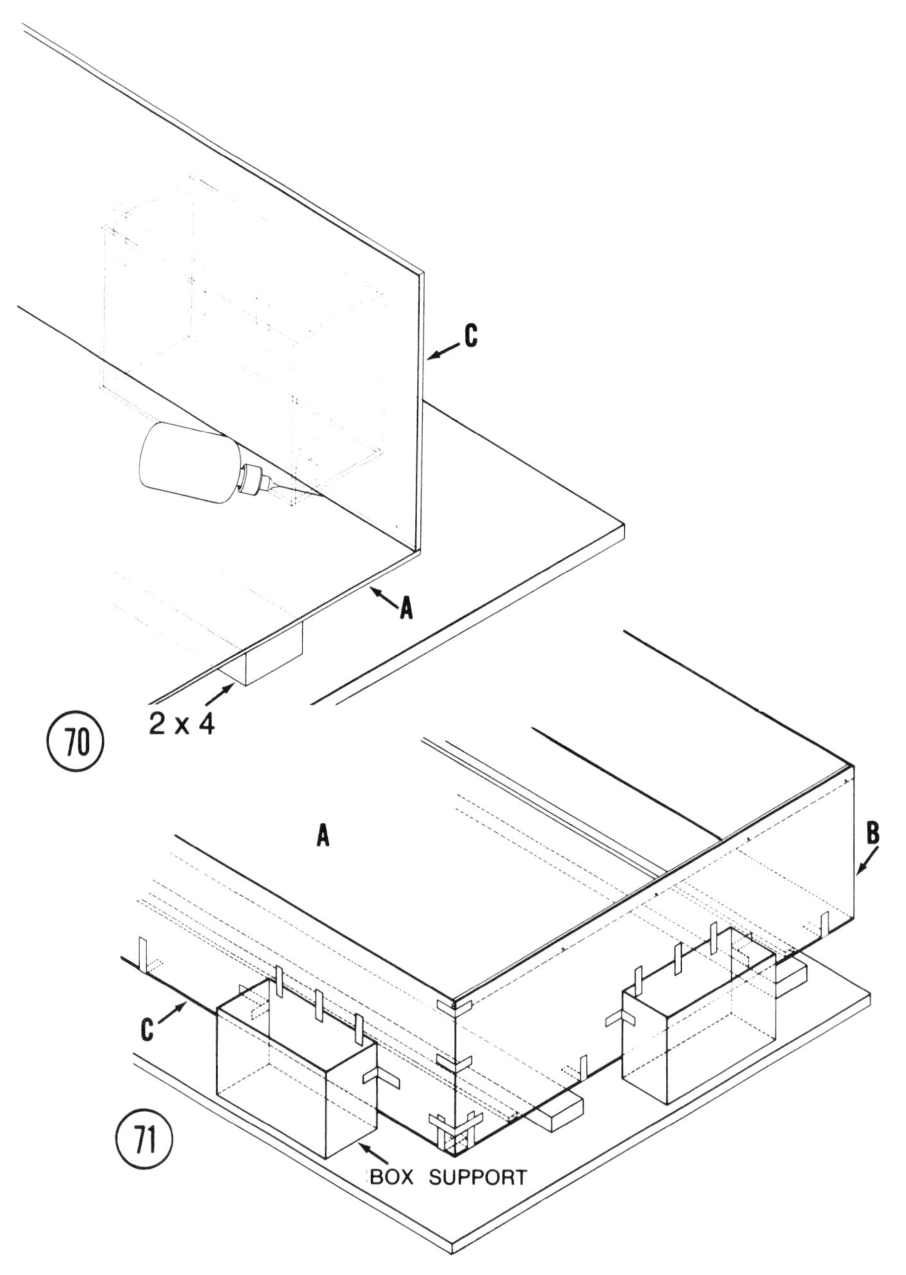

With boxes still supporting C, apply thickened cement to edge of CA and tape B to AC, Illus. 71, 72.

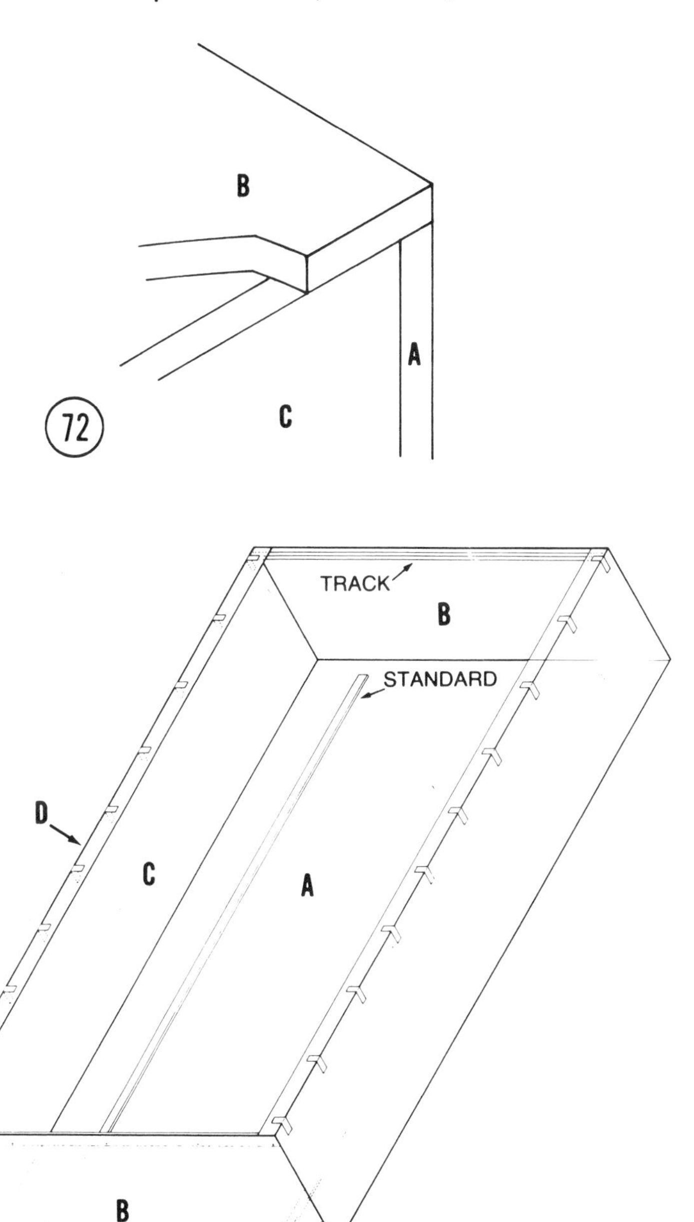

Cut two D, 2 x 75½", Illus. 66. Finish all four edges with a transparent finish. Apply thickened cement to edge of BC and tape D in place, Illus. 68,73.

When all joints have been cemented, or solvent allowed to set, remove tape, Illus. 74.

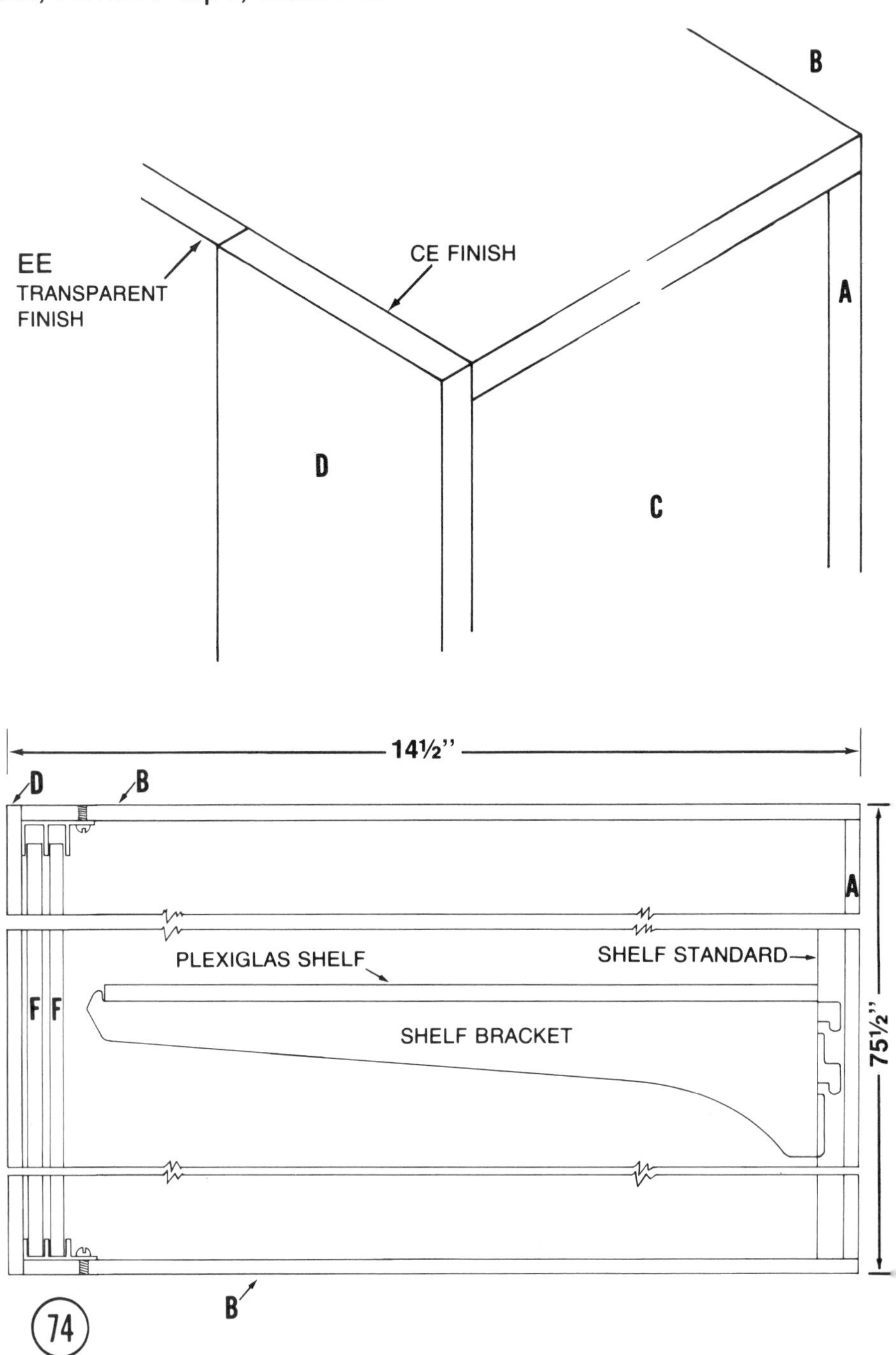

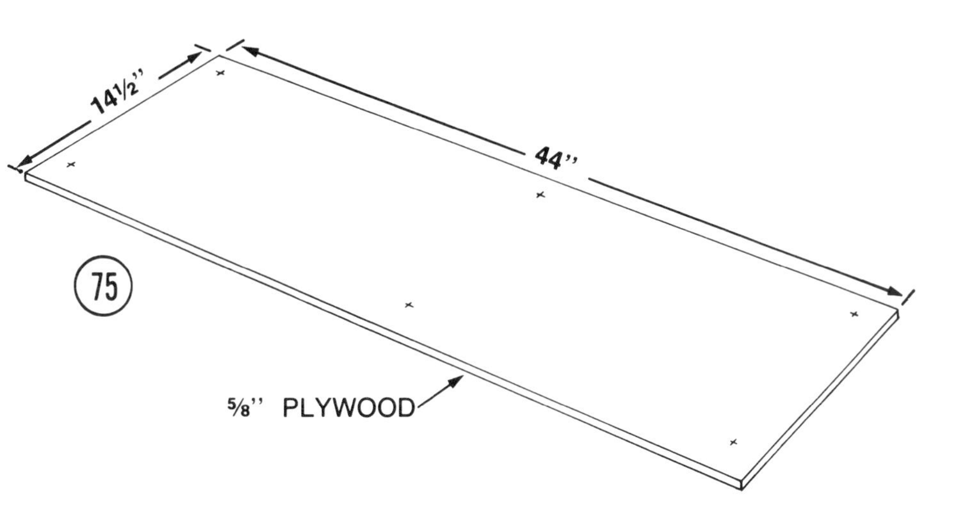

Cut plywood base, ⅝ x 14½ x 44", Illus. 75. Apply 1 x 2 stiffener, Illus. 45, if same is needed. Paint or stain base.

Apply four or six leg brackets, Illus. 76. Install legs.

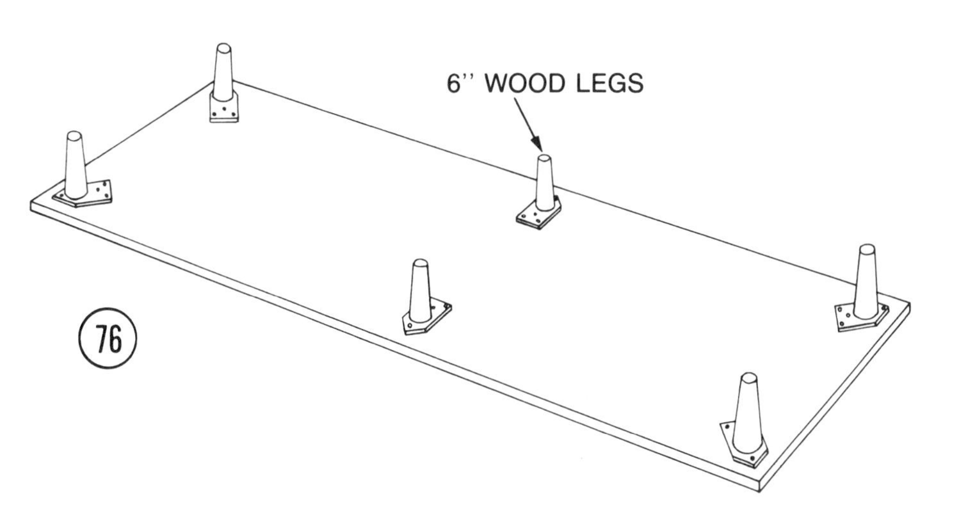

Cut doors F, Illus. 77, to size cabinet requires following directions on page 61. Finish four edges with a transparent finish. Apply door handle stiffeners if same are required.

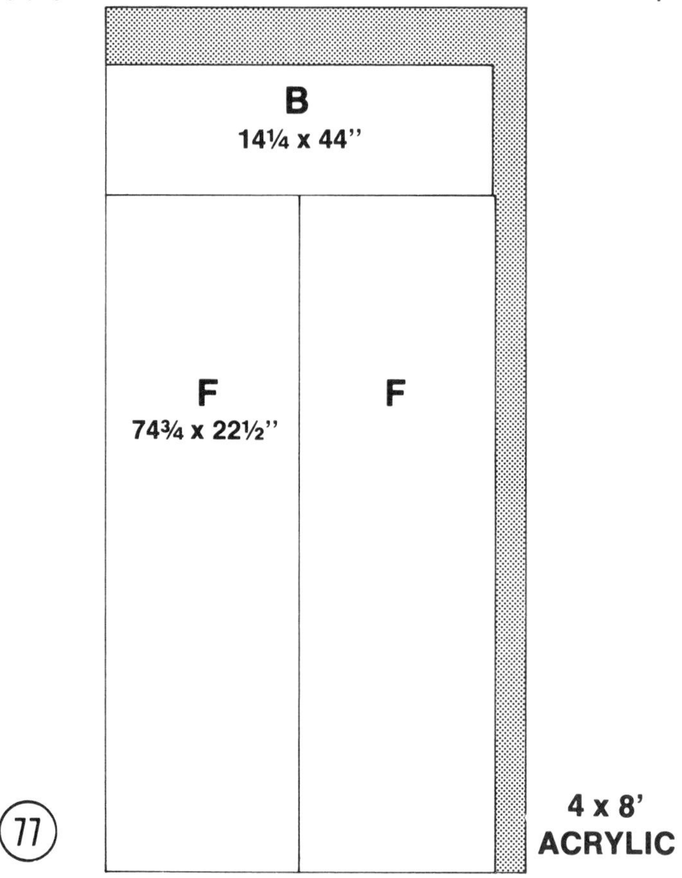

Cut shelves and shelf stiffeners, Illus. 78, to size shown, or to size required. Finish ends of shelves with a transparent finish. Bond stiffener to edge of shelf, Illus. 79, using solvent or cement. Stiffener should be positioned between shelf brackets.

Drill four 11/64" holes through bottom and base and fasten bottom to base with four ⅛ x 1⅛" No. 8-32 machine screws and nuts, Illus. 79a.

Drill a 11/64" hole through each shelf standard and fasten standard to chair rail or to studs in wall, note page 63, with 1" No. 8 round or pan head wood screws. Drill 5/64" pilot hole in chair rail.

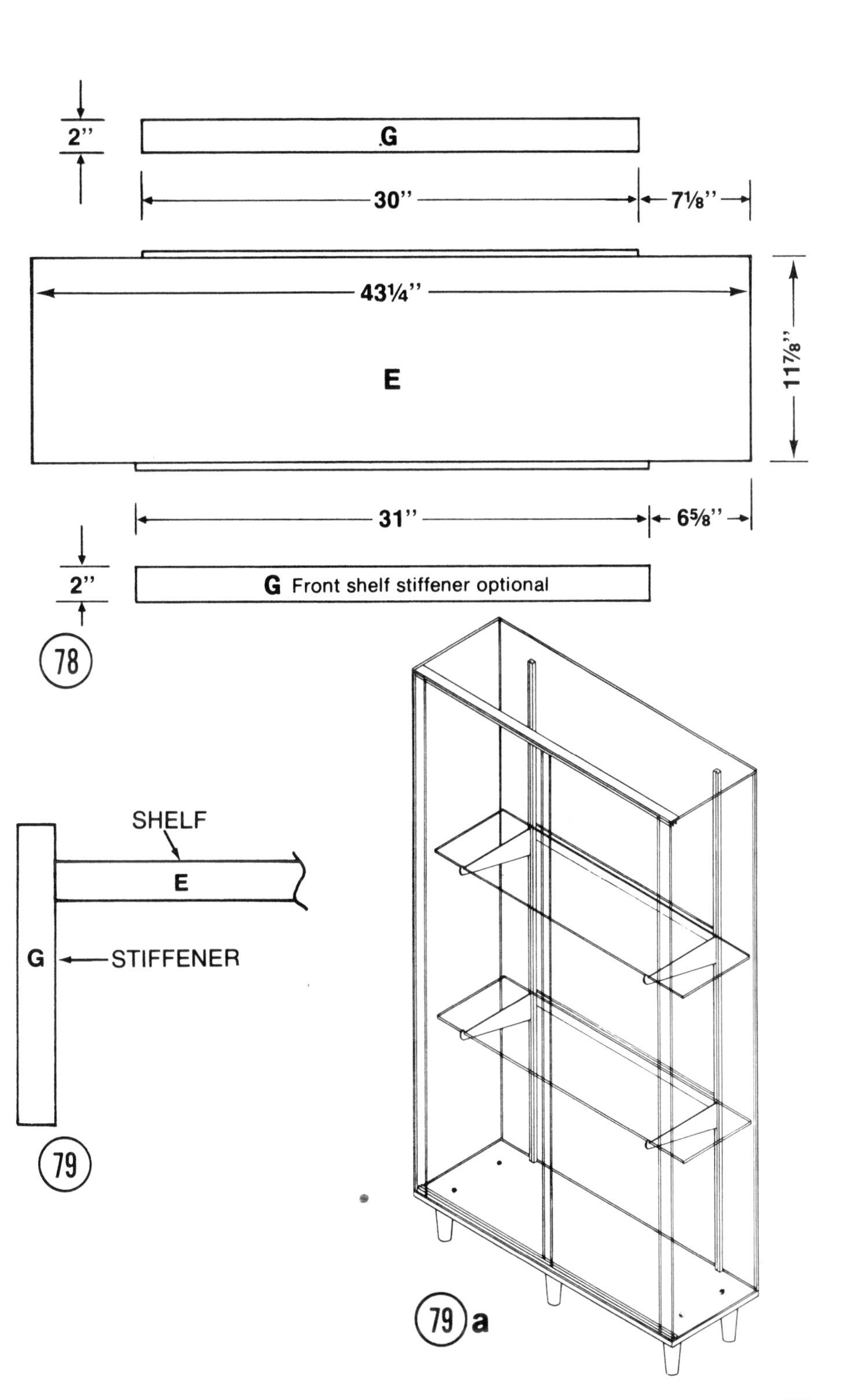
2"
G
30"
7⅛"
43¼"
E
11⅞"
31"
6⅝"
2"
G Front shelf stiffener optional
78
SHELF
E
G
STIFFENER
79
79 a

BASE CABINET

(80)

This handsome cabinet, Illus. 80, measuring 15 x 17 x 36" will complement every article. Collectors frequently position these at opposite corners of a room. The size suggested offers excellent display and storage for records, art books, silverware, a prized vase or bowl. AM-FM stereo enthusiasts find a slightly revised size ideal for equipment. Since many receivers measure 18⅝" or larger, cut back A and shelves to size required.

Directions explain how to build an open faced cabinet. If you plan on placing a statue or other heavy objet d'art on top, reinforce top with a full length stiffener under center of shelf. Always load bottom shelf with sufficient weight to hold cabinet steady.

Retailers find these cabinets extremely useful for floor and window display. Show a sample or a scale model to gift and jewelry store owners, florists, interior decorators, rare book and antique dealers, display managers of fine shops, travel agents, etc. Banks and savings and loan associations that feature free gifts to new depositors find these base cabinets, as well as the all clear 75" cabinet, an ideal way to display many of the gifts offered.

As with the collectors' display cabinets, excessively high crating and shipping costs encourage local fabrication and sale. Always offer to build any size a customer may require.

While directions explain building to 36" height, four foot or taller units can also be built. Install shelves at height required.

NOTE: Only offer to build a taller or larger unit if customer understands the need to load bottom shelf with sufficient weight to anchor and stabilize cabinet. Caution users of the 36" stand to also follow this advice. Unless base is heavily weighted, a prized possession on top shelf may not be safe. As Illus. 80 indicates, art and collectors books on bottom shelf provide ample ballast.

A cabinet measuring 15 x 17 x 36" will require:

LIST OF MATERIAL

1 — ¼" x 4 x 5' acrylic
1 — IPS Weld-On #3 Solvent
Weld-On 16 Thickened Cement

Cut all parts to size shown, Illus. 81. Cut back A, 16½ x 35¾"; top B, 15 x 17"; two sides C, 15 x 35¾"; two shelves D, 14¾ x 16½"; two stiffeners E, 1 x 16½"; one stiffener F, 2 x 16½"; four shelf supports G, 1 x 14¼"; two shelf supports H, 1 x 16½".

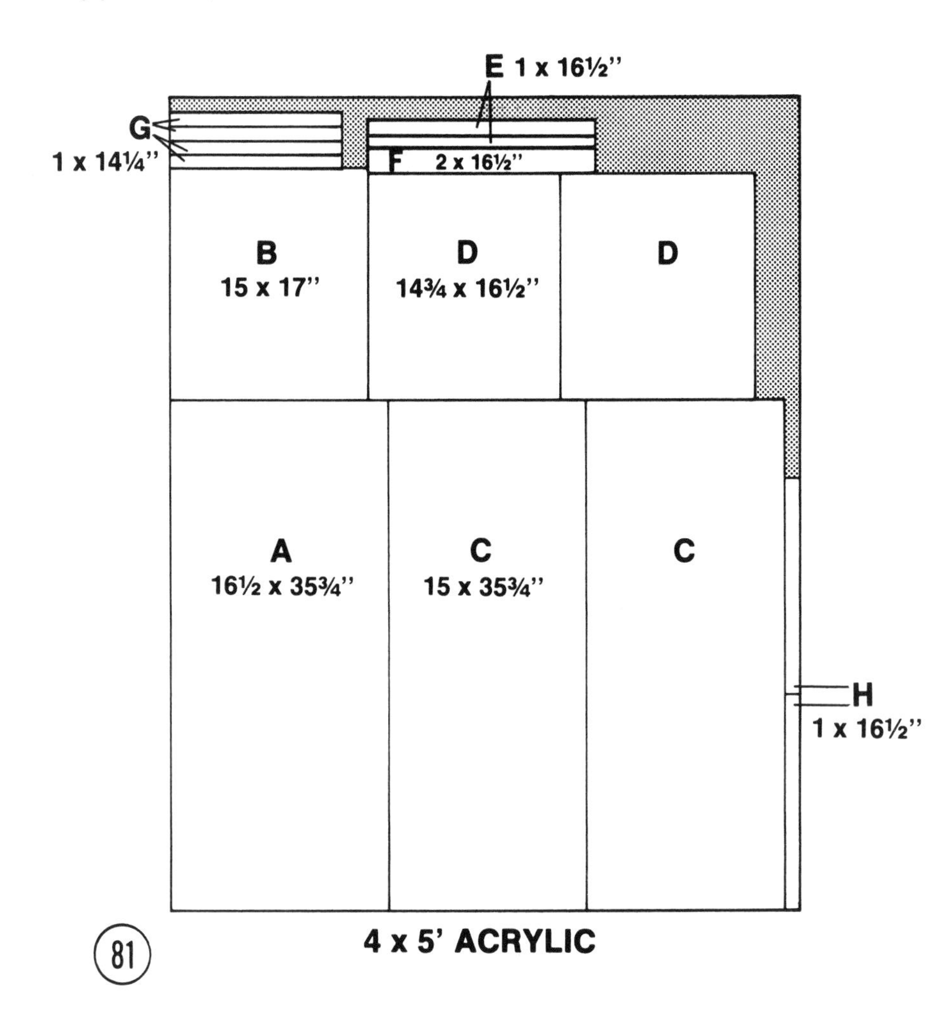

4 x 5' ACRYLIC

Building this cabinet not only requires cutting parts to size required, but also keeping all edges square. Finish those to be bonded with a CE edge; all exposed edges should be buffed to a transparent (EE) finish. After applying a thin ribbon of thickened cement, spread it evenly with a spatula. After applying cement or solvent, allow parts to remain undisturbed following manufacturer's directions.

Cut one A to size specified, Illus. 81. Finish all four edges with a CE finish (60-80, 220-320).

As all four edges of B are exposed, sand and buff to an EE finish (60-80, 220-320, 400-500, plus Disco buffer).

The 35¾" edges of C should be buffed to an EE finish; the 15" edge to a CE finish.

The four edges of shelf D can be buffed to an EE finish.

One 16½" edge of E, and both ends, should be finished with a CE edge. Buff exposed edge to an EE finish.

Bonding all parts with cement simplifies assembly. Use Daybond or IPS Weld-On #16 as manufacturer specifies. Before removing masking, tape parts in position. Inspect to make certain edges are square.

After removing masking, apply a narrow bead of cement to CE edge of E and tape it to B, ¼" from edge, Illus. 82. Or you can bond E to B with solvent, Illus. 30. Fasten E to middle shelf.

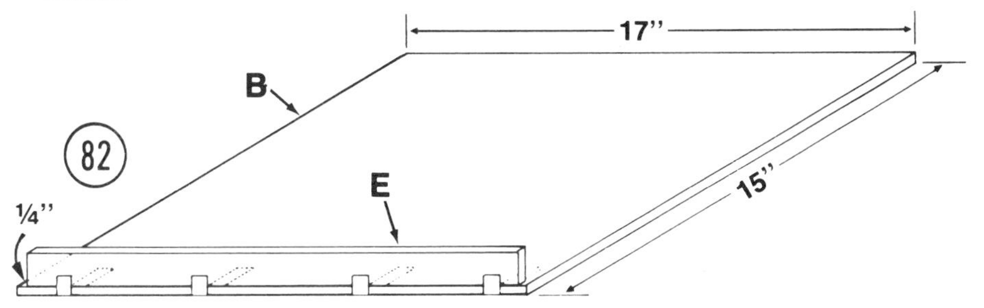

Bond stiffener F to bottom shelf D, Illus. 83. Bond stiffener E to middle shelf.

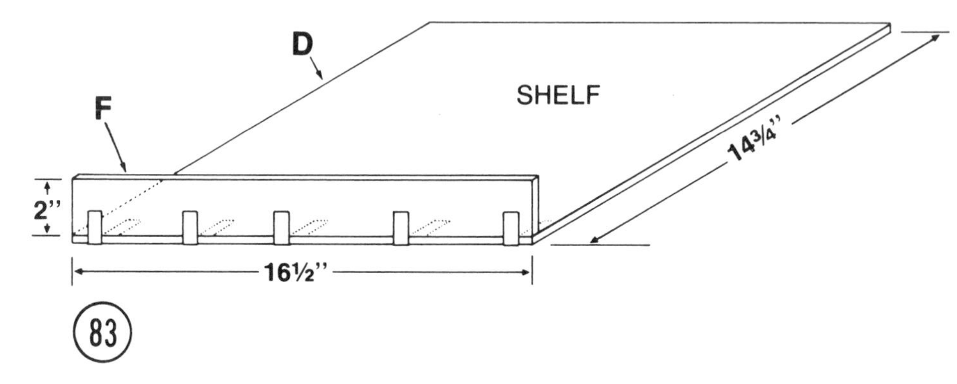

As previously cautioned, always use cement and solvent in a well ventilated area. Allow cemented parts to remain undisturbed for two hours or time directions specify. Under no circumstances inhale fumes. Keep cements and solvents away from flame, children and animals.

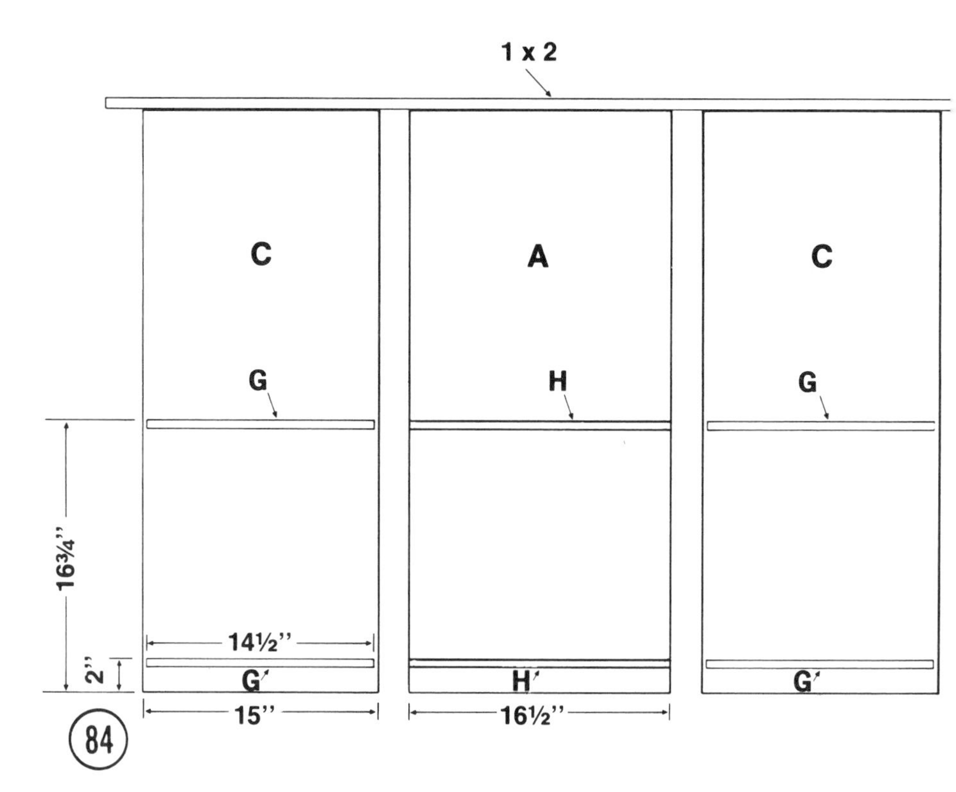

Bond 1 x 16½" shelf support H to A; 1 x 14¼" support G to C. Use a scrap piece of ¼" acrylic to space G proper distance from front edge; ½" from back edge of C. Keep top edge of GH on line, 16¾" up, Illus. 84.

NOTE: G is recessed ¼" from front edge of C and butts against H. Cut G and H to length A and C require.

Using a spatula, spread a thin coating of thickened cement to top edge of A. Place top edge of A against B, Illus. 85. Tape and support A in position. A is recessed ¼" from edge of B, Illus. 86. Check AB with a square. Support A by adding books to box support. Allow AB to remain undisturbed two hours or length of time cement manufacturer specifies.

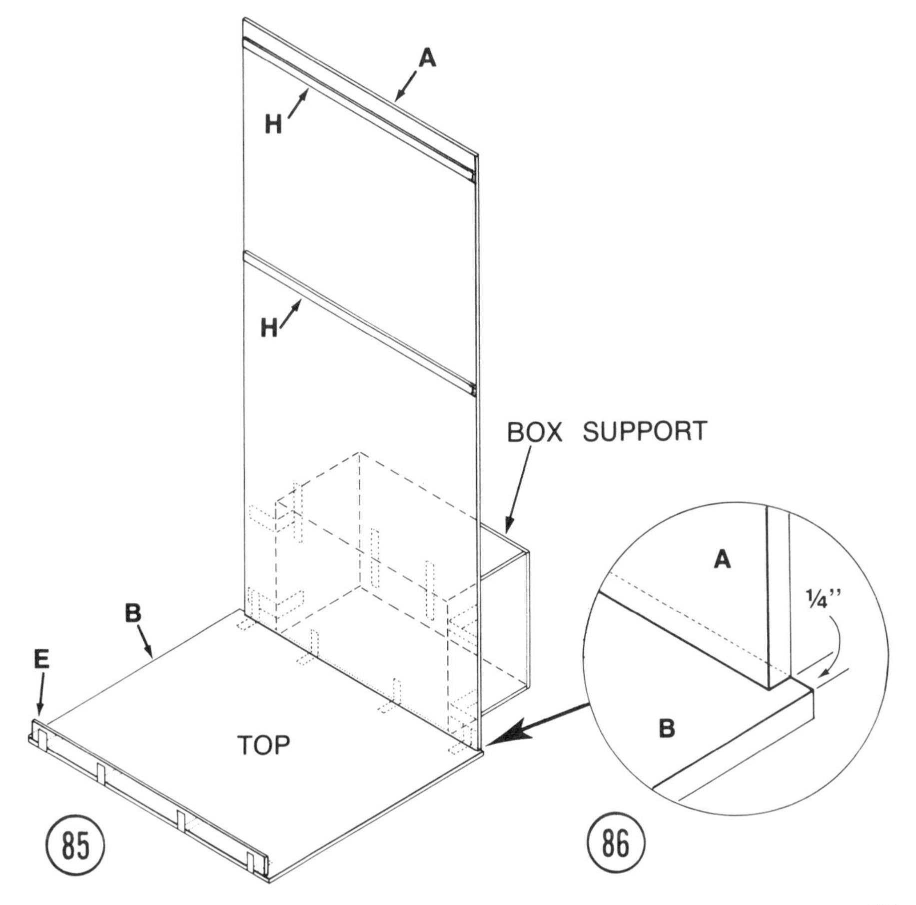

Apply cement to top edge of C and to edge of A. With box supports holding C square and plumb, Illus. 87, bond C to edge of A and to bottom of B, Illus. 88.

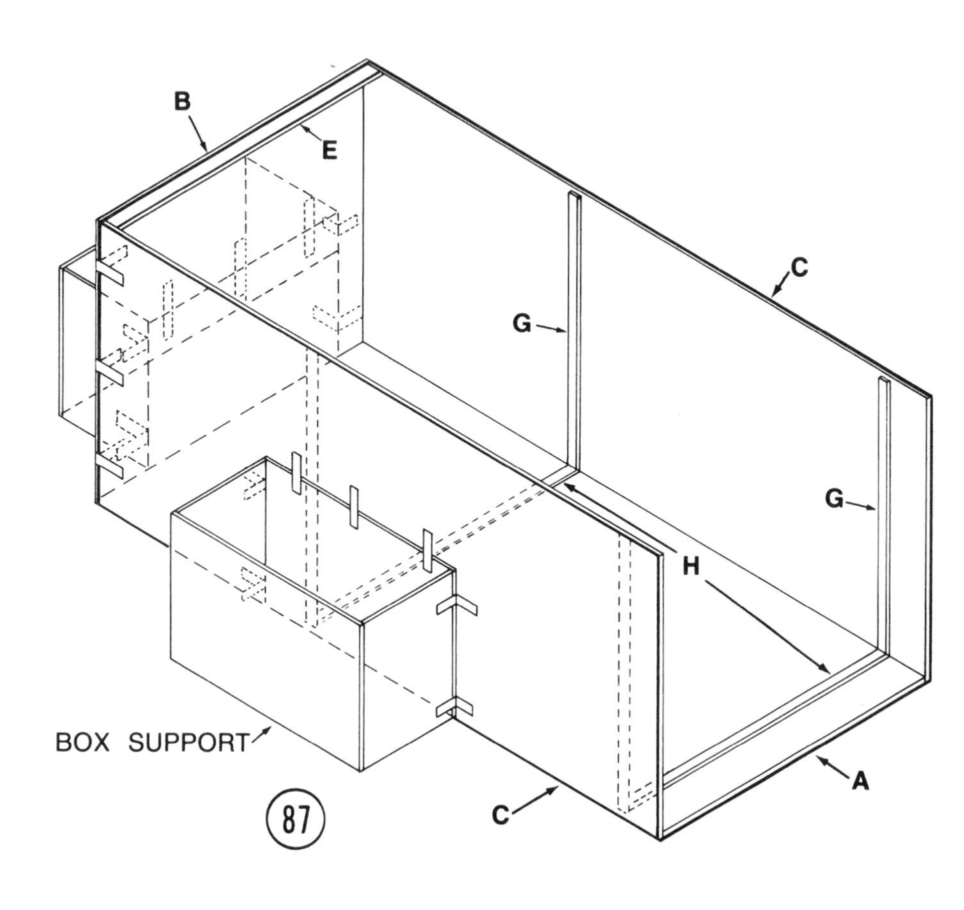

Bond shelves DE and DF to GH. Bond ends of E and F to C, Illus. 88.

If you plan on loading shelves, install a 2" stiffener FF across center of bottom shelf, and a 1" stiffener GG under middle shelf. Notch ends of 2" stiffener to receive G, Illus. 89.

NOTE: To avoid cutting parts inaccurately, check overall length of D,E,F,G,H after cutting A and C.

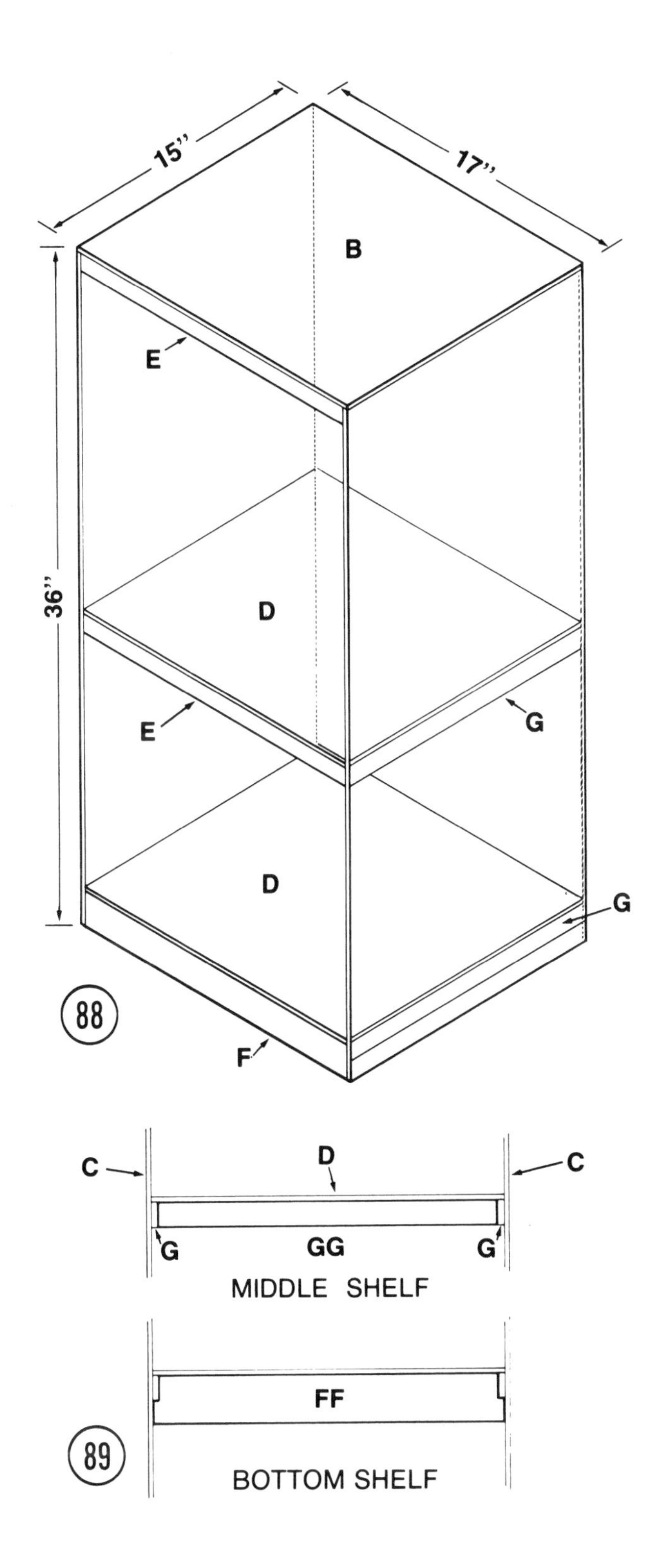
15''
17''
B
E
36''
D
E
G
D
G
88
F
C
D
C
G
GG
G
MIDDLE SHELF
FF
89
BOTTOM SHELF

INDIVIDUAL SHOWCASES

Display fine crystal, a vase, antique clock, tin toys, collectors books, doll or statue in a showcase, Illus. 90,91,92, and you create a handsome, dustproof decoration. When estimating overall size, allow 1½ to 2'' clearance at top, a minimum of 2'' at sides.

90

A table or cabinet top showcase can be made up to 24'' in height using ⅛'' acrylic. Museums use 3/16 or ¼'' thickness. Always buff edge of top and all exposed edges to a transparent (EE) finish.

Considerable savings in material costs can be effected if you can buy shorts. Shop around and you may find a source with an abundance of small pieces ideally suited for every size showcase.

91

92

The case shown, Illus. 91,93, measuring 9 3/16 x 7⅛ x 12", was made from 3/16" acrylic. The base, cut from cedar or pine, measures 5/4 x 8¾ x 13¾", Illus. 94.

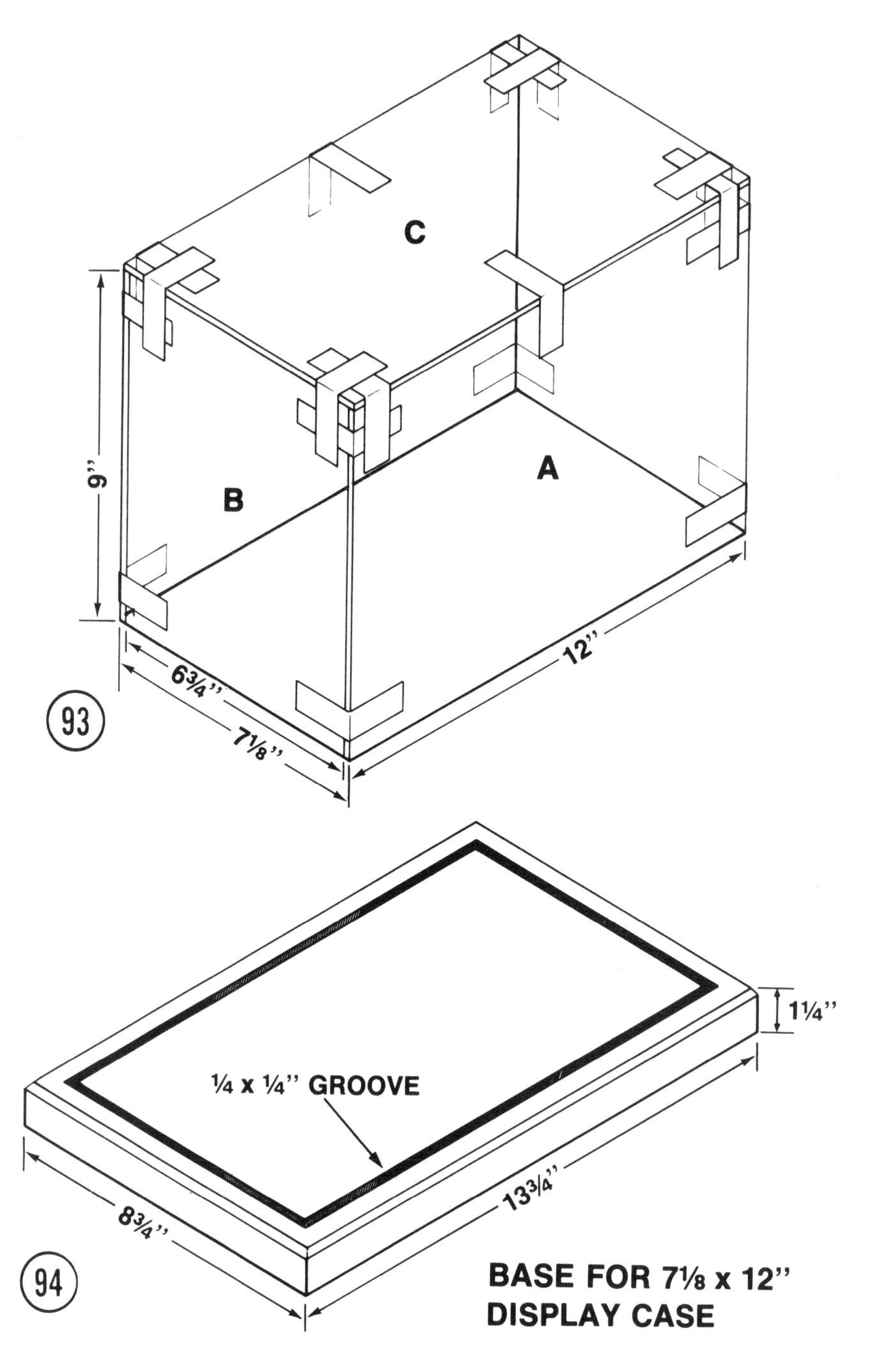

When 3/16" acrylic is used, cut A, Illus. 95, 9 x 12"; B - 6¾ x 9". Finish edges of B with a CE edge. Cut top C, 7⅛ x 12". Buff four edges of C to a transparent (EE) finish. If you use solvent, tape A to B, C to AB, Illus. 93. Place parts in horizontal position, Illus. 30, if you use solvent or parts can be joined with thickened cement.

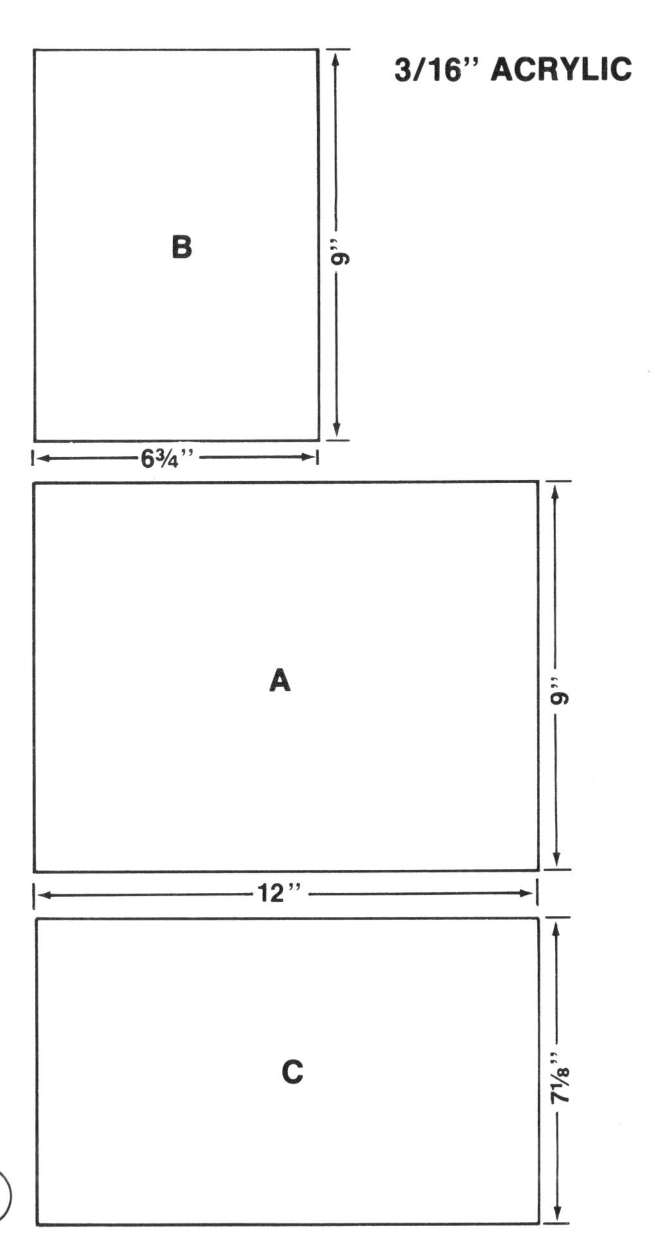

Place assembled showcase on base and draw outline. Use a router bit same size as or 1/16" larger than thickness of acrylic.

Set router guide so bit routs ¼" deep slot, Illus. 96.

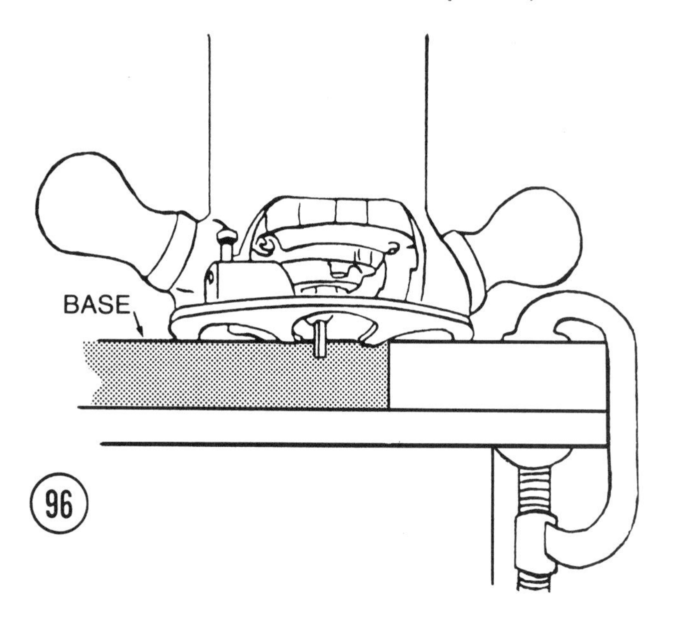

Bevel outer edge of base to a 45 or 50° angle, Illus. 97.

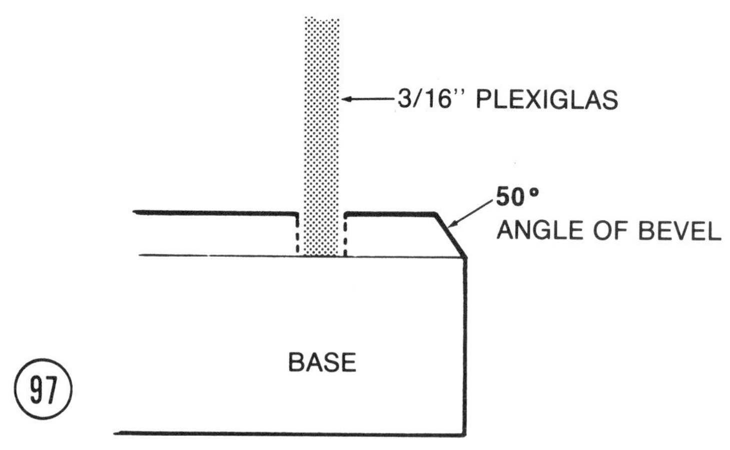

Finish base by sanding, staining or with an application of polyurethane. Use a finish that complements table or cabinet where it will be placed. Glue a piece of felt to bottom of base.

When enclosing a single doll, Illus. 90, glue stand holding figure to a piece of 1/8" hardboard, cut to size that fills showcase.

Allow 1½ to 2" clear space at top and sides when estimating overall size of enclosure.

Illus. 98 shows typical parts needed for a single figure display case. Apply a CE finish to four edges of 6⅞" ends; to top of 7⅛" sides. Apply an EE finish to 22" edge of sides and to four edges of top.

1/8" ACRYLIC

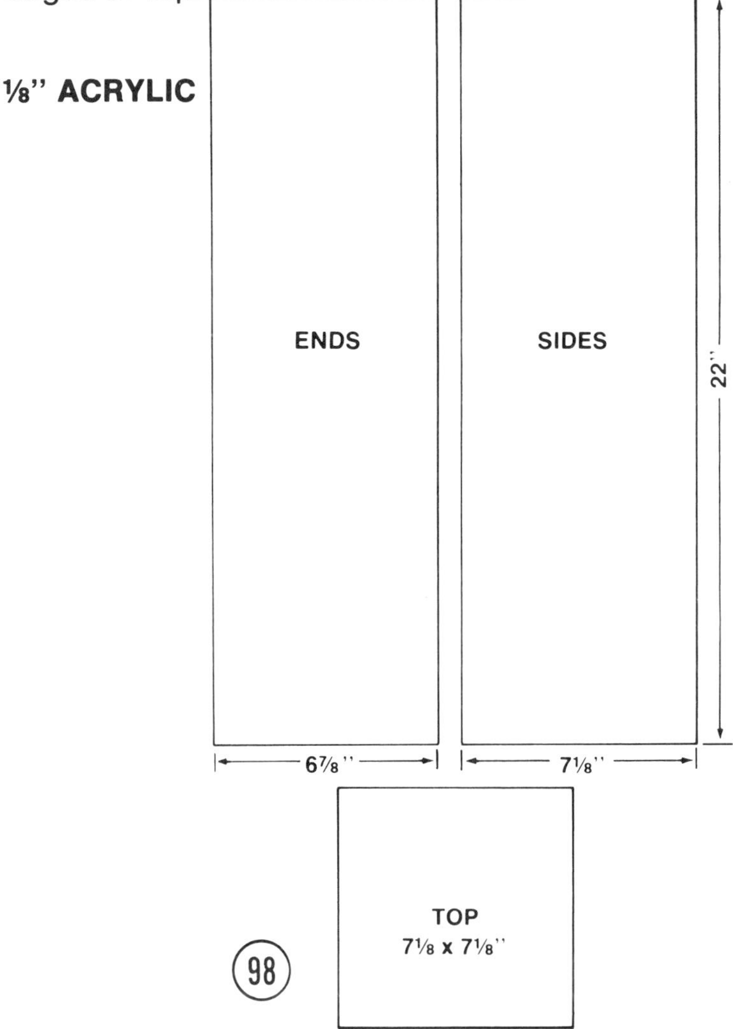

If you plan on installing a turntable, Illus. 101, before removing masking paper, drill two ¾" holes in one 7⅛" side, Illus. 99, then saw or file opening to shape shown in exact position switch on turntable requires.

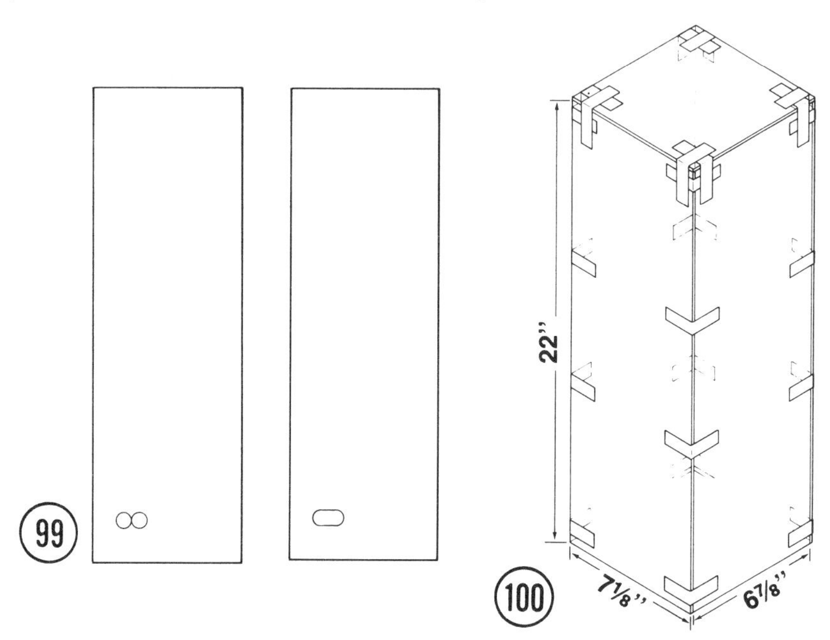

Apply thickened cement to 22" edge of the 6⅞" panel. Tape panels together, Illus. 100. Apply thickened cement to top edge and tape top in place.

When displaying carved figures, animals, birds or other objects that may shift position when the case is moved, consider anchoring these to a base, a piece of acrylic or ⅛" hardboard. Apply glue or tie figure down with a fine wire and a brad.

If you want to create an outdoor scene, place and mark location of each figure, then remove same. Carefully spread a thin coating of white glue over area where you want soil, shrubbery, rocks, trees, etc. Sift soil through a fine screen and sprinkle on the wet glue. For a winter scene, spray trees and shrubbery with glue and sprinkle artificial snow. Anchor figures in position.

ADD A TURNTABLE

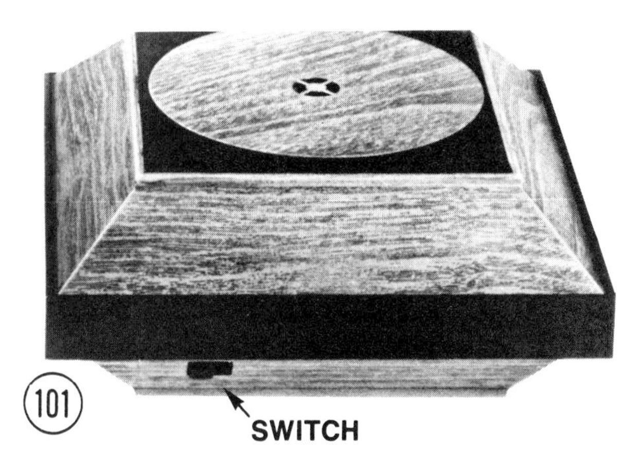

(101)

If you build for store or museum display, consider adding a battery powered turntable, Illus. 101. This low cost unit adds considerable appeal. Turning at a speed of three revolutions per minute, the disc, riding on ball bearings, will support a load up to 8 pounds. Quiet in operation, it creates considerable attention.

When operated eight hours a day, the two flashlight batteries will run the turntable for over three months.

To create a memory a child will never forget, build a showcase for a new doll. Place it over a turntable. Set up a camera so you can take a once in a lifetime shot. Before the child wakes, switch on turntable. Title picture PURE JOY.

Measuring 6½ x 6½", the turntable will fit enclosure shown, Illus. 90,98.

THE SHOWCASE

All through life we choose what we like, and buy what we can afford. As the years flash by, much of what we possess increases in value. Storing fine china, silverware, steins, a collection of wine or water glasses out of sight negates the vibrations that inspired purchase. The same holds true of gifts received and treasured. When they are displayed in an acrylic cabinet, you not only provide safe storage and easy access, but also enjoy the pleasure of its company.

Two handsome cabinets can be constructed. The wall cabinet, Illus. 102, provides open shelving for glassware, cups, plates or a combination of both.

When shelves on a standing cabinet are cut to width articles require, it makes an attractive showcase. Alter size of shelf to fit a stereo, bookcases, etc. When used as a bar fixture, build to dimensions suggested.

When the showcase is built for store display, use black or bronze acrylic. This creates a dramatic display for linens, towels, glassware, china, clocks, jewelry, bar supplies, gourmet foods, perfumes, cosmetics, etc. Every druggist, doctor, dentist and self employed sales agent of specialty products find these cabinets handy for the storage or display of needed samples and inventory.

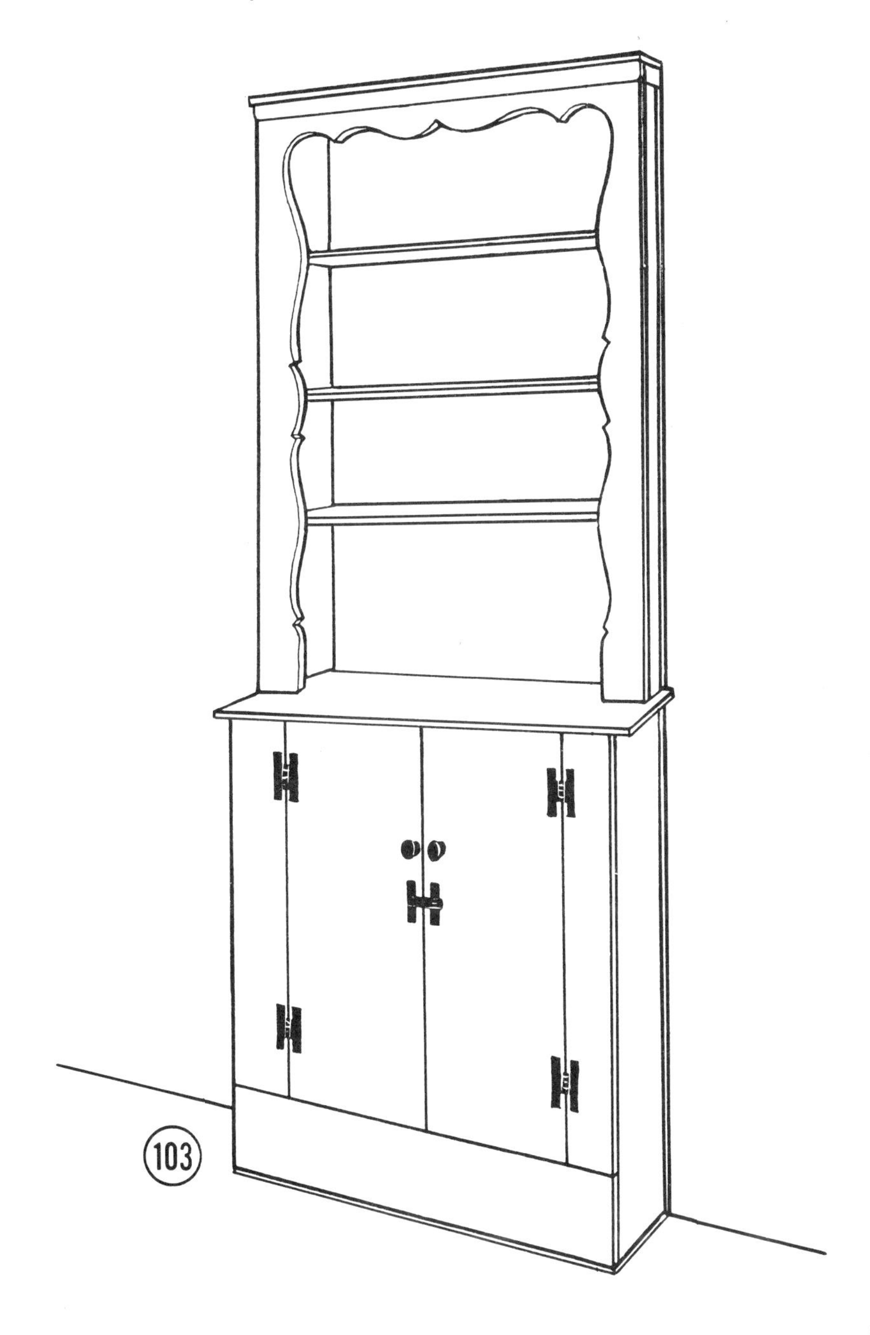

Everyone faced with a major home improvement, i.e., installing an extra bathroom or lavatory, or making repairs to an existing one, experience a sinking spell when they see a plastered wall ripped open so supply, waste and heating lines can be installed or repaired. With skilled plasterers in short supply, replastering a wall frequently runs into big money.

Building a cabinet from floor to ceiling or door trim height offers a low cost solution.

Covering up badly damaged plaster with a cabinet, built to height required, offers excellent display space.

Use black or colored acrylic over damaged area. If you prefer clear, cut a piece of wallpaper to exact size of back. Be sure pattern matches adjacent design. Using a clear silicone cement, tack wallpaper to back. This holds paper in position until cabinet can be fastened to studs in wall.

The cutting chart, Illus. 105, and material list, permit cutting top #1, one inch wider than 4" shelves and sides. If you alter width of shelf and side, the top should still be cut 1" wider. Use a 1 x 6 to cut a 4" shelf. While this width is ideal for miniatures, plates on edge, etc., the dolls shown in the recessed cabinet on page 14 require a 10" shelf. Step-by-step directions and cutting chart explain building cabinet with ¼" acrylic.

LIST OF MATERIAL
1 — ¼ x 40 x 40" bronze, black, clear or color selected
1 — ⅛ x 30 x 39" back

Cut all parts, except back, from ¼" acrylic, Illus. 105. Cut back from ⅛", Illus. 106.

Parts #4 and #5 can be cut to shape shown or applied with a straight edge. Most dentists, doctors and other professionals prefer this cabinet with a straight edge. After cutting to size specified, apply an EE finish to all exposed edges.

Bottom shelf optional when used with base cabinet, Illus. 131.

NOTE: Those building the base and wall cabinet, Illus. 103, should cut a panel of ⅛" to overall size back requires.

For a recessed cabinet, use plywood or lumber S4S. Use 1 x 4, 1 x 6, 1 x 8 or 1 x 12" cut to width shelves, side and top require. Always cut top 1" wider than width of shelves.

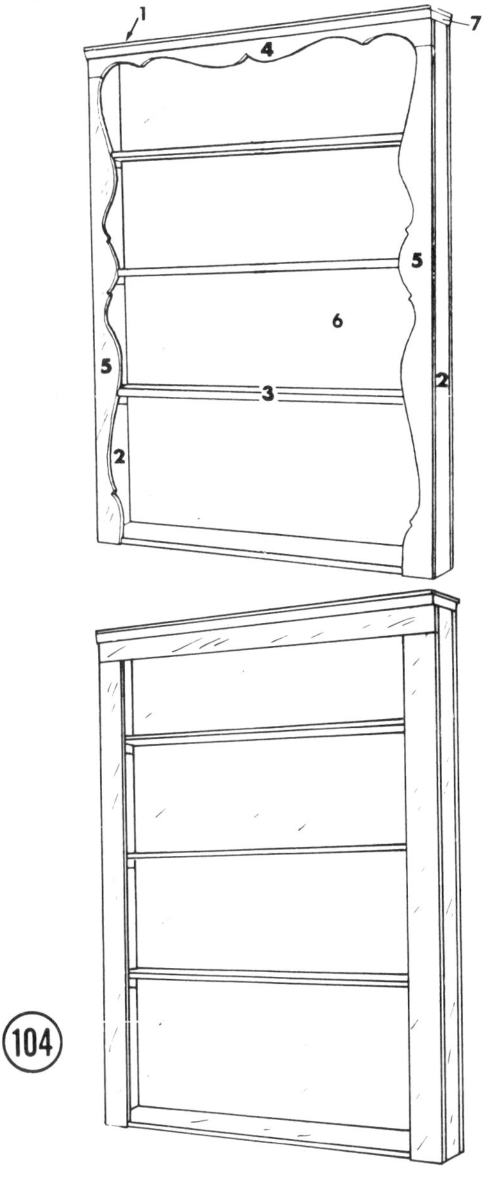

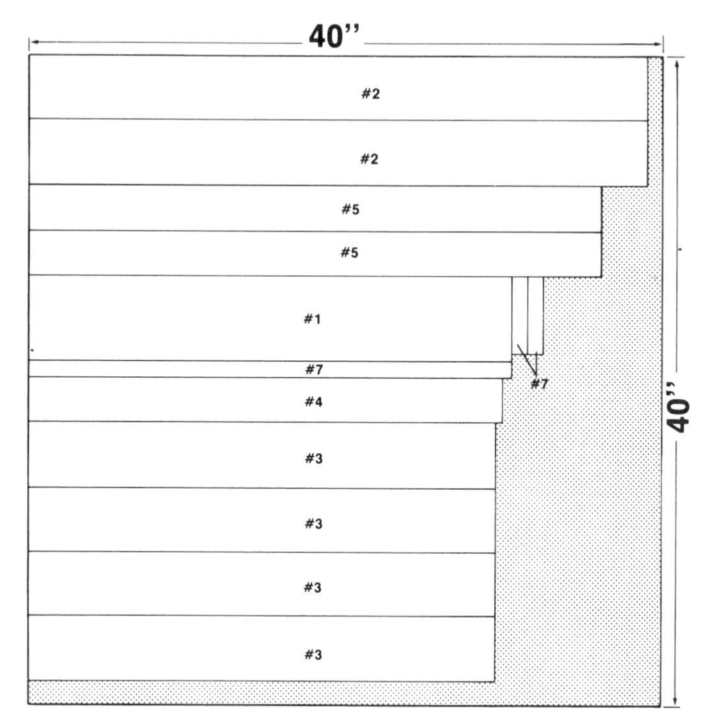

¼" ACRYLIC

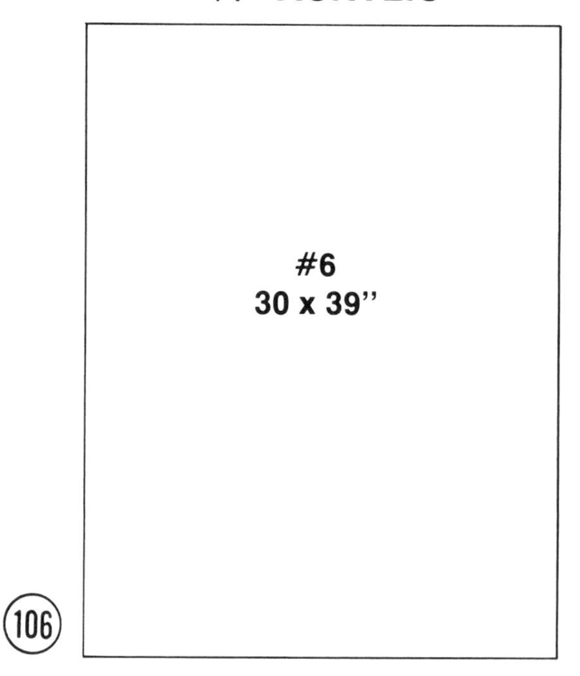

⅛" ACRYLIC

Cut top #1, Illus. 107, 5 x 31''. This allows #1 to project ¼'' over #7 at ends and front.

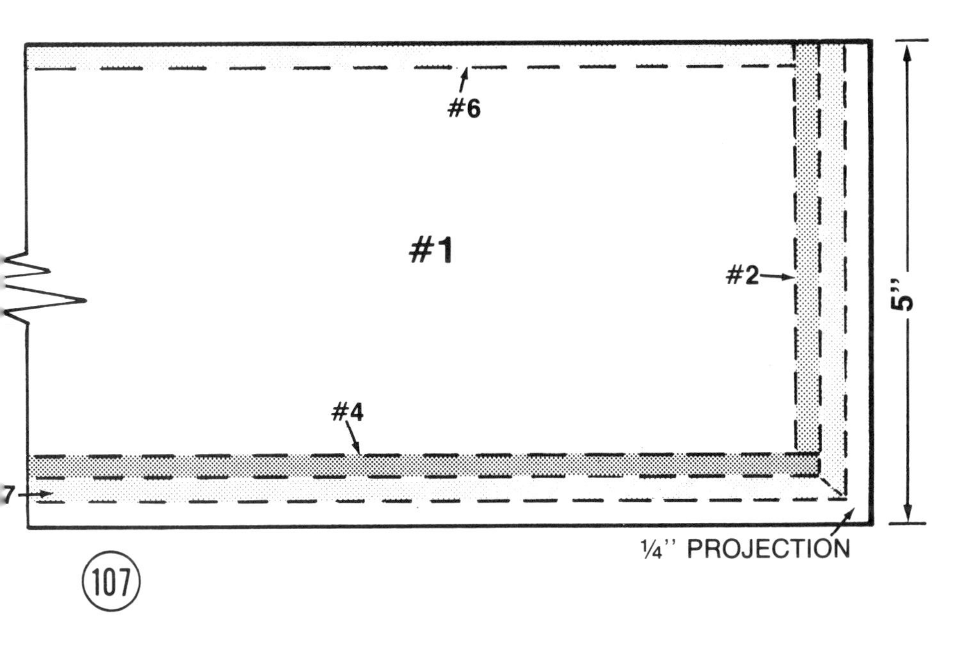

Round front edge and two ends to a transparent (EE) finish, Illus. 108.

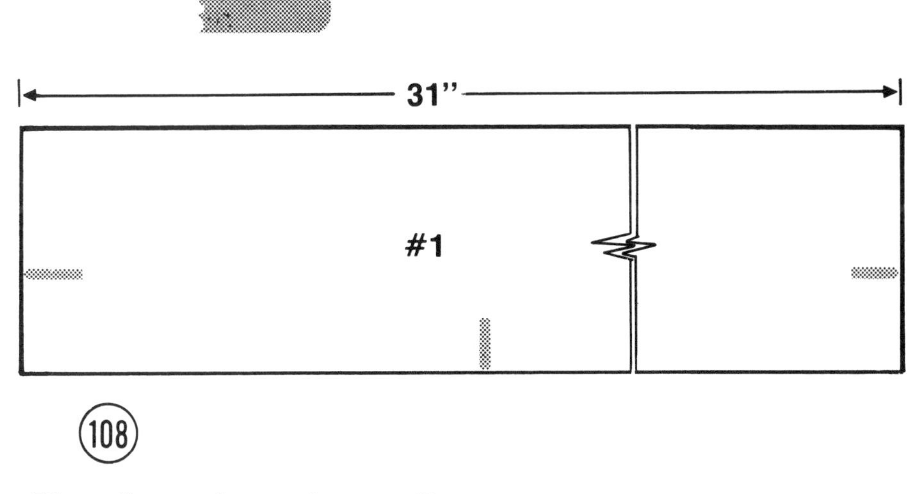

The dimensions shown, Illus. 107, 108, 109, 110, 111, permit building a showcase with 4'' wide shelves. A recessed cabinet on page 14 requires a wider shelf.

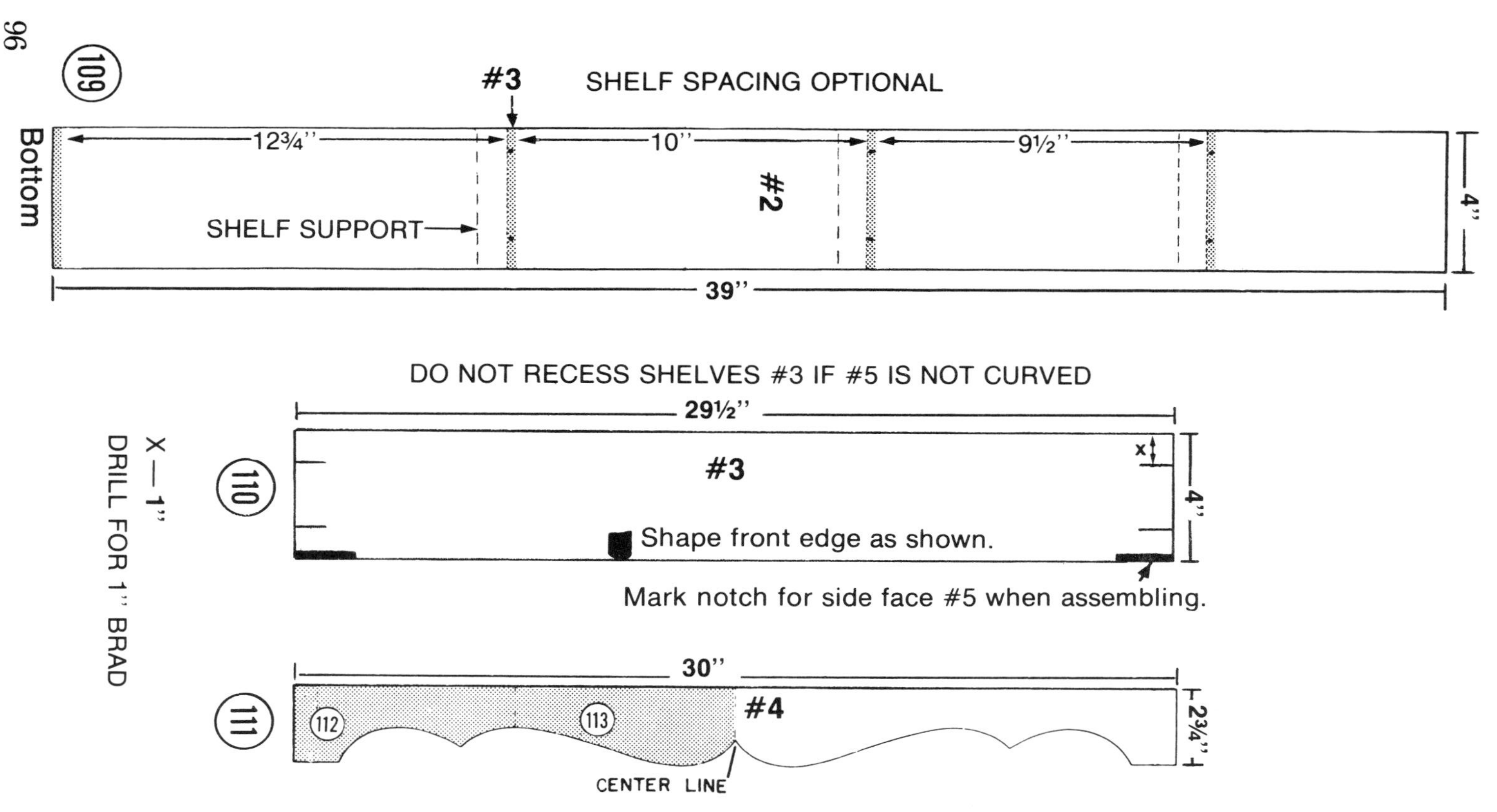
109
#3
SHELF SPACING OPTIONAL
Bottom
12¾''
10''
9½''
#2
SHELF SUPPORT
4''
39''
DO NOT RECESS SHELVES #3 IF #5 IS NOT CURVED
29½''
110
#3
x
4''
Shape front edge as shown.
Mark notch for side face #5 when assembling.
X — 1''
DRILL FOR 1'' BRAD
30''
111
112
113
#4
2¾''
CENTER LINE
Shaded area indicates section of full size pattern supplied.

Cut two sides #2, ¼ x 4 x 39", Illus. 109. Apply a CE finish to all edges.

Cut four shelves #3, ¼ x 4 x 29½", Illus. 110. Apply a CE finish to back edge and ends. Do not shape front edge or notch ends at this time.

Cut one top face #4, Illus. 111, ¼ x 2¾ x 30". Illus. 112 and 113 provide a full size pattern for one half. Join at T. Trace one half. Flop it over and trace other half. Use a coping saw with a spiral, metal cutting blade or a saber saw with a green blade, Illus. 15. Apply an EE finish to curved areas and to ends; a CE finish on edge where #4 butts against #5; also on top edge where #4 butts #1.

Parts #4 and #5 can also be cut to shape shown using a metal cutting compass or keyhole saw; or with a spiral, metal cutting, hacksaw blade. First use the blade on scrap. Keep it free of shavings. If the blade fills, clean it with acetone available in drug stores.

Cut two side facing #5 to shape shown, Illus. 114, and to length required. Using carbon paper, trace outline of each pattern, Illus. 115,116,117,118,119, in position shown, Illus. 120, on a sheet of paper. Cut to shape, then trace pattern on masking paper. Apply a CE finish to top end where #5 butts against #4. Apply an EE finish to curved edge and to exposed 36" edge.

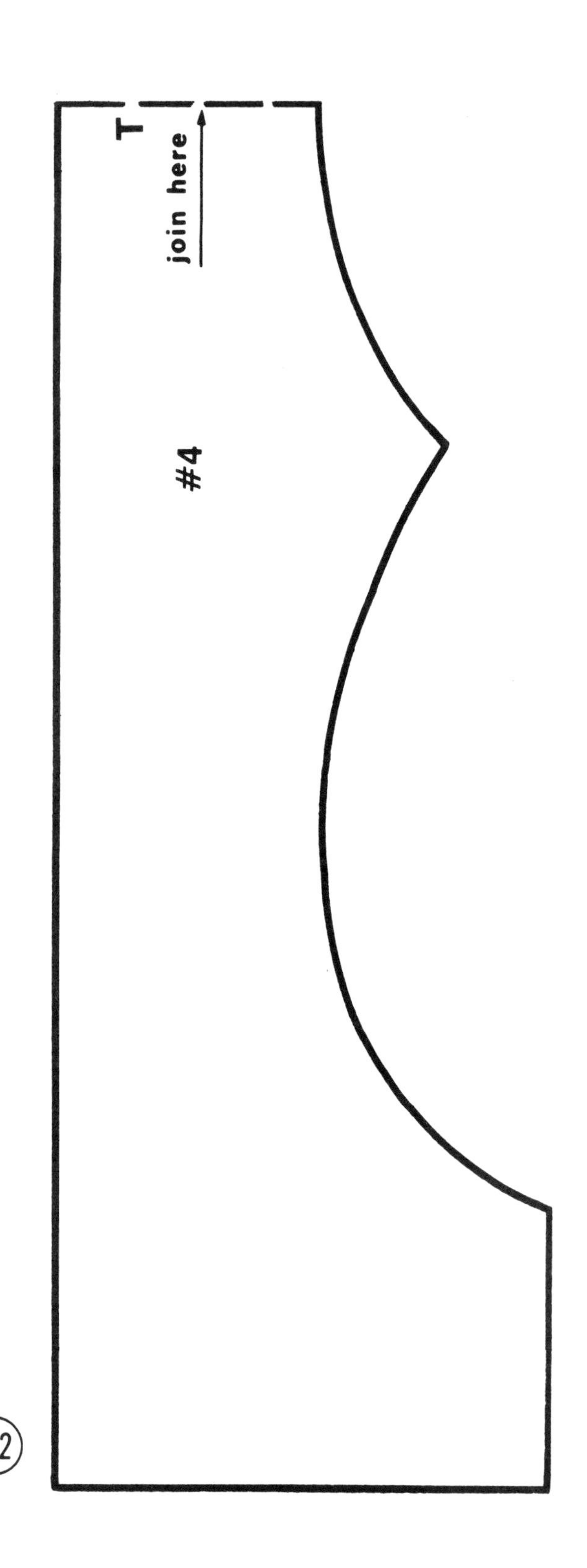
T
join here
#4
112

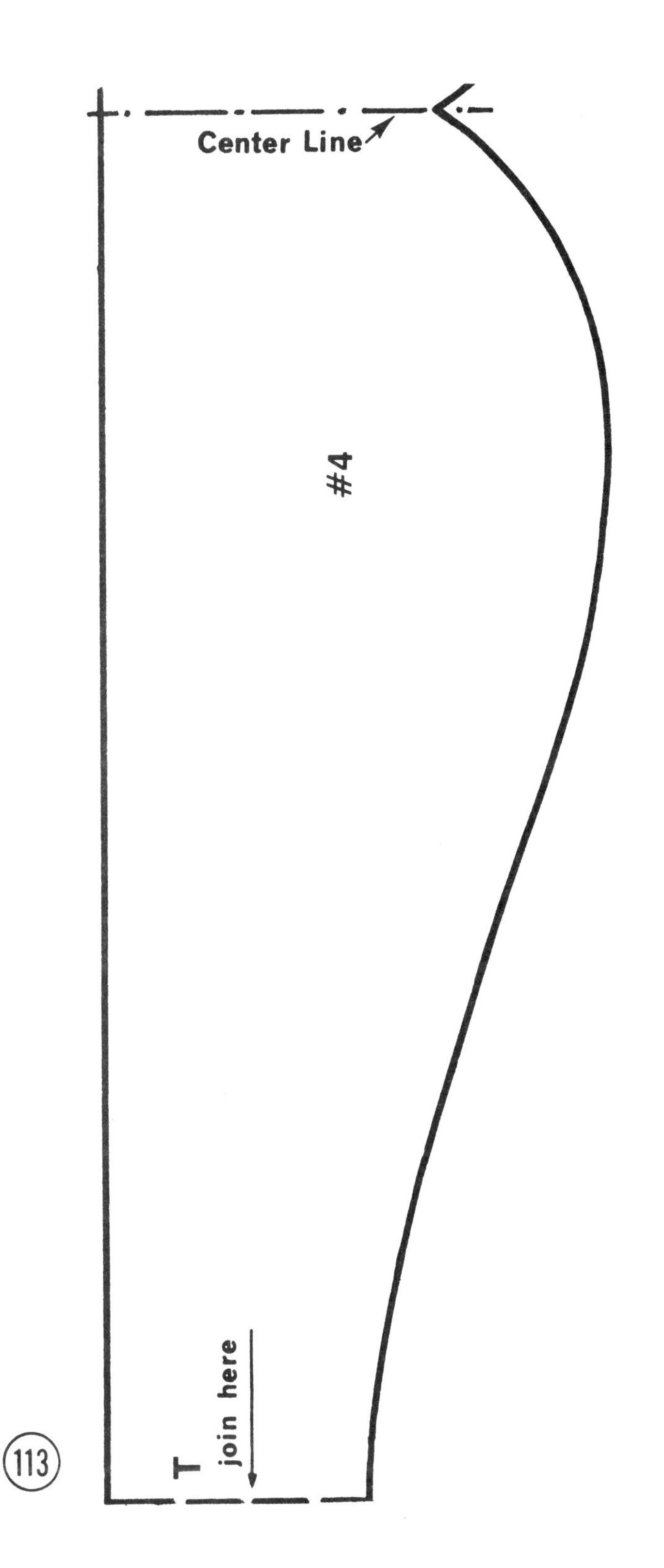
Center Line
#4
join here
T
113

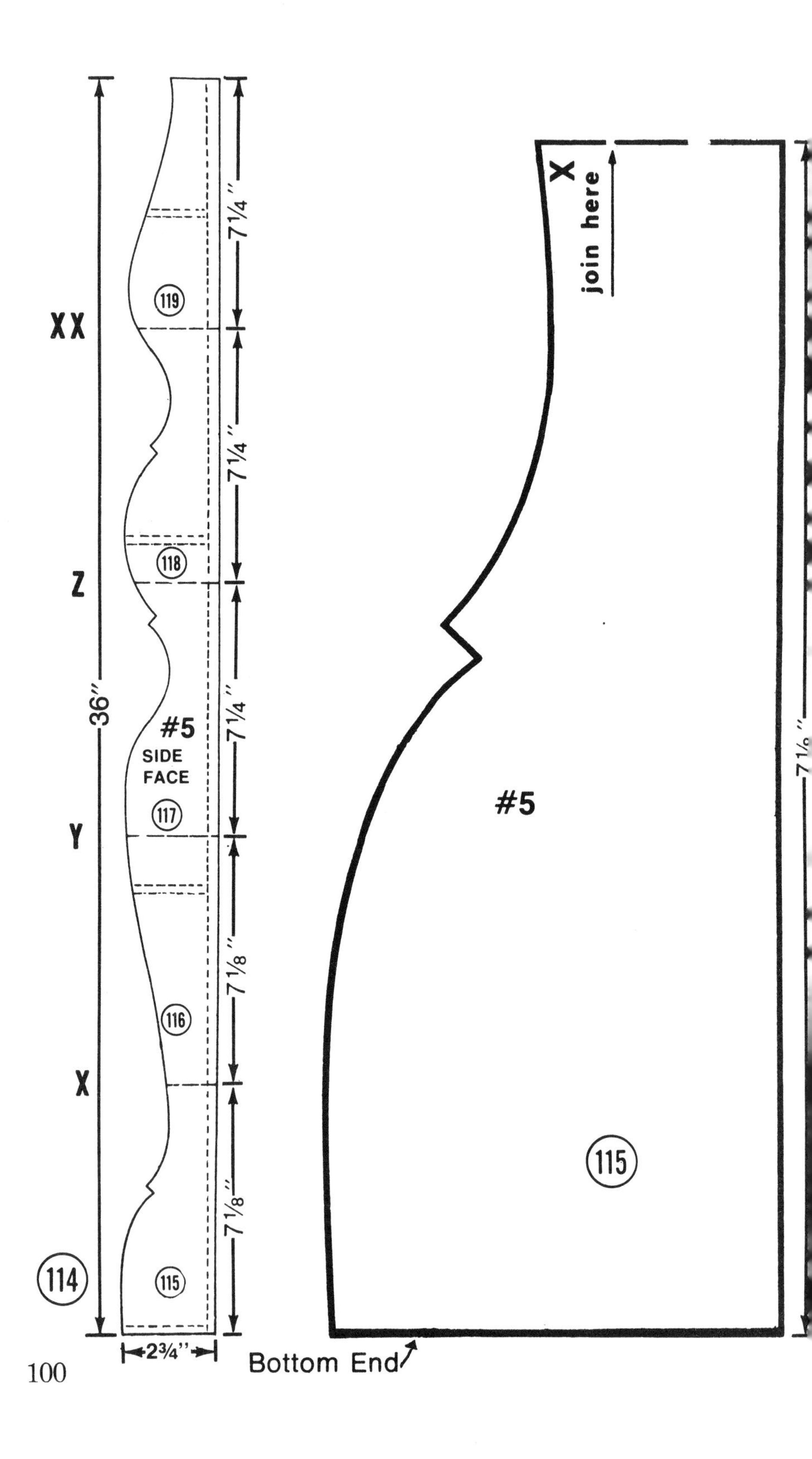
XX
Z
36"
Y
X
114
7¼"
7¼"
7¼"
7⅛"
7⅛"
119
118
#5
SIDE
FACE
117
116
115
2¾"
X
join here
#5
115
Bottom End
7⅛"

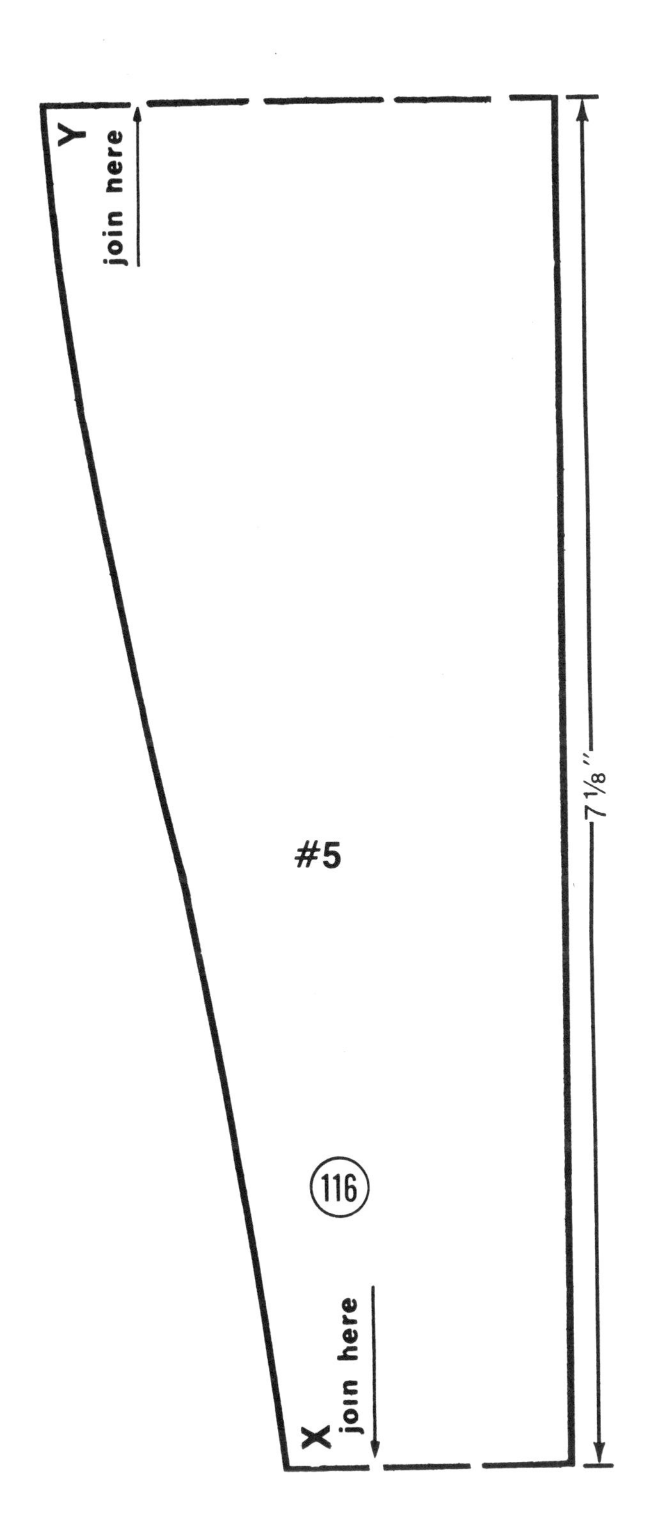
Y
join nere
#5
7 1/8"
116
X
join here

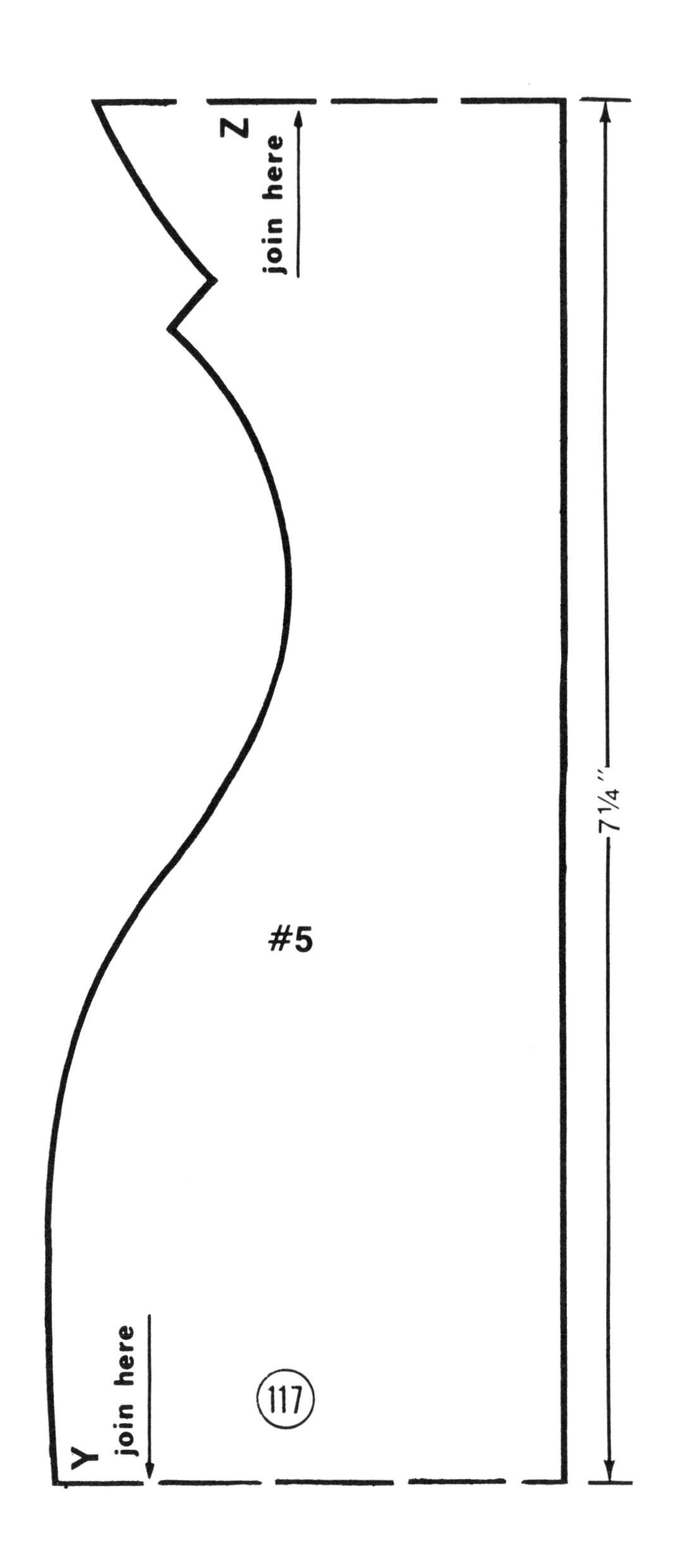
Z
join here
#5
Y
join here
117
7¼″

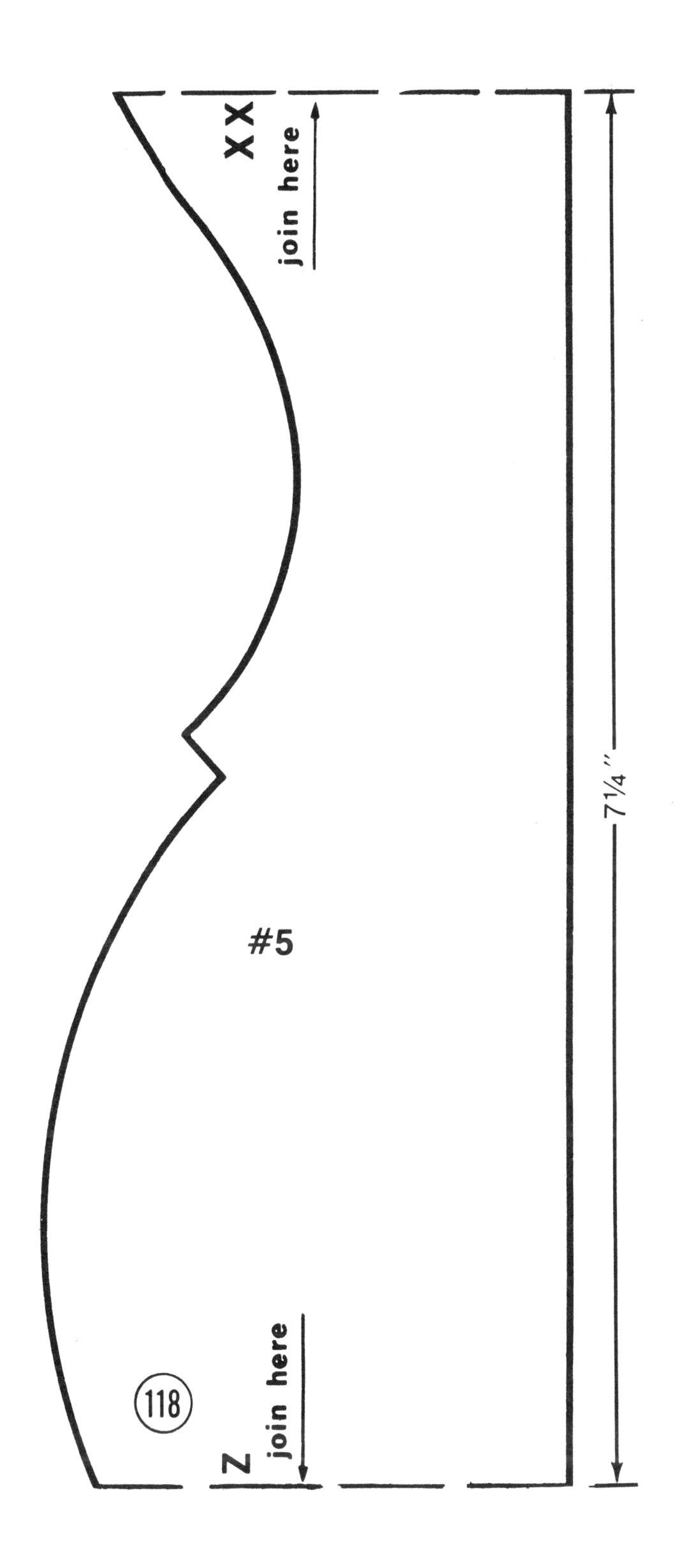

XX
join here
#5
7¼″
118
Z
join here

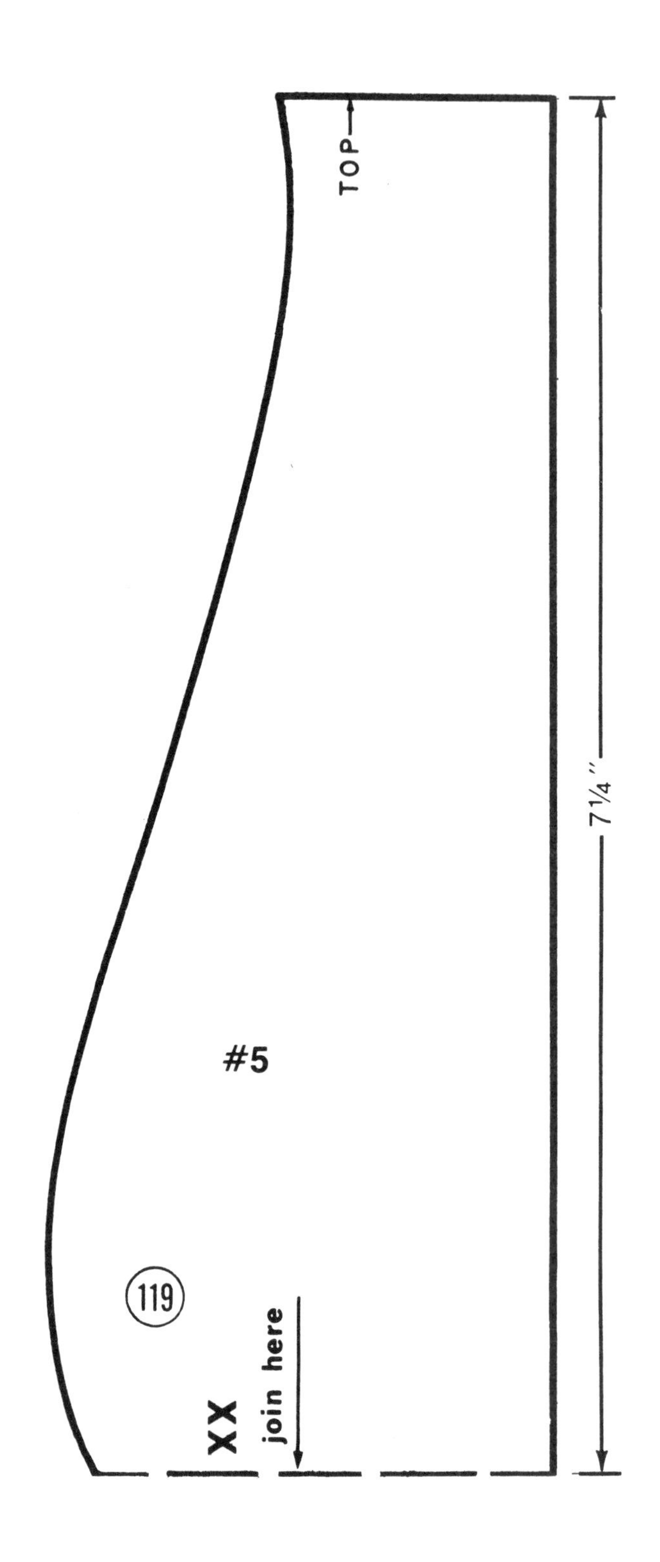
TOP
7¼″
#5
119
XX
join here

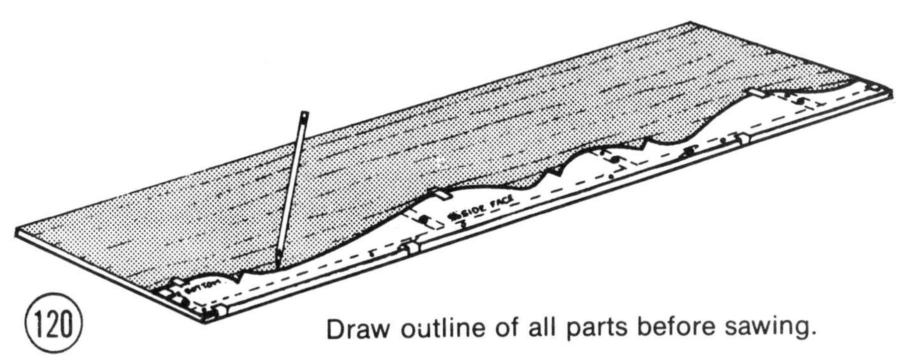

(120) Draw outline of all parts before sawing.

Draw position of each shelf on side facing #5 and on #2. Place each shelf in position against #5. Mark edge of #5 on top and bottom of #3, Illus. 121.

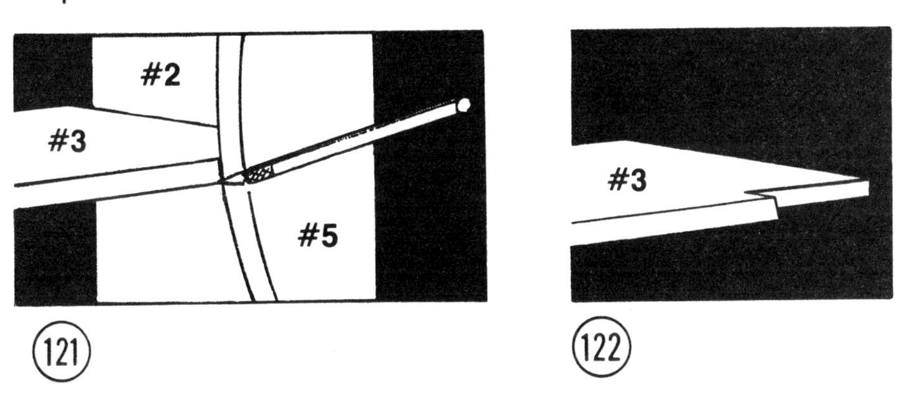

(121) (122)

With back of #3 flush with back of #2, notch each shelf to receive #5, Illus. 122. Apply a CE finish to these notched areas. Round front edge of shelf, Illus. 123,124*, and apply an EE finish. Remove masking paper from #2 and #3.

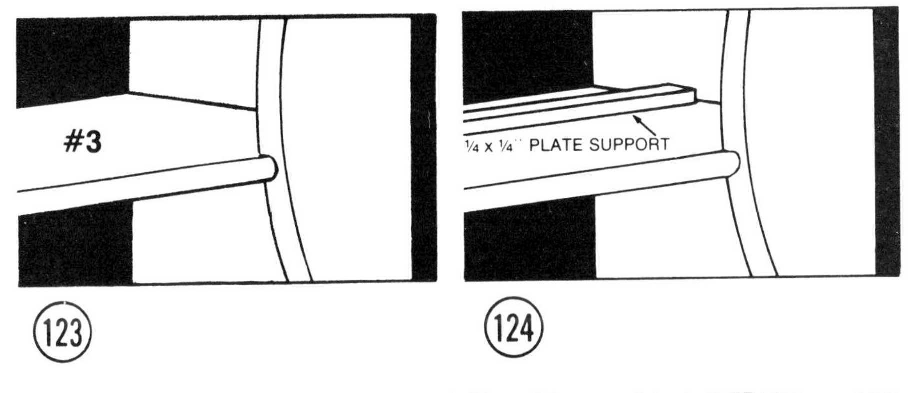

(123) (124)

* Apply ¼ x ¼" strip of acrylic cut to length needed for a plate support. Apply an EE edge to top, a CE edge to bottom. Bond strip to each shelf, if plates are displayed on edge.

Shelves can be supported with ¼ x 1 x 4" shelf supports, Illus. 109, or you can eliminate these and use 1" brads or 2 penny finishing nails. If shelf supports are used, apply a CE finish to top edge, an EE finish to bottom edge. Remove masking from shelf support and #2 and bond support to #2. These must be positioned an equal distance from bottom and at right angle to edge of #2 to provide a level shelf.

#3 can also be fastened to #2 with cement and 2 penny nails. Those who have an electric drill or motor tool, Illus. 129, should now drill two holes through #2, in position each shelf requires, Illus. 109, use 1/16" bit, Illus. 130.

If you have a motor tool and router base, only fasten the clamp of the base to the tool. Fasten tool in vise. Check with level. Build up top of workbench with plywood so acrylic, with masking paper still on, can be fed into 1/16" bit,* Illus. 129. Nail 1 x 2 blocking and straight edge in position so acrylic is fed into bit. Position 1 x 2 A so it positions bit 1" from edge. Position 1 x 2 B so it allows bit to drill into acrylic depth needed to receive a nail or brad through #2. Because acrylic shavings tend to jam up bit, feed shelf in and out of bit. Remove masking. Apply cement to end of #3 and to brad before driving into #2 and #3. Head of brad finishes flush with #2.

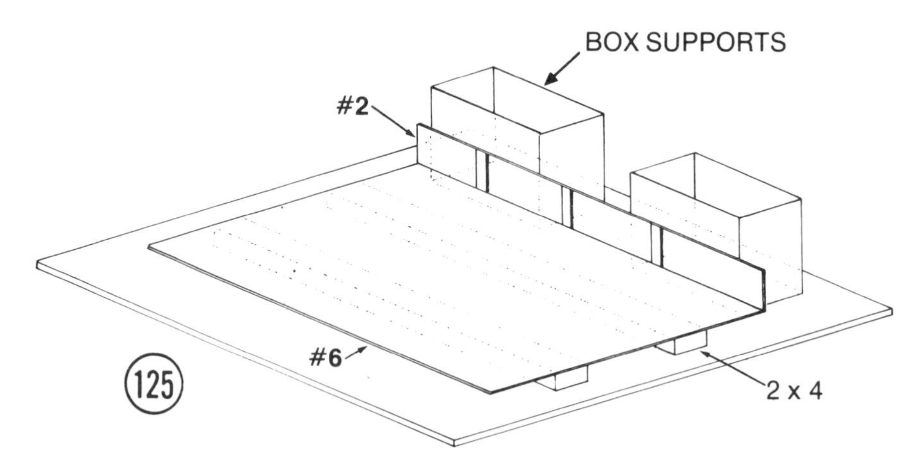

TAPE #2 TO #6, HOLD #2 IN PLACE WITH BOX SUPPORTS

*Depth of hole through #2 and #3 must equal full length of nail.

Cut a ¼" black or bronze back #6, 30 x 39". Check same with a square. Remove masking paper. Apply thickened cement to back edge of #2. Bond #2 flush with edge of #6, Illus. 125. Check with square. Allow cement to set. It's essential to tape, clamp or apply sufficient weight to hold parts together until cement sets.

Apply cement to top edge of #6, to top end of #2. Bond #1 to #6 and #2. Apply cement to end of #3; to top edge of each shelf support. Bond #3 to #2.

Apply cement to edge of #2 where it butts against #4, and to top edge of #4. Bond #4 to #2 and #1, Illus. 126.

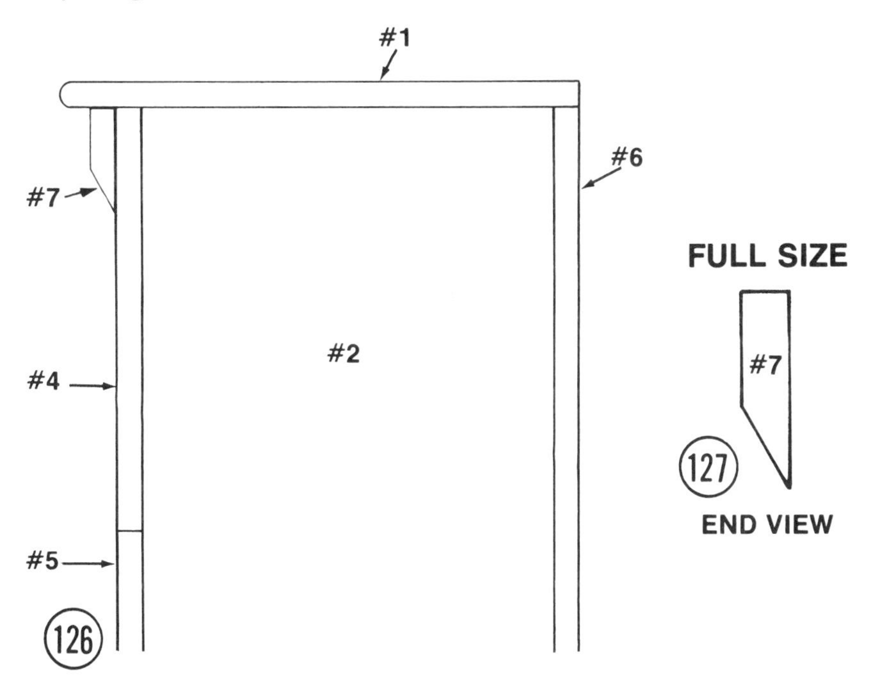

Apply cement to top end of #5, to edge of #2, to notches in #3. Bond #5 to #4, #2 and #3.

Bevel bottom edge of a ¼ x 1 x 30½" strip #7, Illus. 127. Miter cut ends. Apply thickened cement to top edge and back. Bond to #1 and #4. Allow ¼" miter to project at each end. Measure and miter cut piece for ends. Bond in position.

Tap wall to locate two studs. Position cabinet on line with door trim or at height convenient to user. Apply tape to front and back and drill four 3/16" holes through back in position studs indicate, Illus. 128. Remove tape and fasten back to wall with 1½" No. 8 oval head screws and countersunk washers.

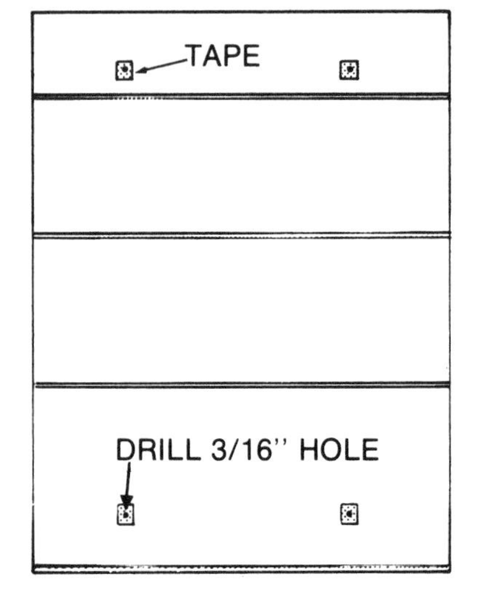

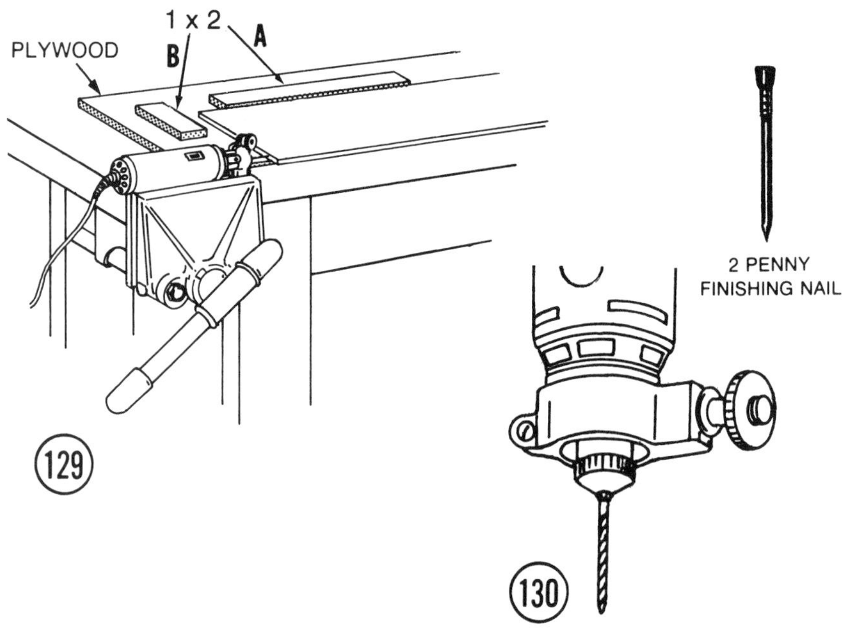

1/16" DIAMETER DRILL

Use size bit brad or nail requires

STANDING CABINET

To build a free standing base and wall cabinet, Illus. 103, with or without doors, requires assembly of the wall cabinet as previously described with one exception. Cut ⅛" acrylic back 30" wide by overall height of the combined unit. Since open faced shelving is continually in demand by retailers for both storage and display, we recommend building the base to 36, 42 even 44" height. Most doctors, dentists, veterinarians and other professionals prefer a countertop at height that's convenient to their examining chair or other equipment.

Show professionals and retailers a scale model made from ⅛" black, bronze or clear acrylic. Make the model to style shown, Illus. 131. Show each potential customer a 6 x 6" piece of ¼" colored acrylic and explain color selected will be used for all parts.

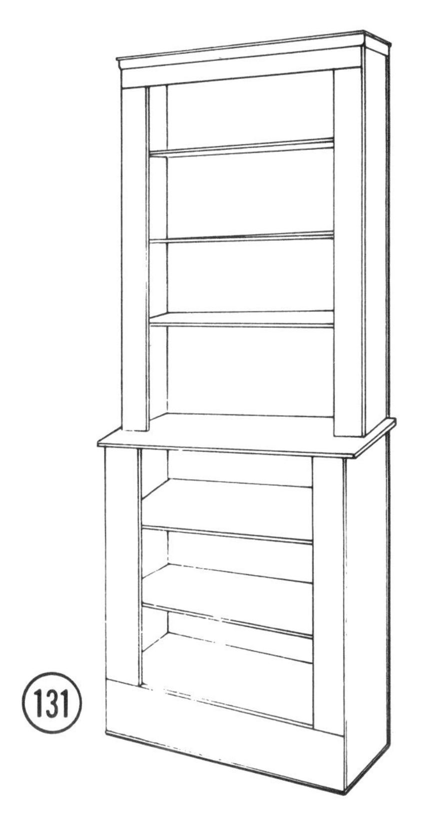

131

To build a 7⅞" deep base, 30" wide, with countertop at 36" height, cut parts to following size. Note cutting chart, Illus. 132.

LIST OF MATERIAL

1 — 30 x 75" back A (use ⅛")
2 — 7½ x 35¾" sides B
2 — 1½ x 29½" supports C
2 — 1½ x 7" " D (cut three if door is installed)
4 — 1 x 29½" " E*
4 — 1 x 7" " F
1 — 5½ x 30" base G
1 — 7⅞ x 30" bottom H
2 — 3½ x 30¼" columns K
1 — 8¼ x 30½" countertop L
2 — 11½ x 30" doors M (optional)
2 — 7½ x 29½" shelves N

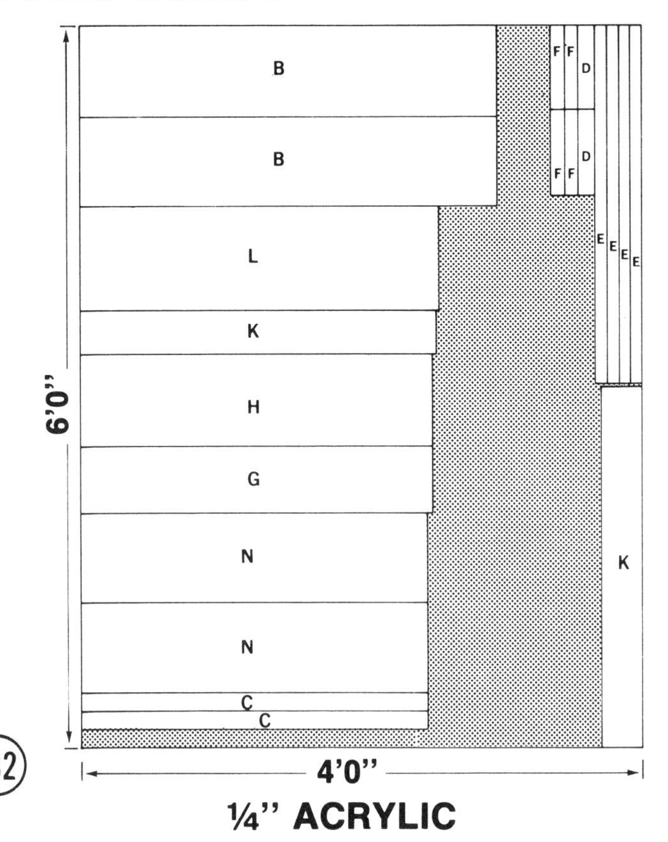

132

¼" ACRYLIC

*Applying E to front of middle shelf is optional.

Cut one back A, ⅛ x 30 x 75". Apply an EE finish to three edges; a CE finish to bottom edge.

Cut two B, 7½ x 35¾". Apply a CE finish to four edges, Illus. 133.

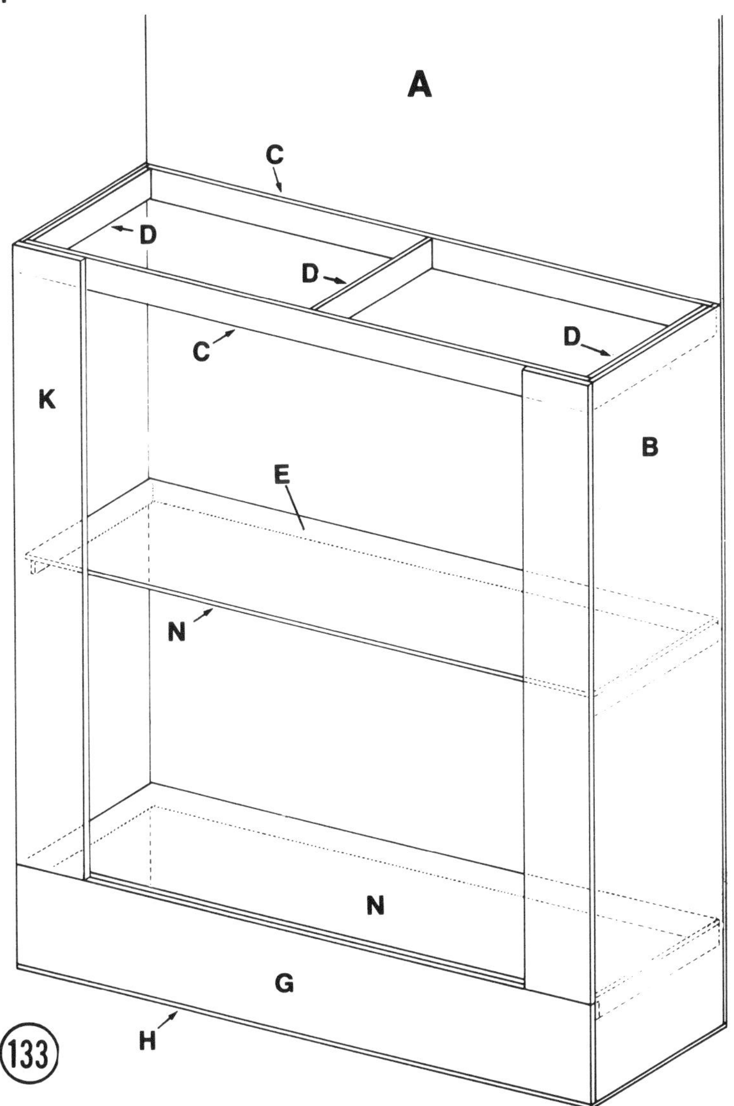

Cut two C, 1½ x 29½". Apply a CE finish to top edge and ends of C,D,E,F.

Cut two D, 1½ x 7". Cut a third D if doors are installed.

Cut three E, 1 x 29½". Cut four F, 1 x 7". Cut one G, 5½ x 30". Apply a CE finish to 3½" top edge of G indicated by shaded area, Illus. 134, and to bottom edge; an EE finish to exposed top edge.

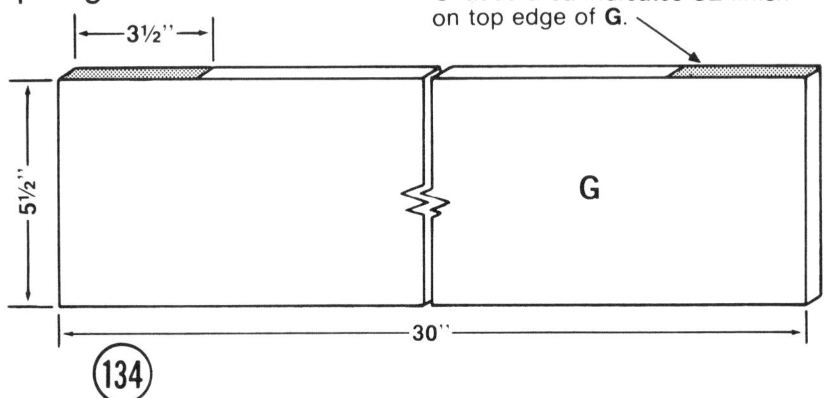

Cut bottom H, 7⅞ x 30". Apply an EE finish to four edges. Cut two ¼ x 2 x 6" stiffeners. Apply cement and bond stiffener to bottom face. Drill holes through stiffener and H to receive Domes of Silence or casters, Illus. 135.

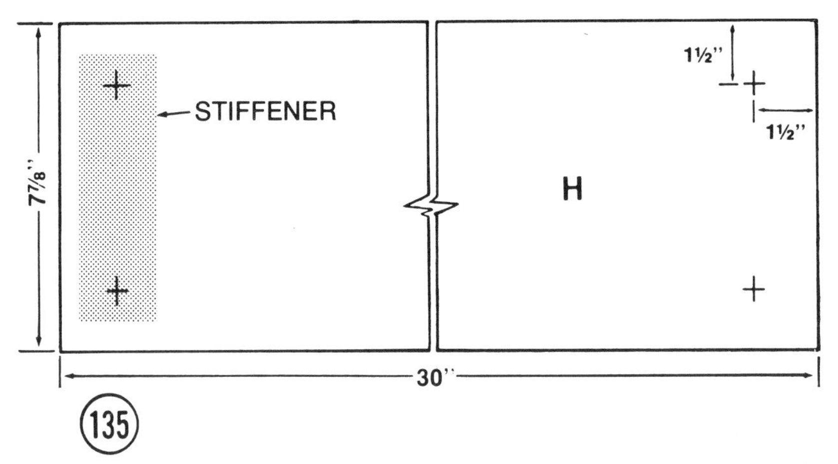

Cut two K, 3½ x 30¼". Apply a CE finish to top and bottom ends; an EE finish to vertical exposed edges.

Cut one countertop L, 8¼ x 30½". Apply a rounded EE finish to front and ends, Illus. 108; a CE finish to back edge.

Cut two doors M. Apply an EE finish to four edges.

Apply thickened cement and bond C and E to A in position shown, Illus. 136.

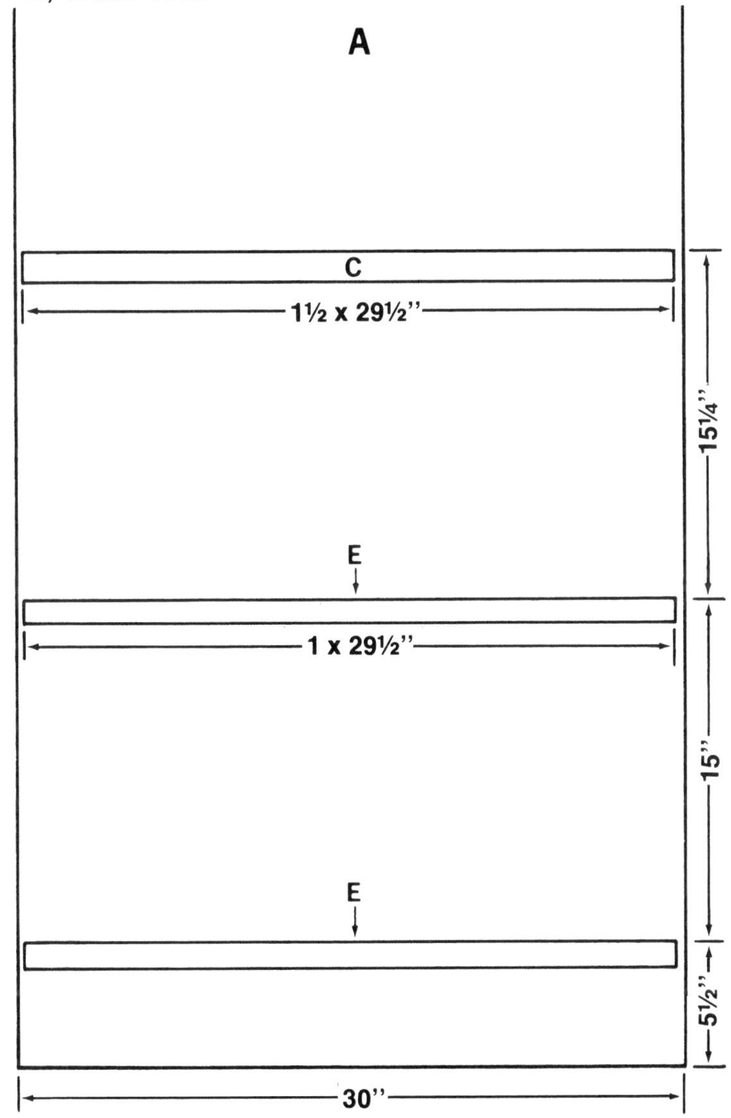

Bond E flush with top edge of G, Illus. 137.

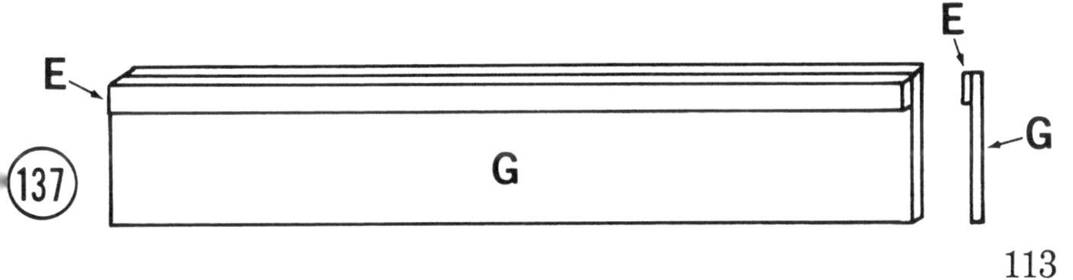

Bond D and F to B in position shown, Illus. 138.

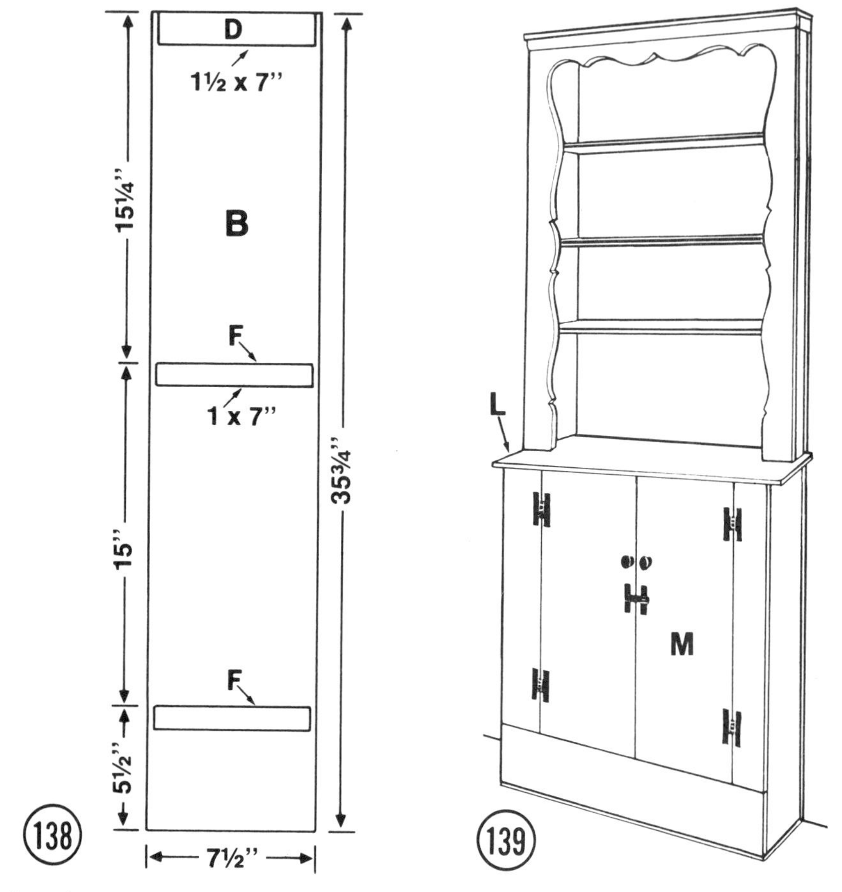

Apply cement to back edge of B and to ends of CDEF. Tape ABDEF in position, Illus. 133.

Bond G to front edge of B and end of E to F.

Cut two shelves N, 7½ x 29½" or to size required. These can rest on EF or be bonded to top edge with cement.

Bond bottom H to ABG. Fasten Domes of Silence or equal to H in position shown, Illus. 135.

Apply cement to top edge of CDK and to back edge of countertop L. Bond countertop in position. L projects ¼" over front and ends, Illus. 139.

Doors are optional. Cut doors M to fit opening. Doors are hinged to K with two pairs of H hinge or style hinge acrylic distributor recommends. Allow door to clear G and L by 1/16". Drill 3/32" holes, or size hole screws require. Test drilling in scrap. Fasten hinge to scrap with screws provided. If these are too long for ¼" acrylic, saw screws to length needed. Again drill a hole and test screw in scrap before drilling holes in door.

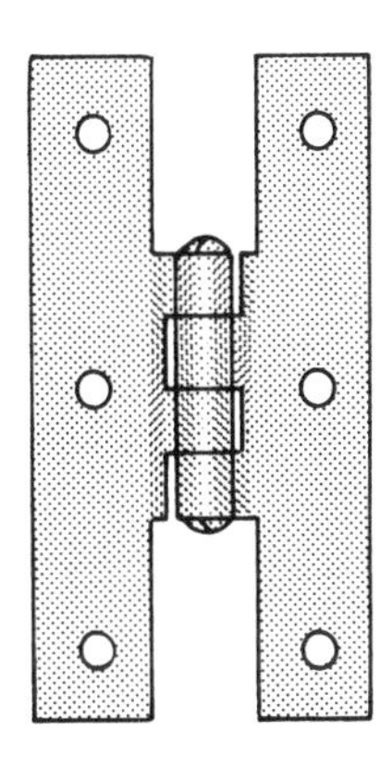

"H" HINGE

Apply cement to back edge of #1, #2 and to bottom end of #2 and #5. Tape assembled wall cabinet in position and allow to remain undisturbed until cement sets.

If customer plans on using cabinet in display work that necessitates constant moving, suggest using casters instead of Domes of Silence.

SHELVING AND CLOTHES STORAGE

When additional shelf space or a clothes rack is urgently needed, this open sided, single, Illus. 140, or double unit, Illus. 141, provides two very convenient, practical and economical solutions.

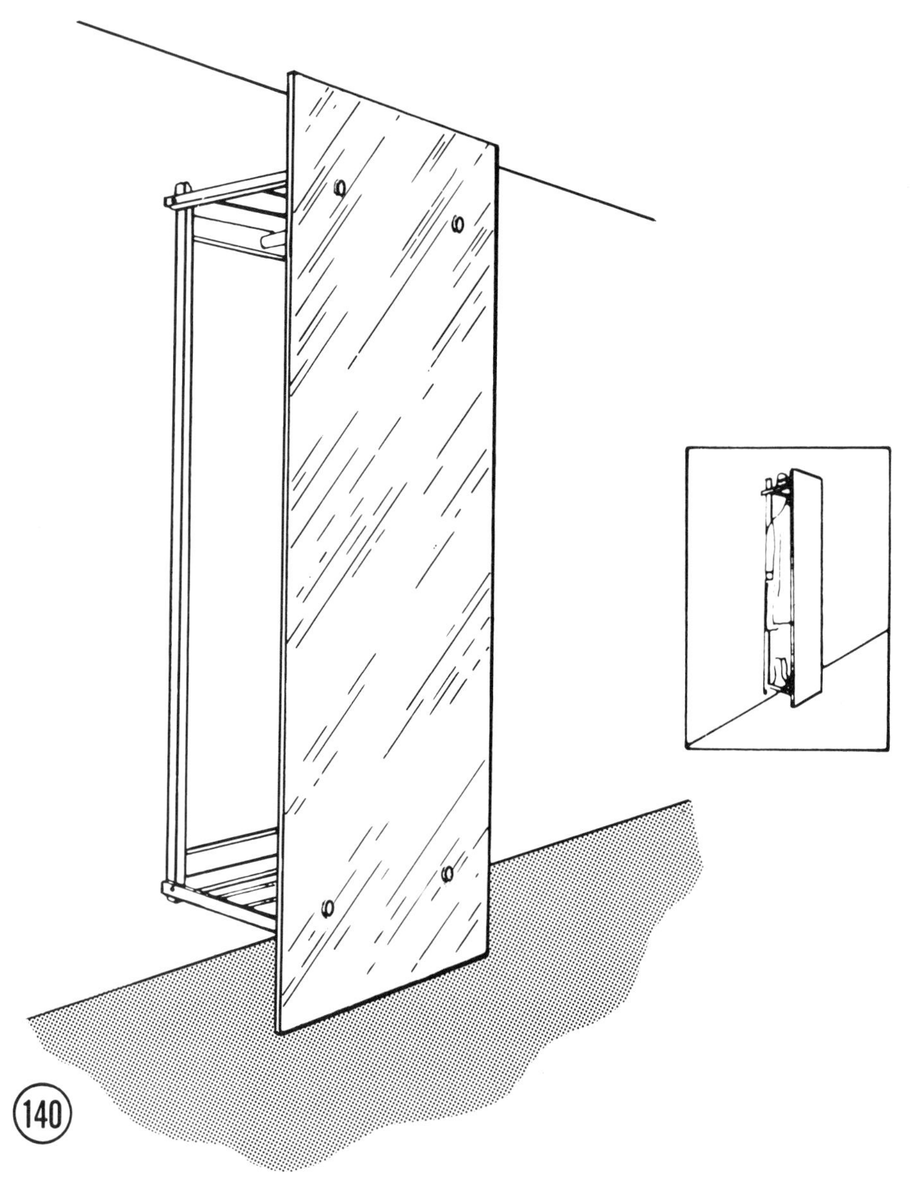

Projecting little more than 12" into room, each provides easy to reach storage. A single unit requires a ¼" x 2 x 6' bronze, black or other colored acrylic. The double unit requires a ¼" x 4 x 6' sheet. Like the showcase, Illus. 131, this unit solves a storage problem for every type of business and professional.

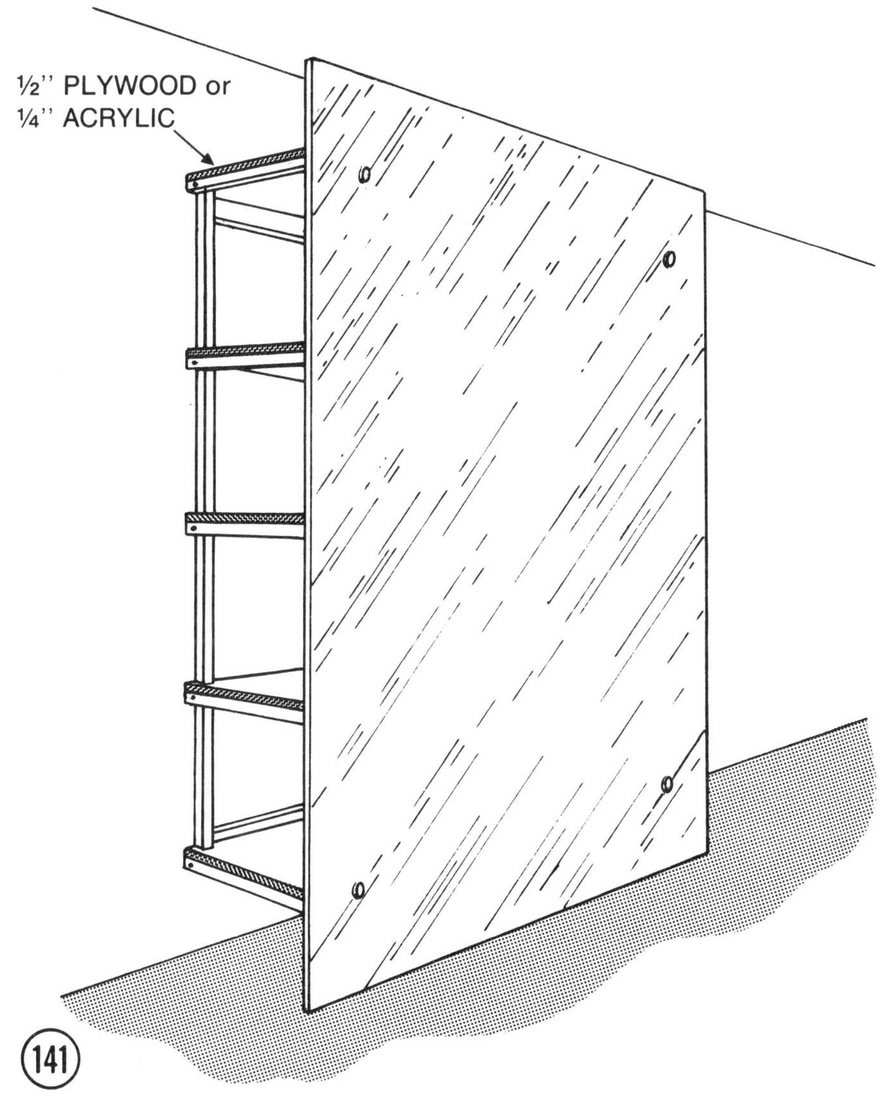

Step-by-step directions explain how to build the single unit as a clothes storage wardrobe. This can also be built with shelving as shown in Illus. 141.

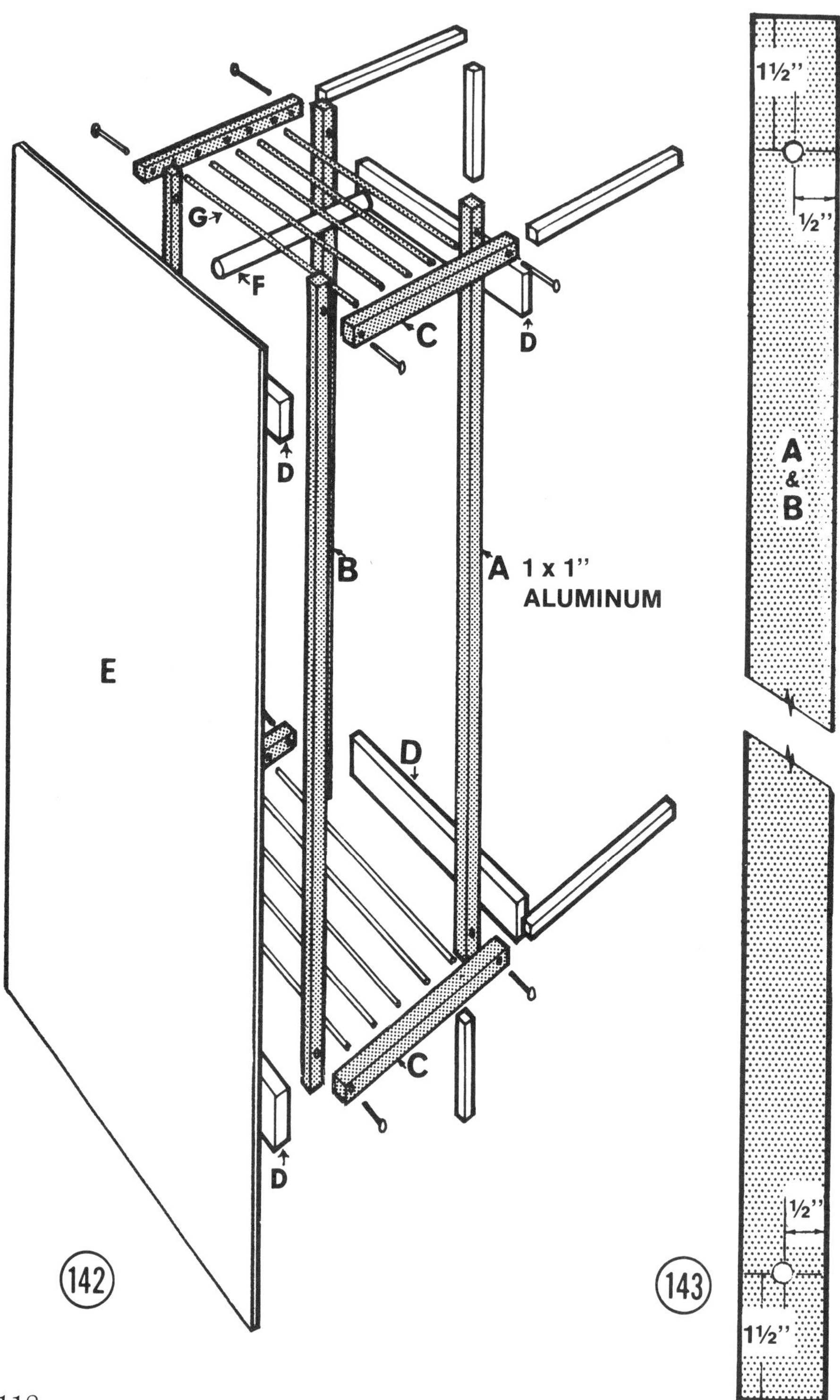
G
F
C
D
D
B
A
1 x 1"
ALUMINUM
E
D
C
D
142
1½"
½"
A
&
B
½"
1½"
143

LIST OF MATERIAL FOR SINGLE UNIT

1 — ¼" x 2 x 6' acrylic. Select color desired.
4 — 1 x 1" x 6' square aluminum tubing ABC
5 — ⅜" x 3' aluminum rods (for clothes storage)
1 — 1 x 2 x 4' filler
1 — 1 x 3 x 6' D
1 x 12" aluminum pipe F

Cut four 1 x 1 x 60" square aluminum tubing for A and B, Illus. 142.

Drill ¼" holes at center of A and B, 1½" from ends, Illus. 143.

Cut eight ¾ x ⅞ x 6" (or size required) filler blocks from 1 x 2. Insert in ends of A and B, Illus. 144.

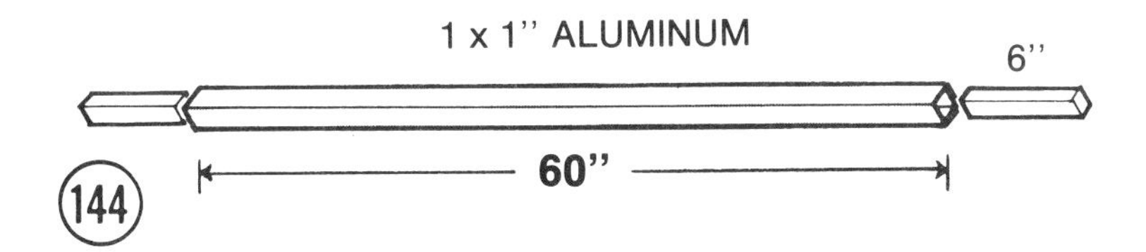

Use four 1 x 1 x 12" tubing cutoffs for C, Illus. 145. Cut four ¾ x ⅞ x 12" filler blocks. Insert in C.

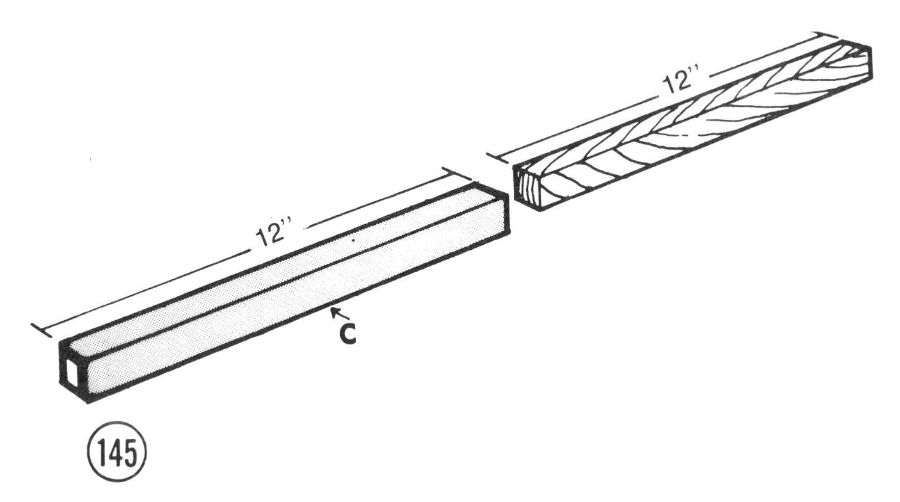

Drill ⅜" holes, ¼" deep in C in position indicated, Illus. 146.
Drill two 5/16" holes through C, ½" from ends.

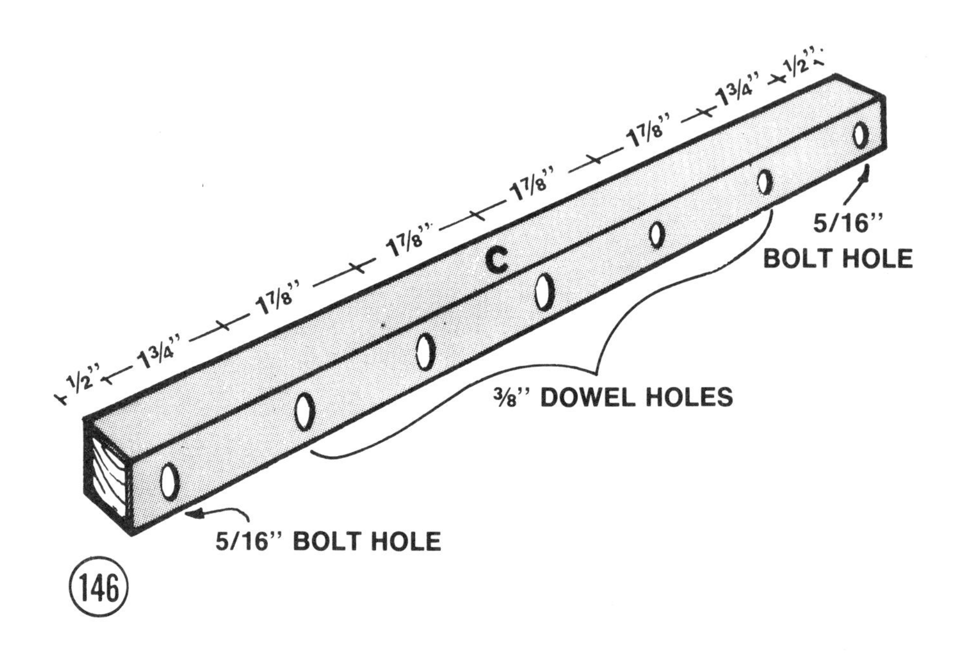

Cut ten ⅜ x 18" aluminum rods G, Illus. 147.

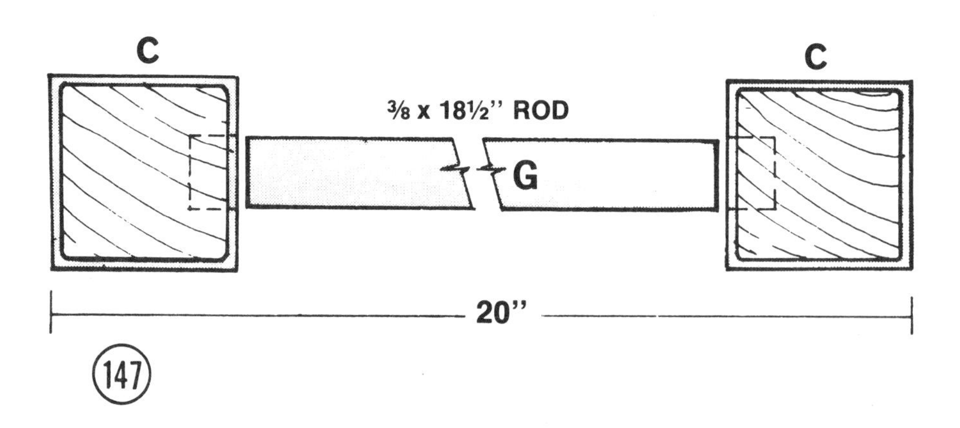

Cut four 1 x 3 x 15½" for D, Illus. 148.

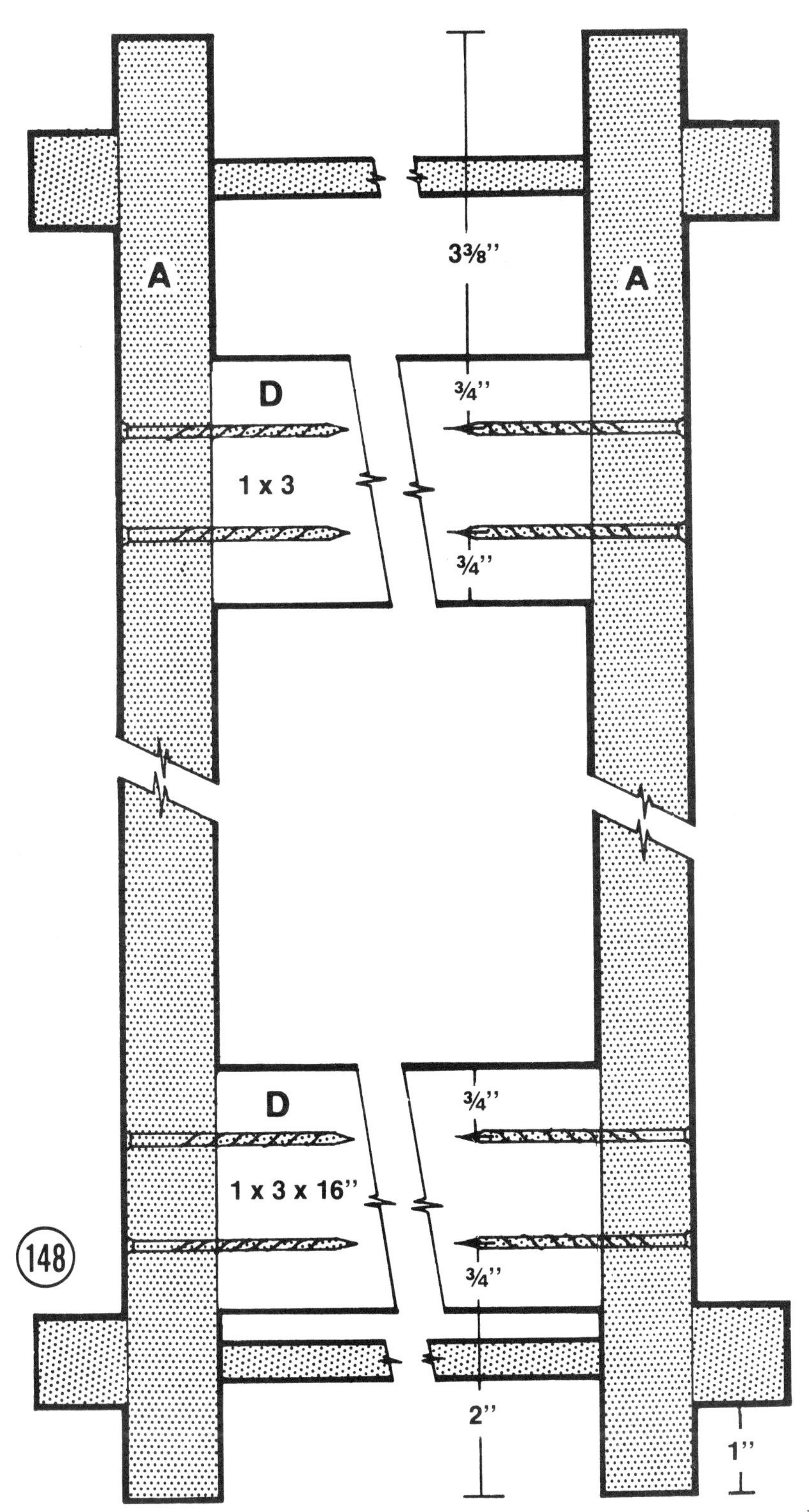
A
A
3⅜''
D
¾''
1 x 3
¾''
D
¾''
1 x 3 x 16''
148
¾''
2''
1''

Drill 1" hole through center of two top D to receive 1" pipe F, Illus. 149, if you are building a clothes rack.

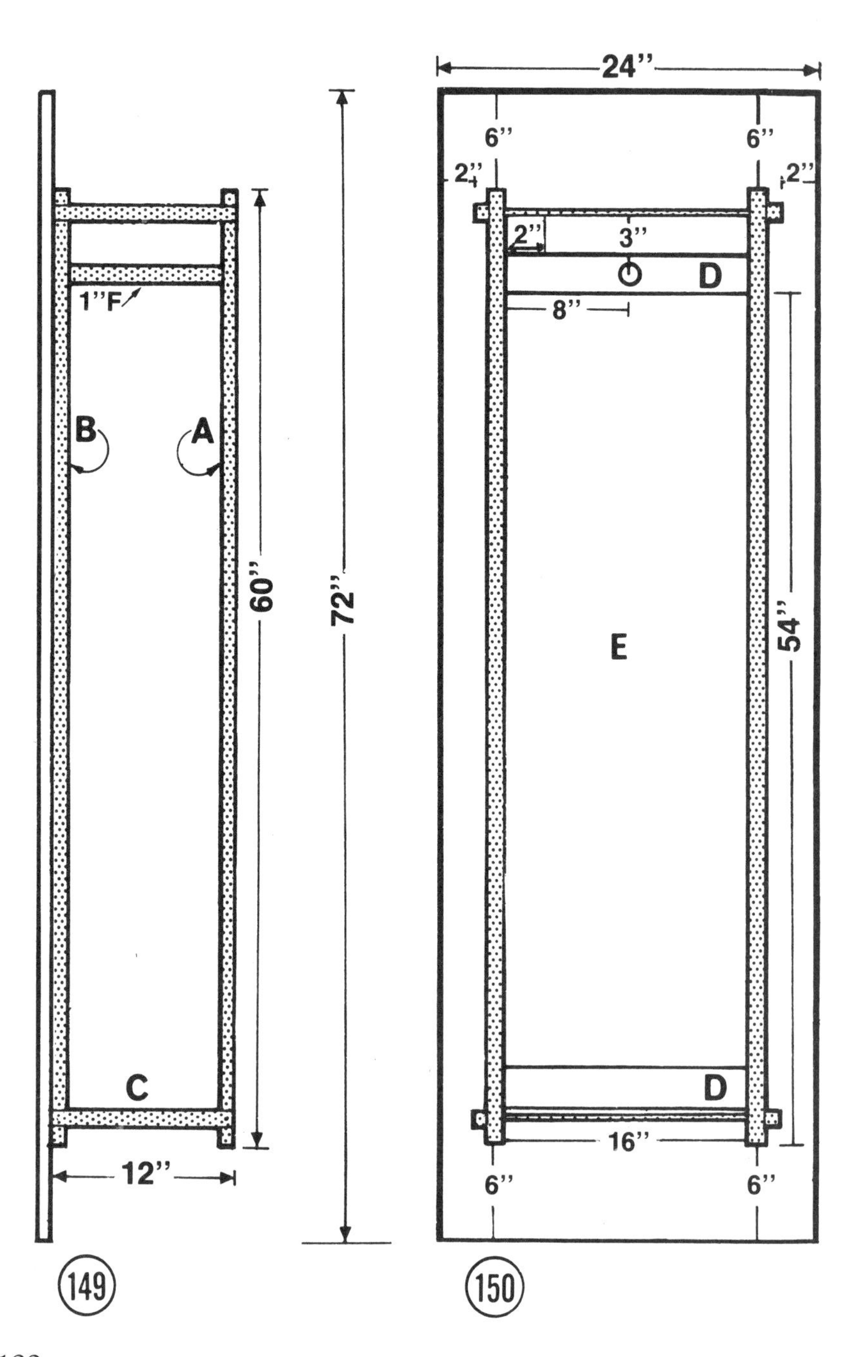

Drill four 9/64" holes through AB in position indicated, Illus. 148. This permits nailing A to D, B to D with 8 penny aluminum Stronghold or equal nails.

Tap wall to locate a stud or note where baseboard was nailed. Fasten D to a stud in wall. Nail one D approximately 8" from floor, the top D in position indicated, Illus. 150. Check D with level before driving second nail. Studs are usually spaced 16" on centers. Measure from corner to locate one, then measure over every 16" to locate the one desired.

Drill four 9/32" holes through E and D. This size hole permits fastening E to D with medallion head saw screws, Illus. 151, or buy screws, glass or plastic rosettes from a mirror or glass retailer.

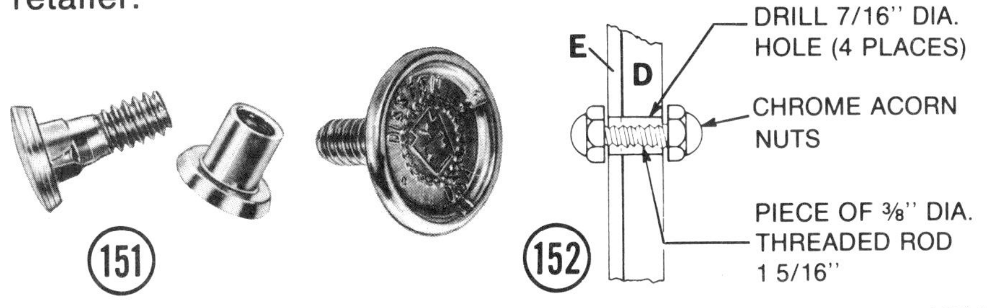

151

152

You can also fasten E to D with ⅜" chrome acorn nuts and ⅜" diameter threaded rod, Illus. 152. Drill 7/16" holes through ED. Cut threaded rod 1¼ to 1 5/16" or to length ED requires. Only tighten nuts to a snug fit. Excessive tightening will crack the acrylic.

Insert ⅜" rods G in C, Illus. 147.

Fasten C to A and B with ¼ x 1¼" chrome or zinc chromate finished carriage bolts, Illus. 142. Drill a slightly larger hole in C if needed to receive shoulder of bolt.

Drive 8 penny Stronghold or equal aluminum nails through B into D fastened to E.

Place 1" pipe F in D. Place assembled unit in position. Nail through A into D.

To build this unit for wall storage, cut as many C, Illus. 145, as you need shelves. Drill 5/16" bolt holes, ½" from ends, Illus. 146. No wood fillers are required. Drill two 5/16" bolt holes in position shown, Illus. 153.

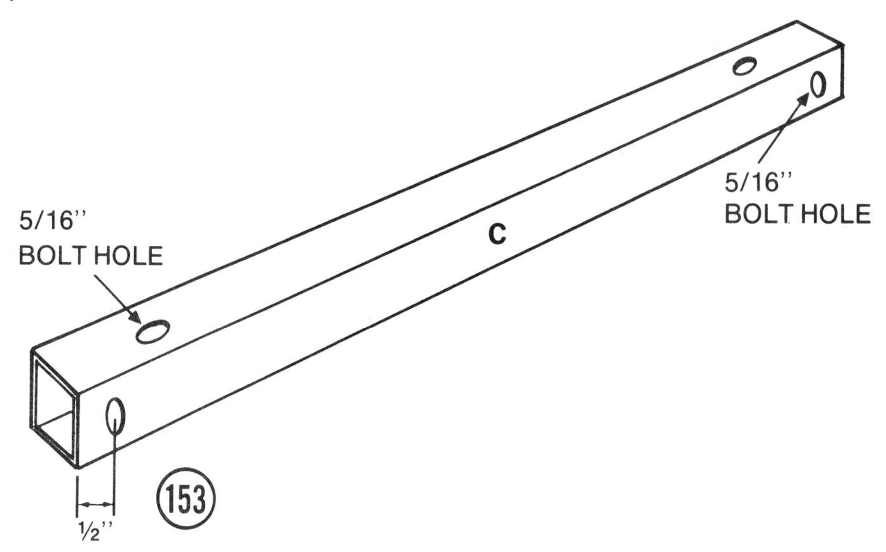

Assemble as previously described without including rods G.

Cut ½ or ⅝" plywood shelves,* 9¾ x 18", Illus. 154. If a wider shelf is desired, notch shelf to fit around A and B, Illus. 154a. Fasten C to A and B, at height convenient to articles to be stored, Illus. 141. Drill 5/16" holes through A and B wherever C is to be fastened. Drill 5/16" holes through shelf in position C indicates. Fasten shelf to C with ¼ x 1¾" or length bolts shelving requires.

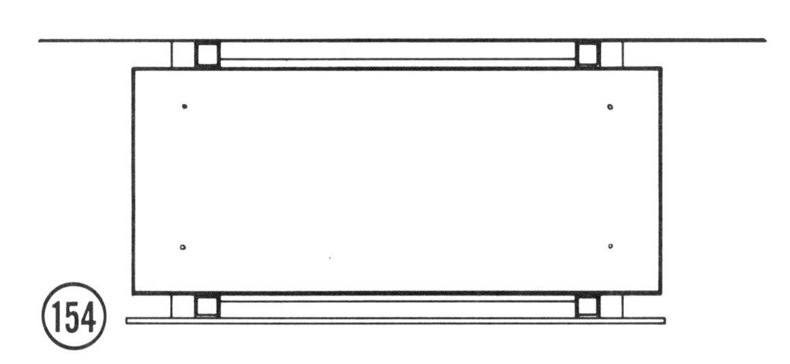

*Or use ¼" acrylic

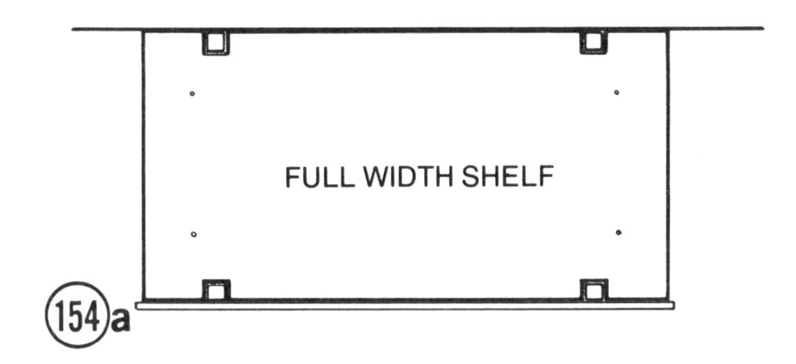

A double unit, Illus. 141, follows same assembly procedure. Use a ¼'' x 4 x 6' acrylic panel. The length of D can be 32'' or up to 42''. Cut shelving to length required.

If you wish to use one half as a clothes rack and the other half for shelving, position A and B as shown, Illus. 142, plus an extra pair of A and B at 32, 36 or 42'' width. If A and B are positioned distance from edge of E, as shown in Illus. 150, and a clothes rack is built to size shown, a considerable amount of shelf space can be gained in a four foot area.

ROOM DIVIDERS, FOLDING SCREENS, PRIVACY PARTITIONS

Since privacy is one of life's most precious possessions, everyone finds a need for a partition, room divider or folding screen. This can take many different forms, shapes and sizes. A panel of clear, bronze or black acrylic can be etched and mounted in a frame to blank off an entry door, Illus. 155, or to screen an examining area in a professional office. Or a deep etched folding screen, Illus. 156, 157, can be used. We call this Etchacrylic. It's a form of creative art that has great appeal.

¼" slot, ¼" deep in position panel requires.

Rout a ¼" slot, ¼" deep in position acrylic panel requires. Insert panel in slots. Measure length required for 5/4 x 6" header. Cut header. Paint or stain framing.

Spike one post to stud in wall. Nail header to joist in ceiling, or use toggle bolts. Insert panel in slot and nail outside post to header. Toenail to floor with 6 penny finishing nails. Countersink heads. Fill holes with wood filler. Or panel can be hung as a free flowing partition from chains.

Etching a design into acrylic is a time consuming endeavor that provides hours of instant escape and relaxation. Any design can be applied using the electric motor tool, Illus. 129. This tool comes with a wide assortment of bits and abrasive wheels, Illus. 158. You adjust cutter in router base so it lightly etches line of design. We call this the Etchacrylic* style of design.

(158) 7/32" DIAMETER BALL CUTTER

¼" DIAMETER x ½"

Full size patterns mentioned on page 176 simplify tracing the actual design. These turn amateurs into pros. The masking paper is removed. The pattern is taped to a flat surface. The acrylic, cut to overall size desired, is taped in exact position over pattern. You can use the ⅛" ball bit, the 7/32" oblong cutter or the mounted abrasive wheel.

The cutter selected is fastened in place. The router table is adjusted to lightly score the design. Only trace the design on the first pass. To gain experience needed, practice on a piece of scrap. Note how each cutter requires a very light touch, how you must go over each line several times to obtain the depth and width of cut desired. As you make each pass, you not only go deeper, but also broaden each line. Since the tool can't handle a deep cut in one pass, you must practice to experience its limitations. Reset the adjustable base as you make each successive pass.

Note the wide variety of cutters and abrasive wheels available at stores selling this router. With a little practice, exceptionally attractive results can be achieved. Each can be applied to screens, room dividers, etc. Lighted nameplates, Illus. 159, can also be etched.

*TM

While the routed area creates a highly decorative design, an additional dimension can be achieved by painting the routed design with silver, white or black acrylic paint. Nine full size patterns not only simplify tracing each design, but also explain how to build the frames to exact size required. While these patterns were originally designed for use on plywood, each is far more attractive when applied to acrylic.

Those who don't wish to Etchacrylic, can, using carbon paper, trace the design on the masking paper. Tape pattern along top edge to masking paper in exact position required. Raise pattern and insert carbon paper. When entire pattern is traced, remove pattern and carbon and broaden each line with a ⅛" wide marking pen. Using an X-ACTO Knife, Illus. 1, draw it along each edge of every line. Apply a bit of pressure so the knife scores the acrylic as it cuts the ⅛" wide strips. Carefully remove ⅛" strips.

Using white, silver or other acrylic color, spray exposed lines. Wait 20 to 30 minutes, or time paint manufacturer specifies, and spray a second coat. Allow to dry thoroughly before removing masking paper. Use care not to damage painted lines. By scoring the acrylic with the X-ACTO Knife, you buttress edge of painted design.

Frames for a folding screen can be assembled with glue and dowels following the same procedure described for building doors on pages 146 to 160. Or frames can be assembled according to the method described in Pattern #930 offered on page 176.

Use clear, bronze or colored acrylic, ¼ x 16 x 60". Cut four equal size panels. Etchacrylic each design in position directions on pattern suggest.

Use 5/4 x 2 x 60" for A, 5/4 x 2¾ x 16" for B, 5/4 x 3¾ x 16" for C, Illus. 160. Drill holes for dowels, apply glue, assemble frame, paint or stain as directions suggest. After applying and finishing design, fasten each panel to frame using ⅜" quarter round. Miter cut ends and nail in place, Illus. 201. Insert panel and apply quarter round to other side. Apply double acting screen hinges in position shown, Illus. 161.

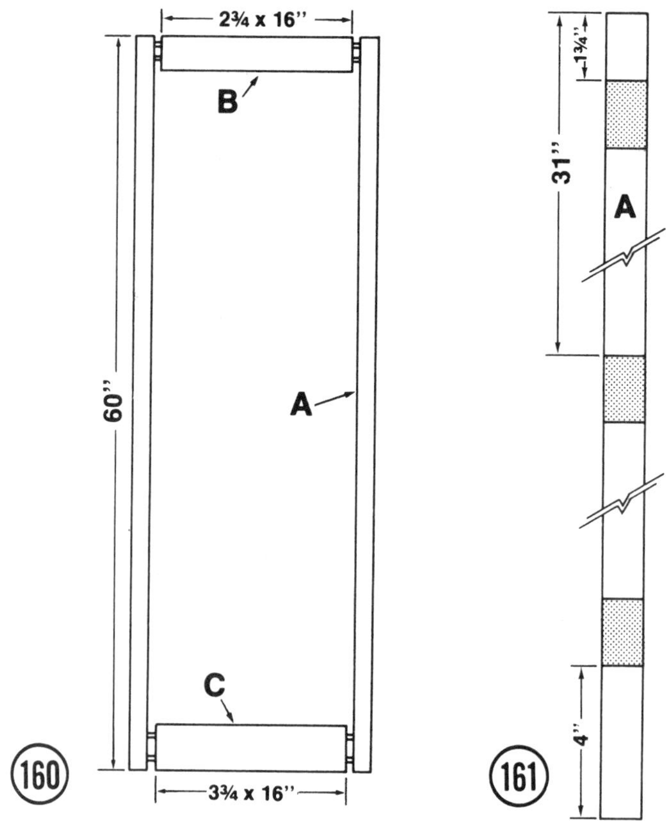

OUTDOOR DISPLAY CABINET

Single pane on front, doors on back.

A free standing see through enclosure, Illus. 162, can attract customers for a wide variety of products and services. To estimate sales potential, show a picture of the cabinet to every business and service organization that has sufficient curbside space to erect one. Each user soon discovers it can prove a money maker for the display of their own products or as a rental unit. Service station operators find these display cases excellent income producers. While some build and rent space for an annual fee, others invite customers to display and sell everything from books, tools, china, toys to posting for sale signs. A 10% sales commission soon shows a profit over the cost of all material.

After making your first installation, photograph same with people studying the goods offered. Show the picture to other, non-competing businesses. If a franchised operator erects one, show it to the same franchise operator in neighboring communities.

With locked doors on one side and a securely fastened ¼" panel on other, the cabinet offers extremely attractive display space. Fluorescent lighting installed in overhead canopy can be operated by a timer.

The following material will be needed to build an outdoor display case measuring approximately 5' wide and standing 7' high.

LIST OF MATERIAL
1 — ⅛ x 30 x 60" acrylic
2 — ¼" x 4 x 5' acrylic
4 — 2 x 8 x 10' - A*, or 2 — 3 x 8 x 10'
2 — 1 x 8 x 10' - B,C
1 — 5/4 x 12 x 5' - D
1 — 5/4 x 4 x 12' - E
1 — ¾ x 4 x 8' - F,G,H, ext. grade plywood
1 — 5/4 x 2 x 10' - J
1 — 5/4 x 6 x 10' - K
1 — 5/4 x 8 x 12' - L,M,N,O,P
2 — 48" fluorescent fixtures
Plus underground cable, junction box, etc., as needed.

Since the posts should be buried 2½ to 3' deep, check site selected to make certain no underground service lines, water, telephone, electric cable or sewer pipe prevents using site. Probe with a crow bar to make certain no rock interferes with excavating to depth required. If you run into a rock formation well below grade, and no comparable site is available, excavate 14" diameter holes to depth of rock. Call a tool rental store and rent a jack hammer, Illus. 163, and a rock drill bit on an hourly basis. Drill holes in rock to a depth of 8 to 12". Select locations for drilling that place reinforcing rods, Illus. 164, 1½ to 2" away from each post.

*We figured 2 x 8 as measuring 1½ x 7¼"; a 1 x 8, ¾ x 7¼".

163

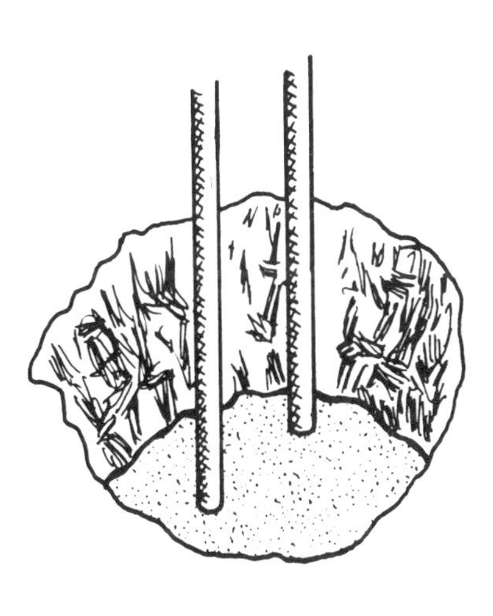

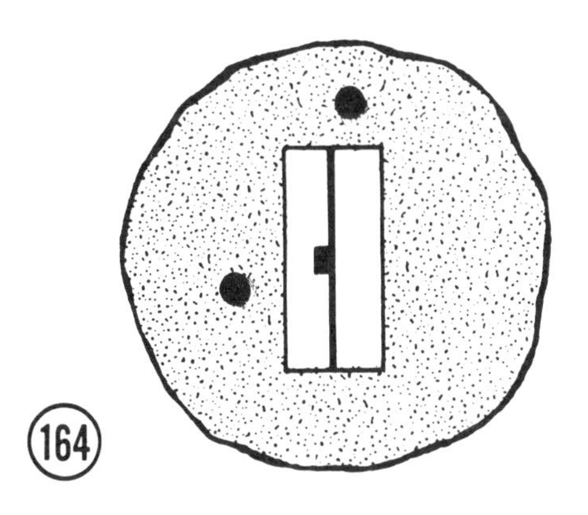
164

Since night lighting is important to the successful use of these enclosures, dig a trench from one post hole to closest point where electric cable can be connected to source. Following directions detailed in Book #694 Electrical Repairs Simplified, lay out a length of underground cable with sufficient overage to run up post to a junction box in canopy.

Cut 14" diameter concrete forms, Illus. 165, to length required to reinforce posts above grade. Cut ⅜ or ½" reinforcing rods to overall height of form plus 6". If holes are drilled 8" deep, rod will drop 2" below top of form. Insert rods in holes. Lock in place with a wet mixture of 1 part cement to 2½ parts of sand.

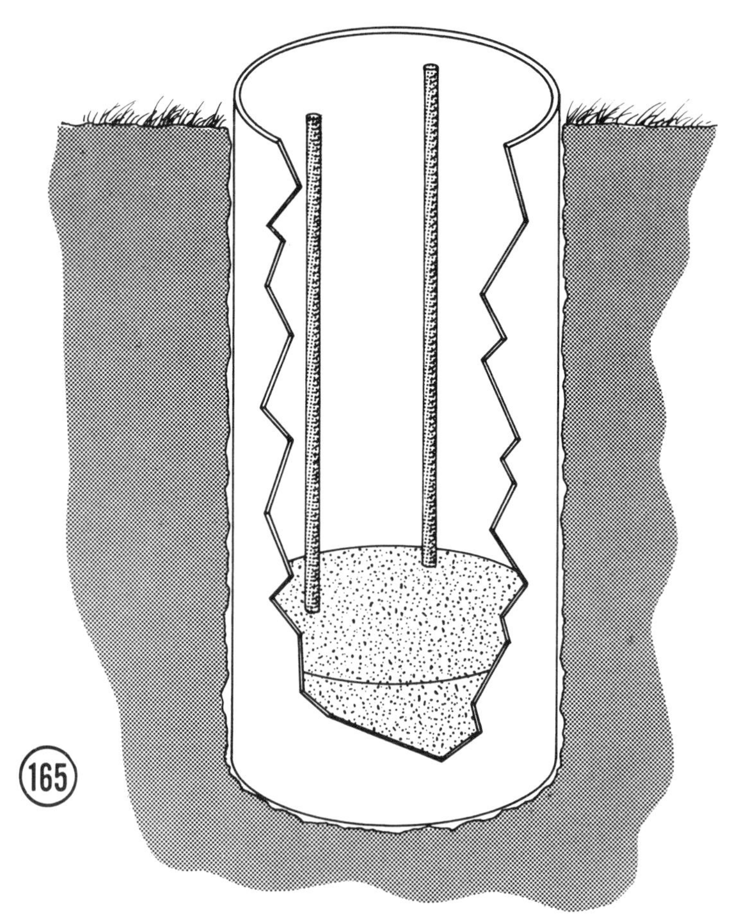

If you use 3 x 8 redwood or cedar for A, make saw cuts, chisel out a ½" slot, Illus. 166, in post. Cut slot to width cable requires. If two 2 x 8 are used for each post, cut a slot on inside face of one 2 x 8 to width and depth needed to receive type UF-NMC cable. After chiseling slot, apply creosote or other waterproofing agent. With sufficient cable extending at top to reach a junction box, and with cable laying in slot, spike 2 x 8's together using 16 penny nails.

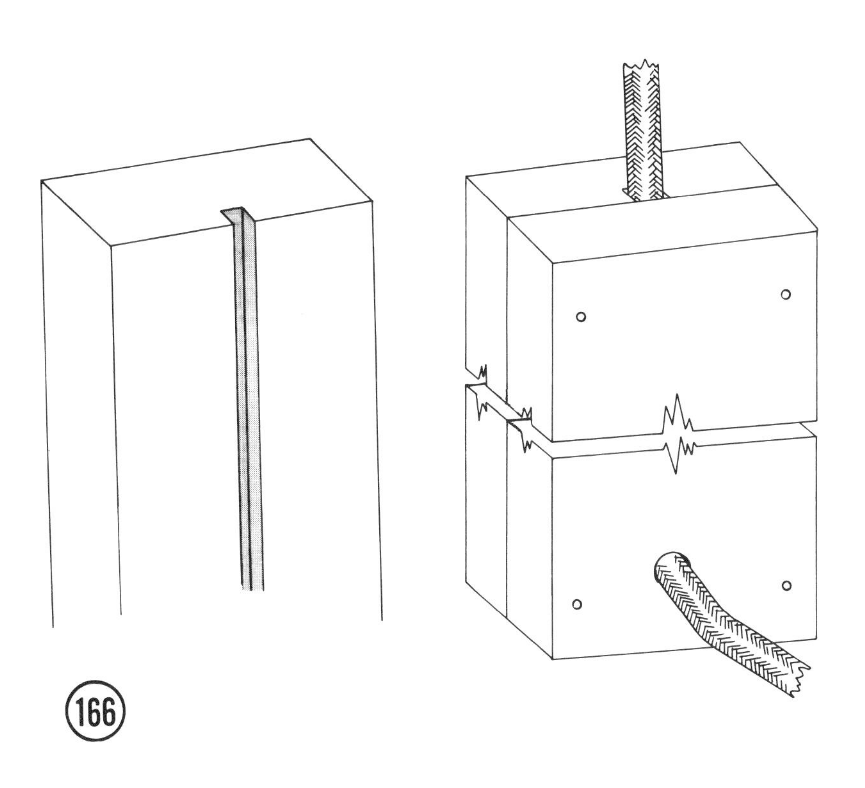

Due to the variance in lumber width and thickness, always measure and cut inner framing members to exact size previously assembled parts require.

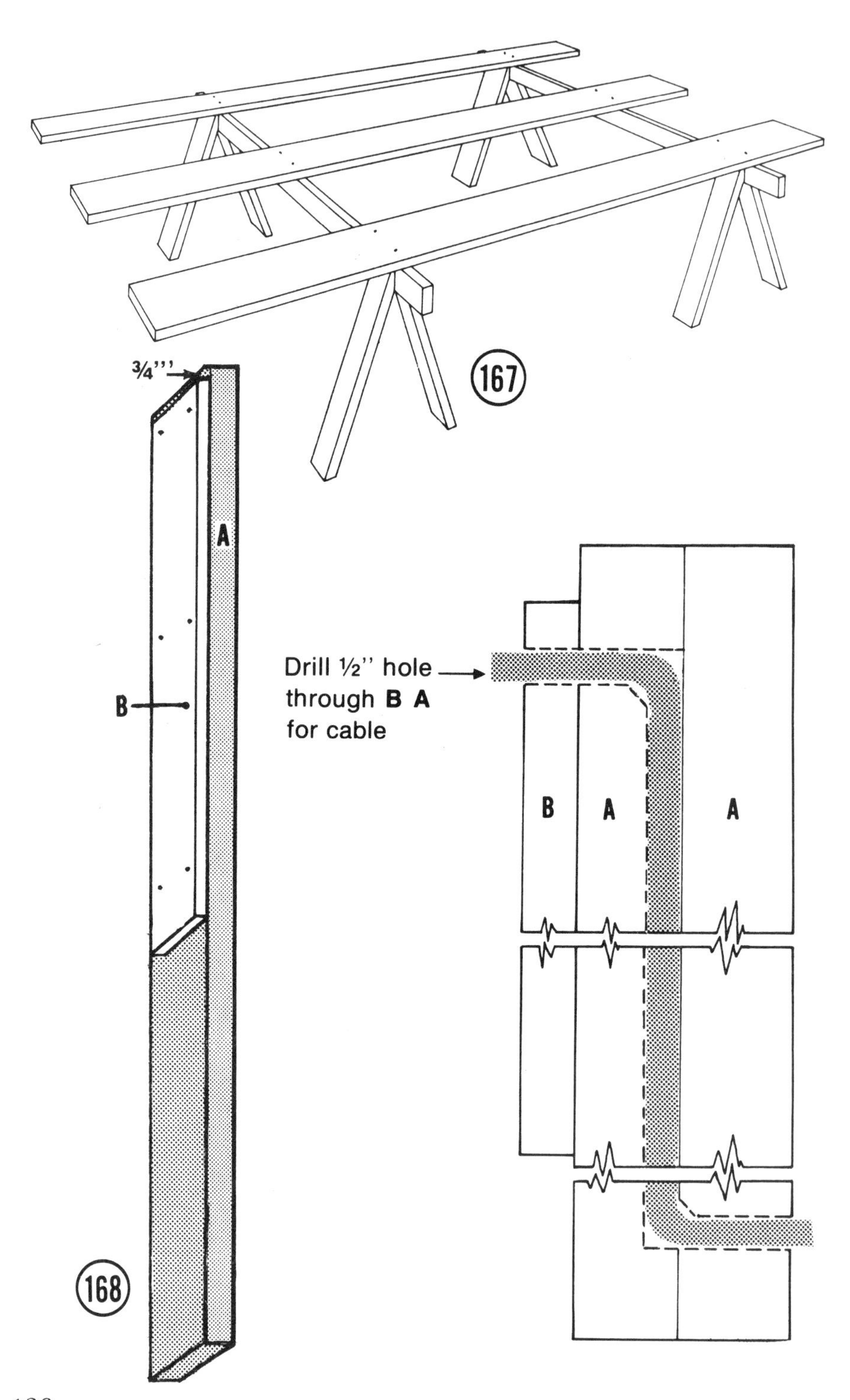
167
¾''
A
B
168
Drill ½'' hole
through B A
for cable
B
A
A

To simplify construction, space two sawhorses 6' apart. Toenail three 2 x 8 x 10' to sawhorses in position shown, Illus. 167.

Cut two B — 1 x 8 x 67¼", Illus. 168. Position B ¾" down from top of A and nail B to A using 8 penny finishing nails.

Cut one C — 1 x 8 x 52¾", Illus. 169. Nail C to B.

Check C and B with a square, Illus. 170.

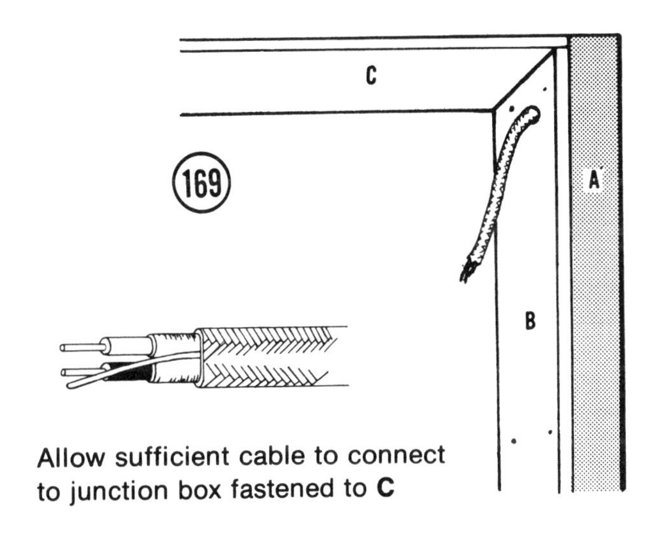

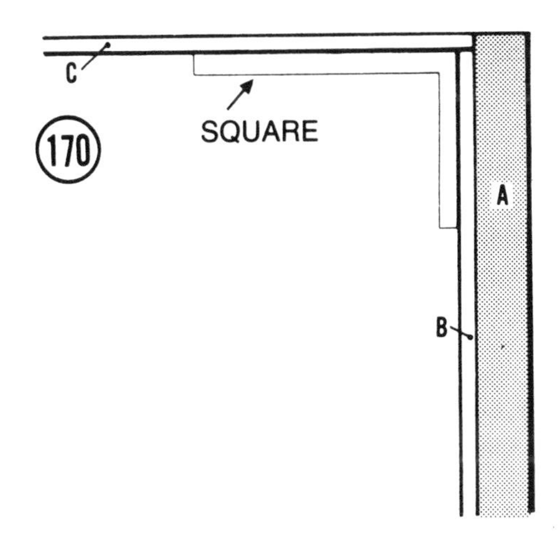

Nail 1 x 2 cross bracing to A, Illus. 171, to hold framing square.

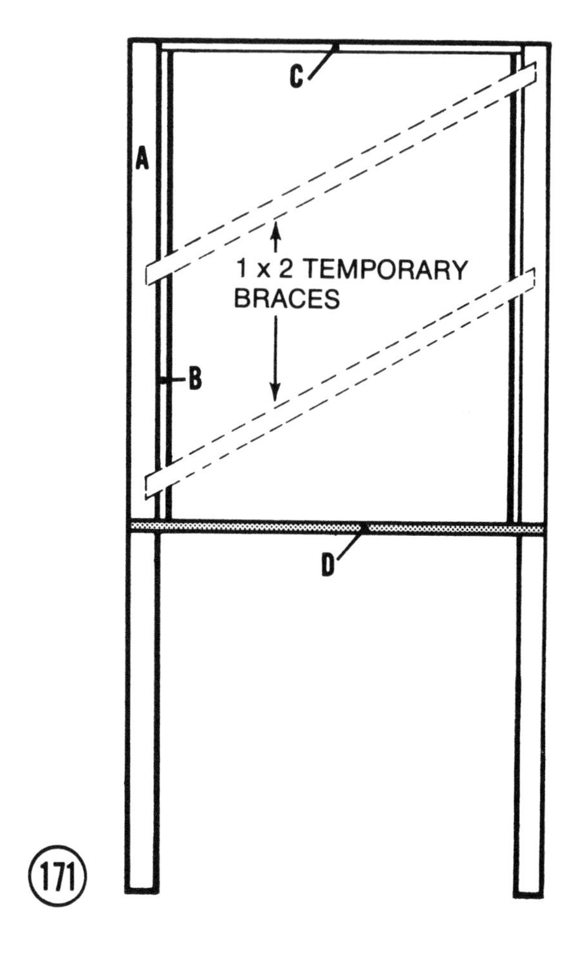

Cut one sill D from 5/4 x 12 x 5'0", Illus. 172. Notch ends of D to receive A. B butts against top of D. Bevel D along front and back edge. End view of bevel is shown, Illus. 173.

Nail through bottom of D into ends of B using 8 penny finishing nails. Nail a ¾ x ¾" stop to D, Illus. 174, on side receiving doors.

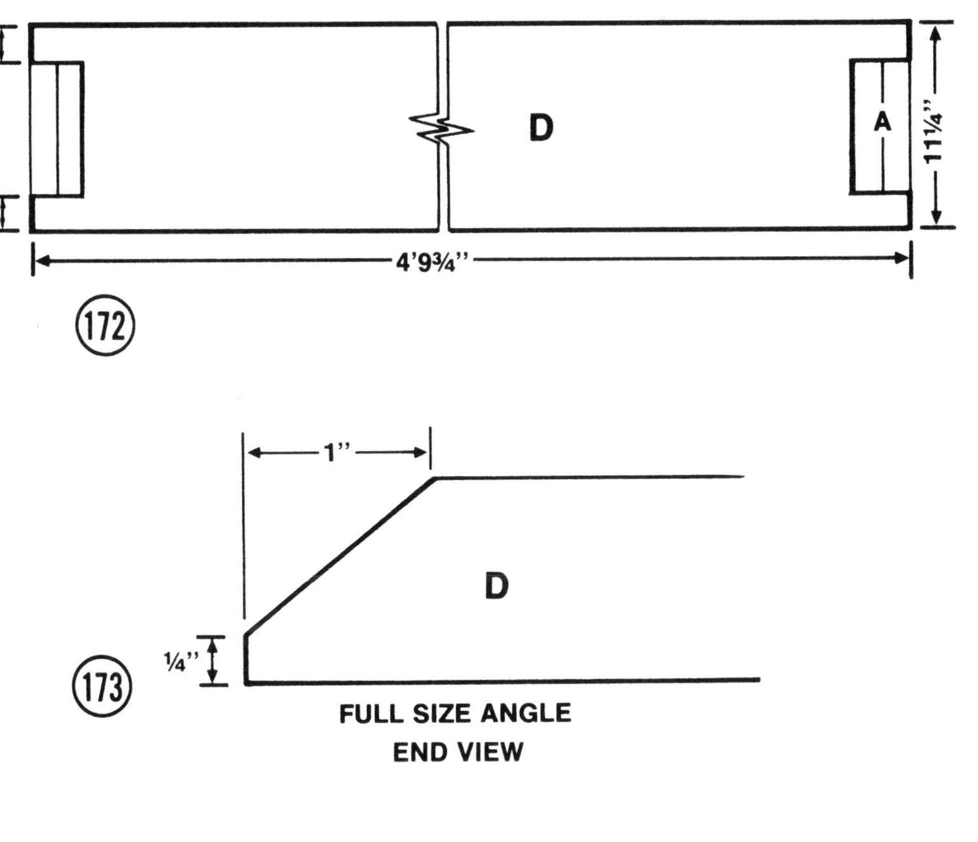

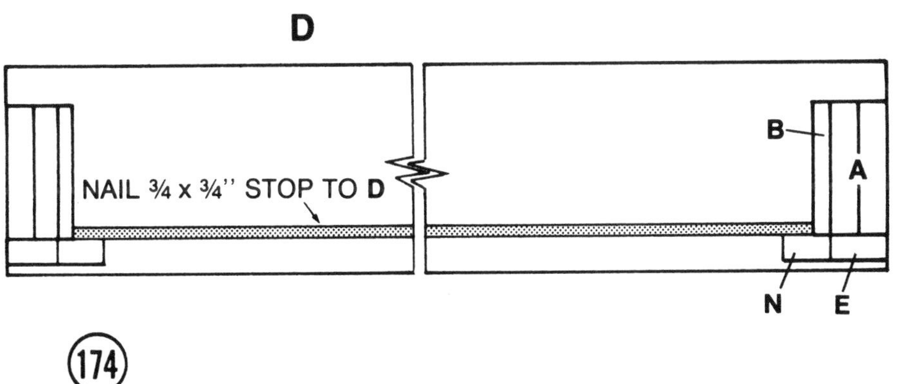

From this point on, apply parts to one face before turning assembly over. Remove 2 x 8 and position sawhorses so assembled unit doesn't rest on beveled edge of D. Note Illus. 185.

Cut four E, Illus. 175, from 5/4 x 4" to width of A. Cut E length required to butt against D and finish flush with top of A.

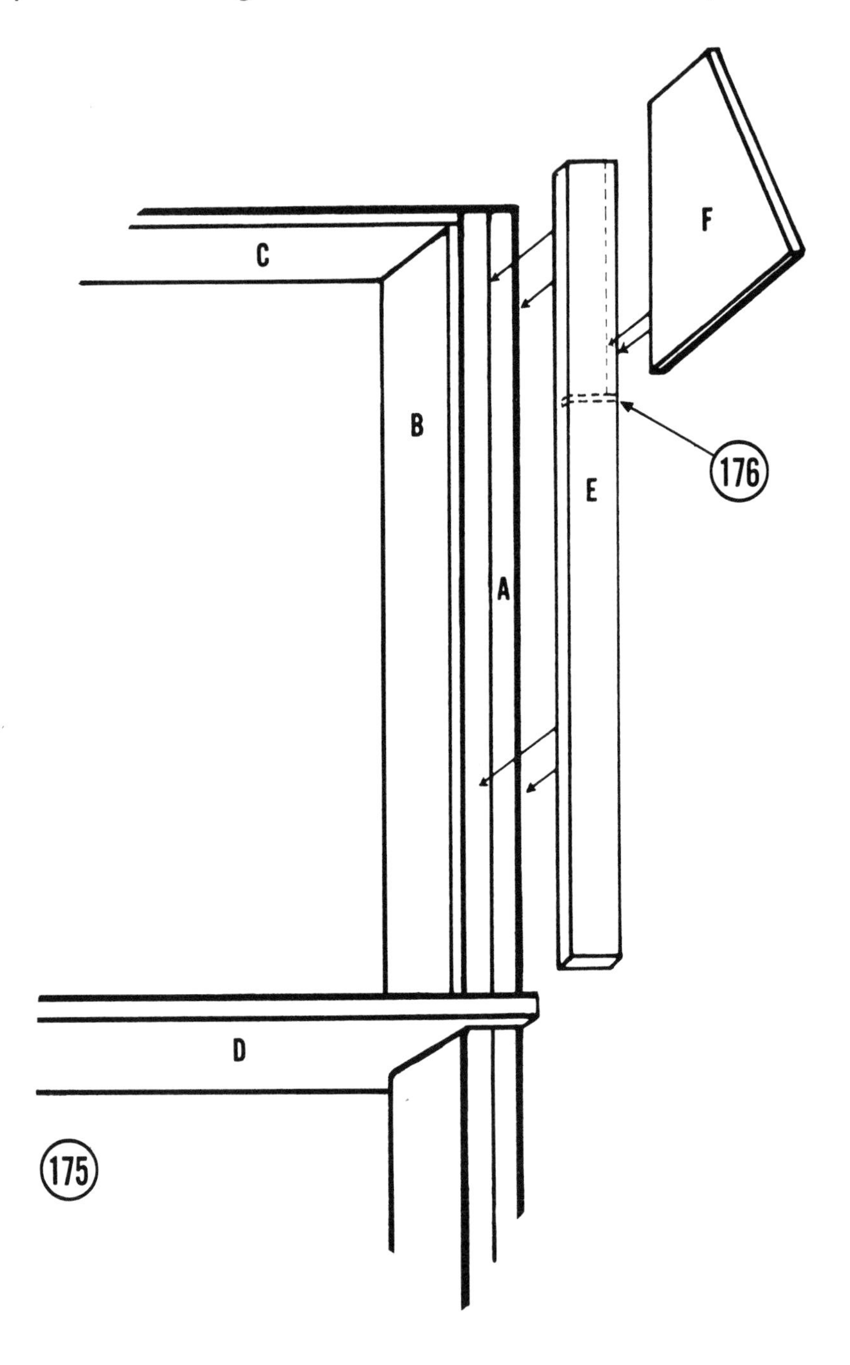

Saw ¾ x 15¾'' notch at top outside edge of E, to receive F, Illus. 175.

Make saw cut across E in position shown, Illus. 176, to receive acrylic ceiling panel. If you use ⅛'' acrylic for ceiling panel, make slot equal width. Nail E flush with edge of A using 8 penny finishing nails.

Cut four F, Illus. 177, ¾ x 12¾ x 16½ x 5¾''. Use exterior grade plywood.

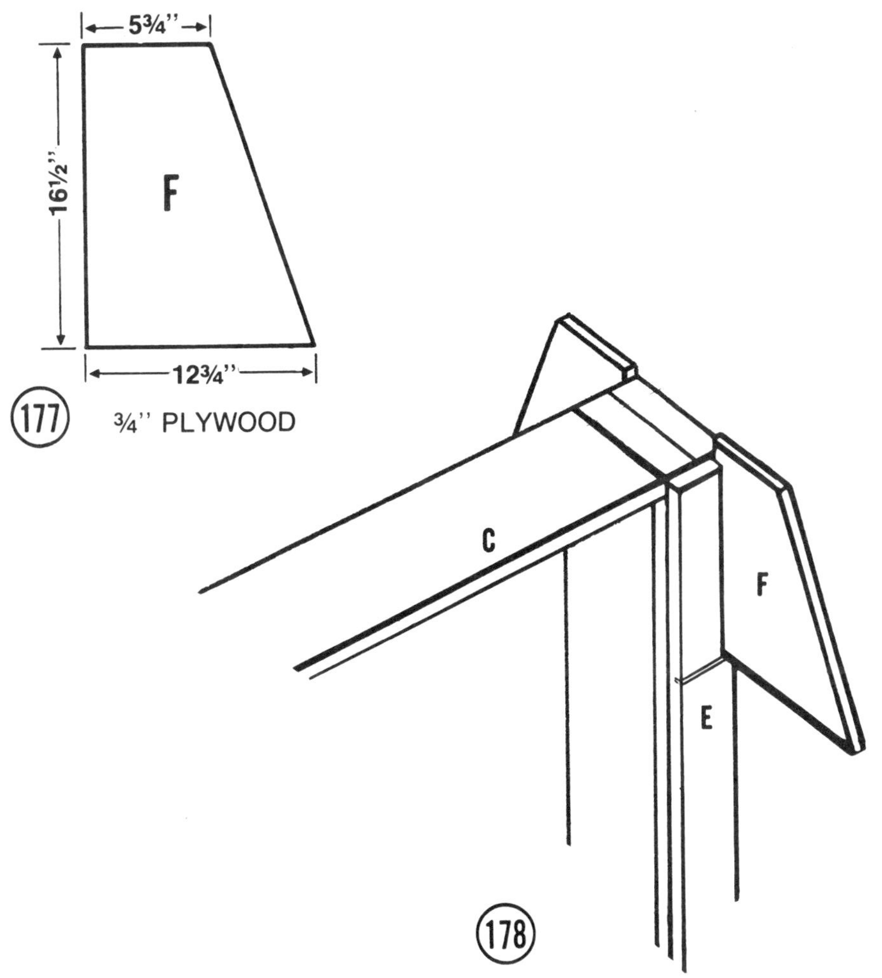

Apply glue and nail F to E, Illus. 178, with 6 penny finishing nails. NOTE: F projects ¾'' above top of AEC.

Using ¾" exterior grade plywood, cut G, Illus. 179, to overall width and length required so leading edge, beveled to angle of F, Illus. 180, is recessed ¾" from F. Notch ends of G to receive F.

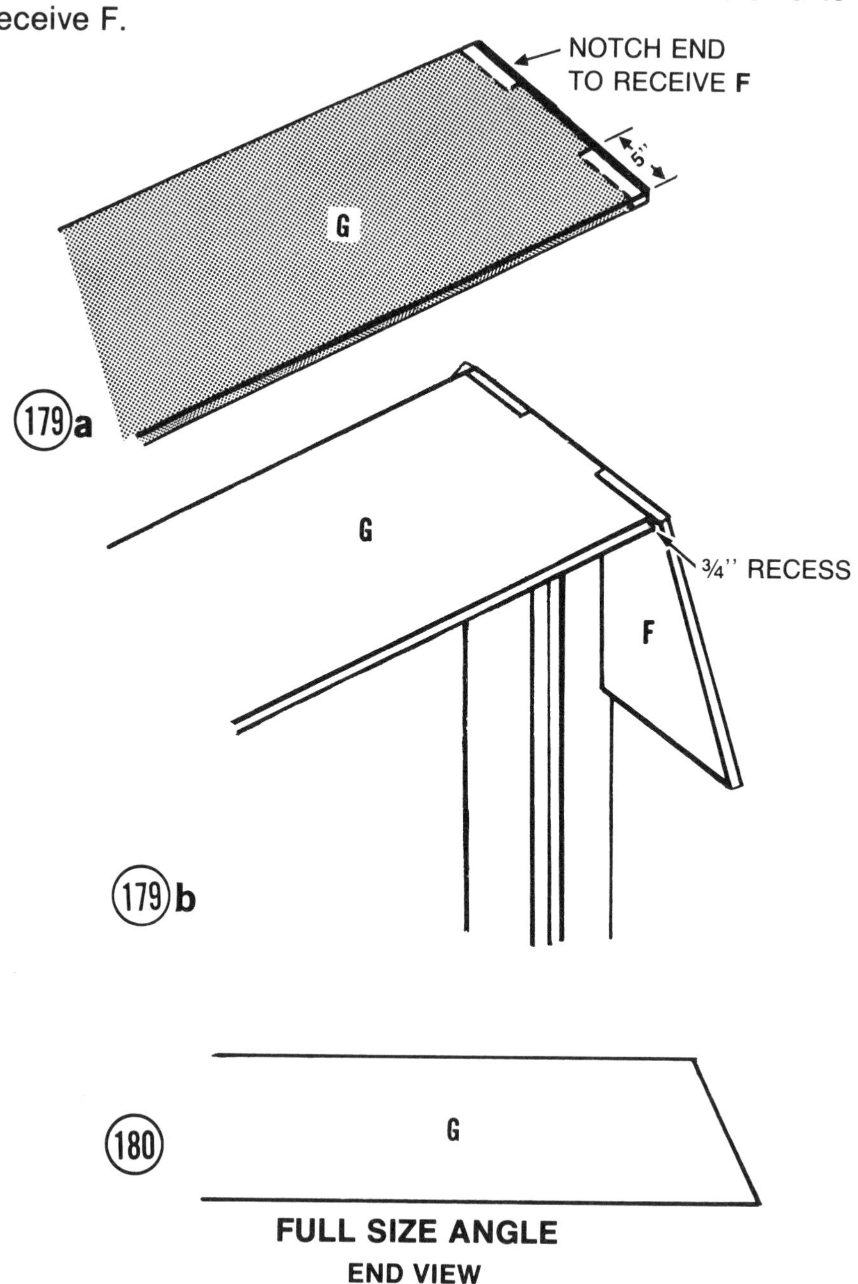

Cut two H, Illus. 181, to overall width and length required to butt against F and G. Plane top and bottom edge to angle shown, Illus. 182, or to angle required. Apply glue to edge of G and to ends of H. Nail F to H with 6 penny finishing nails. Using care, nail through H into edge of G with 3 penny finishing nails. Countersink heads. Fill holes with wood filler.

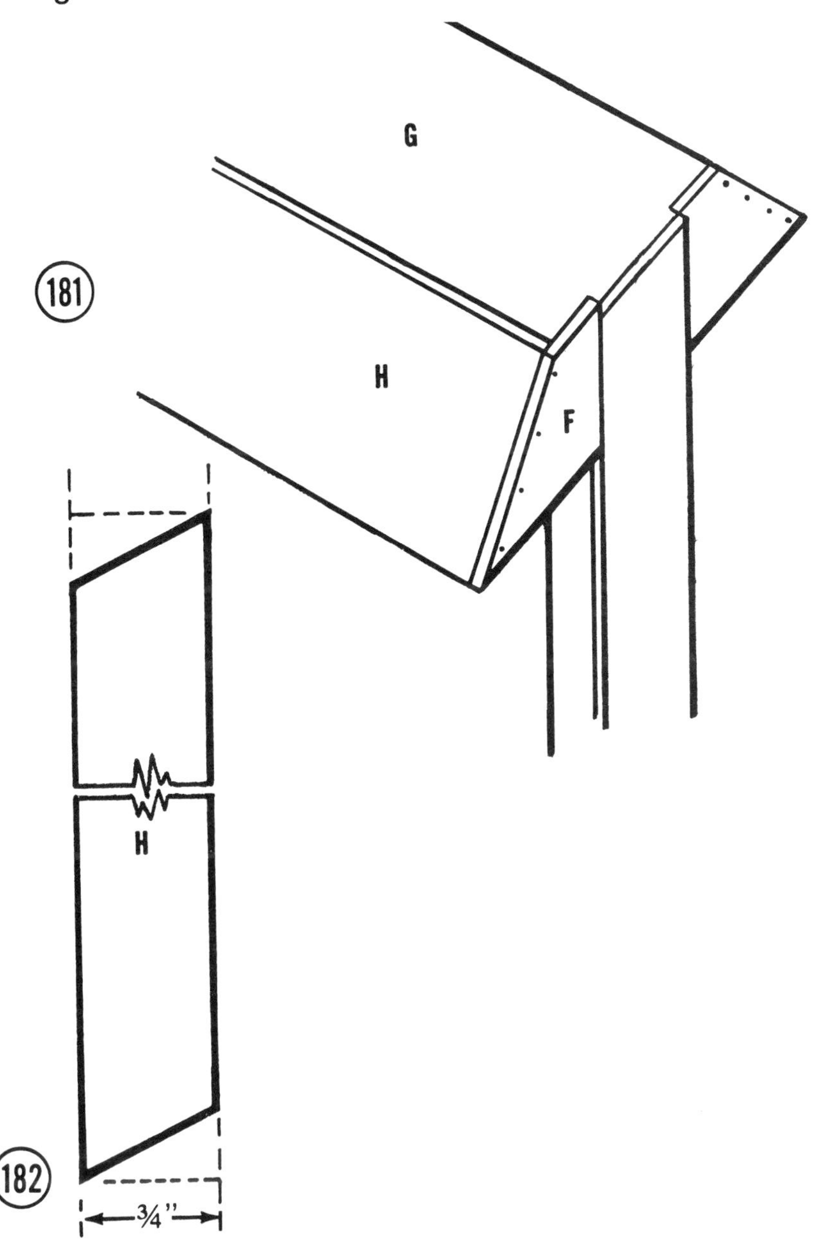

Cut two J, 5/4 x 2" to length required to butt against E, Illus. 183. Apply glue and nail J to B so bottom edge is level with top edge of slot through E. This permits sliding acrylic ceiling into position, Illus. 211. If you use ⅛" acrylic for ceiling, space K ⅛" from J. Use a level to insure nailing J accurately.

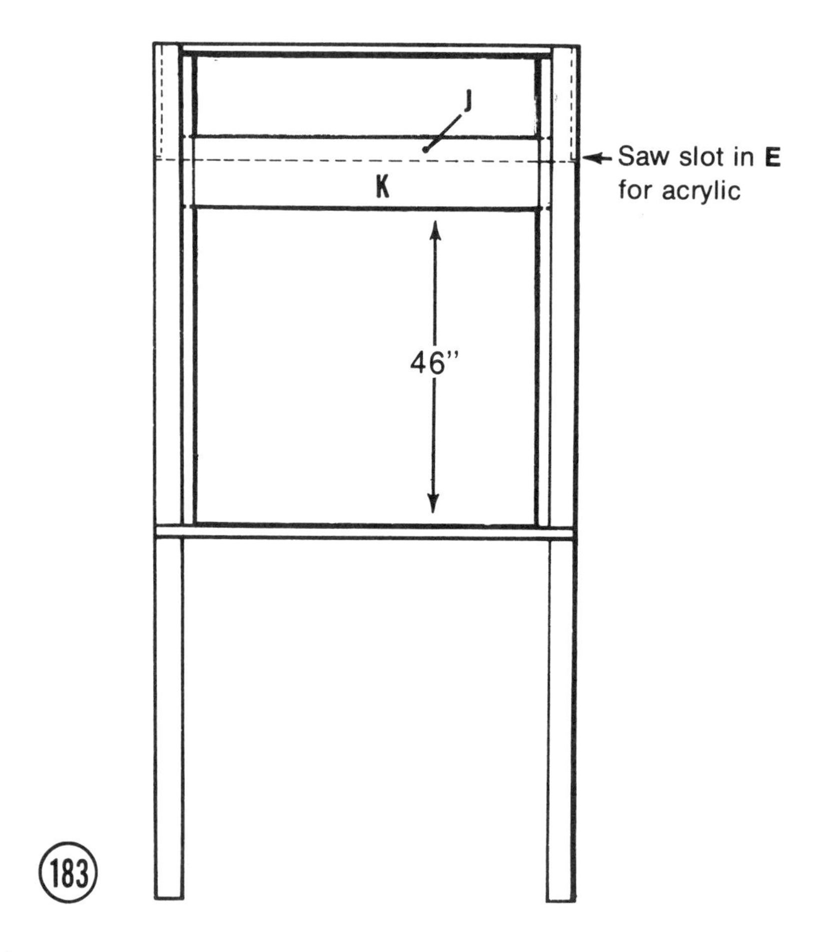

Cut 5/4" K, Illus. 183, 184, to width that allows 46" for doors. Apply glue, check with square and nail K in position. Countersink nail heads. Fill holes with putty.

K provides a good place to apply a nameplate. Apply letters or paint nameplate. Book #607 How to Build Fences, Gates, Outdoor Projects, offers a full size lettering guide.

VILLAGE OF BRIARCLIFF MANOR
184

NOTE: Dimensions provided for door parts are exact size; i.e., N — 5/4 x 2'', requires cutting N 2''.

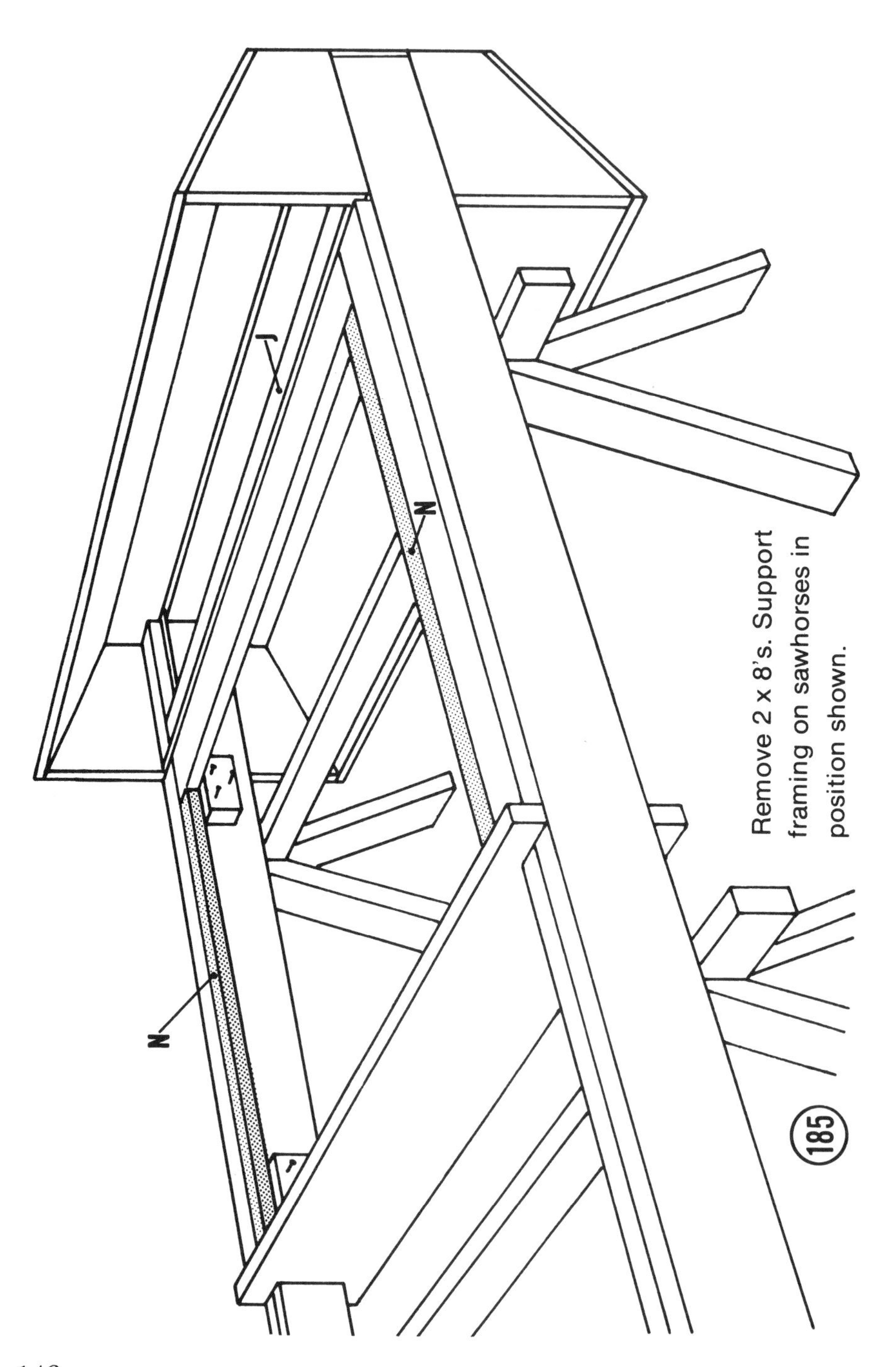

185

Remove 2 x 8's. Support framing on sawhorses in position shown.

To build a pair of doors, cut two stiles N, 5/4 x 2" by length needed, Illus. 185. Tack 1 x 2 support blocks in position to hold door framing N,O,P flush with EK.

Cut center stile O from 5/4 x 2"; stile P from 5/4 x 2¾" by length required, Illus. 186.

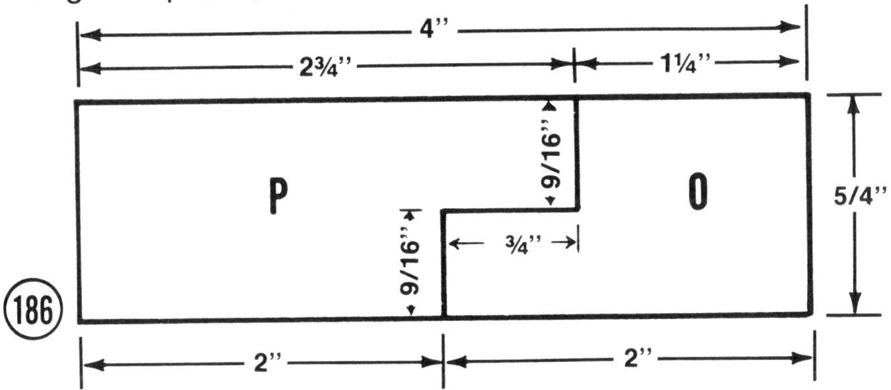

Set table saw to cut ¾" depth. Set fence to permit making a 9/16" cut, Illus. 187. Run edge of O and P through saw.

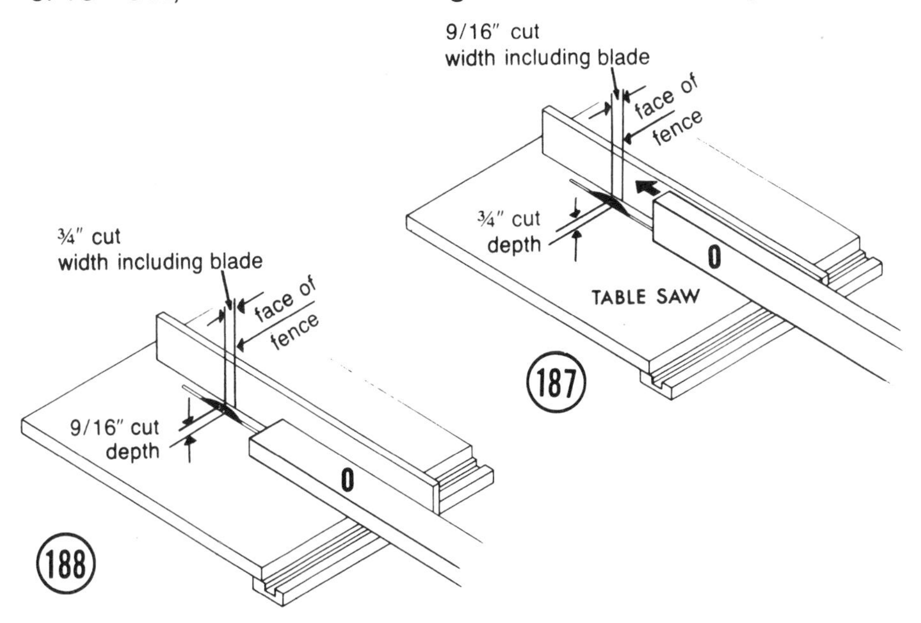

Reset saw for a 9/16" depth cut. Set fence to allow a ¾" cut, Illus. 188. Run O and P flatwise through saw. Cut O and P to length required.

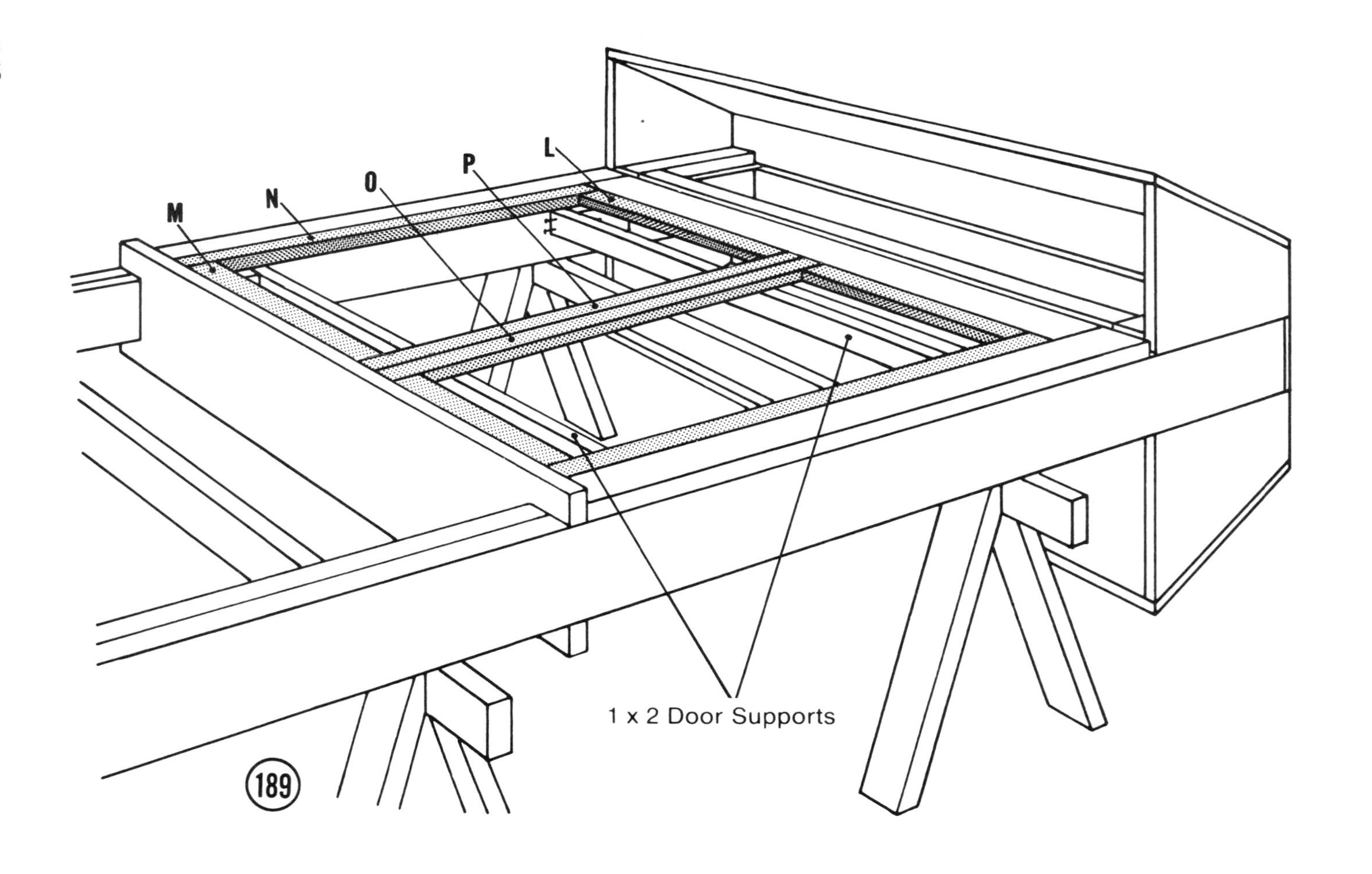
M
N
O
P
L
1 x 2 Door Supports
189

Place OP in position in center of opening, Illus. 189. Cut two top rails L, 5/4 x 2¾" by length required. Cut two bottom rails M, 5/4 x 3¾" by length required. Place in position.

To assemble a door frame with dowels, make a drill jig, Illus. 190. Cut two pieces of ¼ x 3 x 8" plywood, one 5/4 x 5/4 x 8". Position pattern, Illus. 191, over 5/4 x 5/4. Punch centers with a nail. Drill ⅜" holes through 5/4 x 5/4. Nail ¼" plywood to sides.

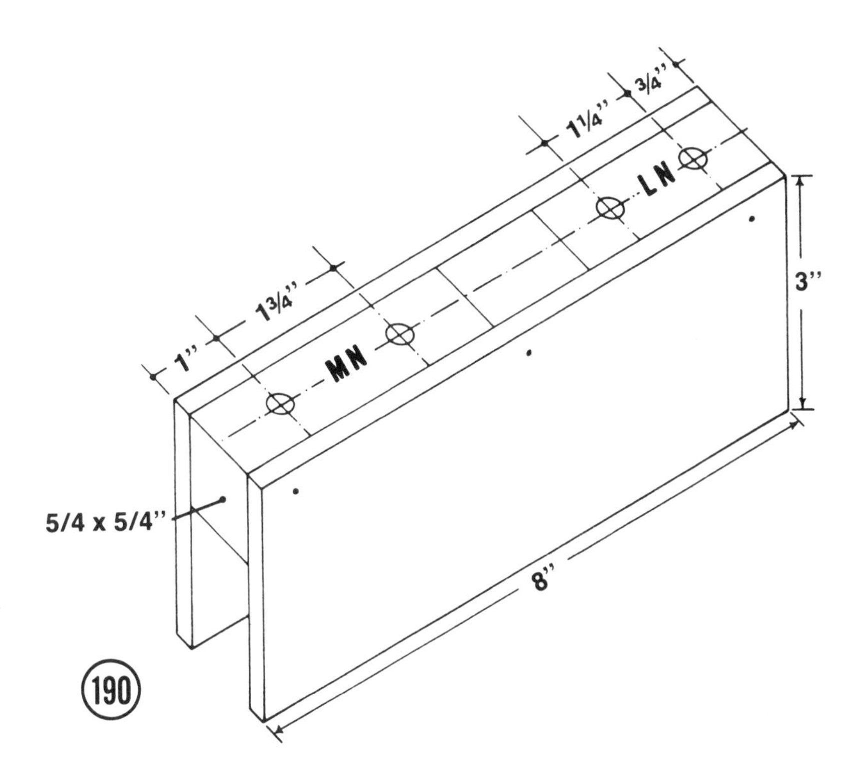

To assemble N to M and L; O to L and M, each joint should be joined with two dowels, Illus. 192. The exact location of these dowels is shown in Illus. 191.

If you are using a hand or electric drill, place N in a vise or bench clamp, Illus. 192, with the LN edge up. Place jig flush with end of L and drill holes spaced as shown, Illus. 193. Reposition jig and drill holes for MN.

FULL SIZE PATTERN

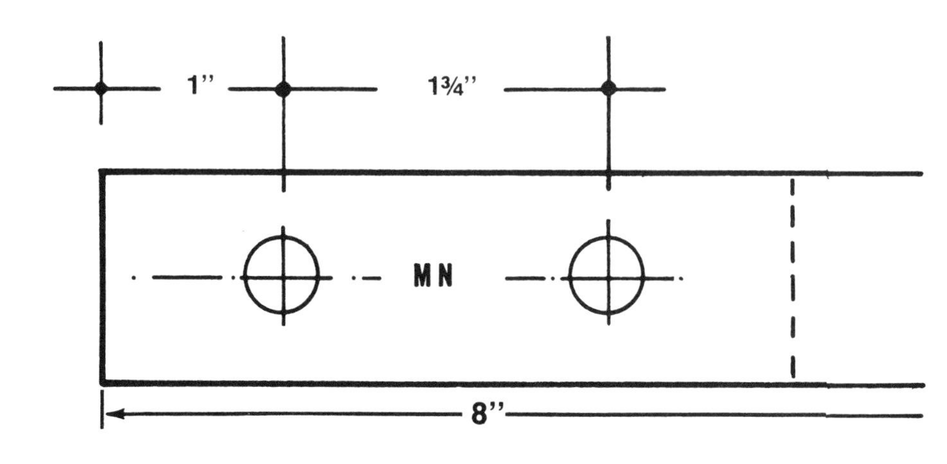

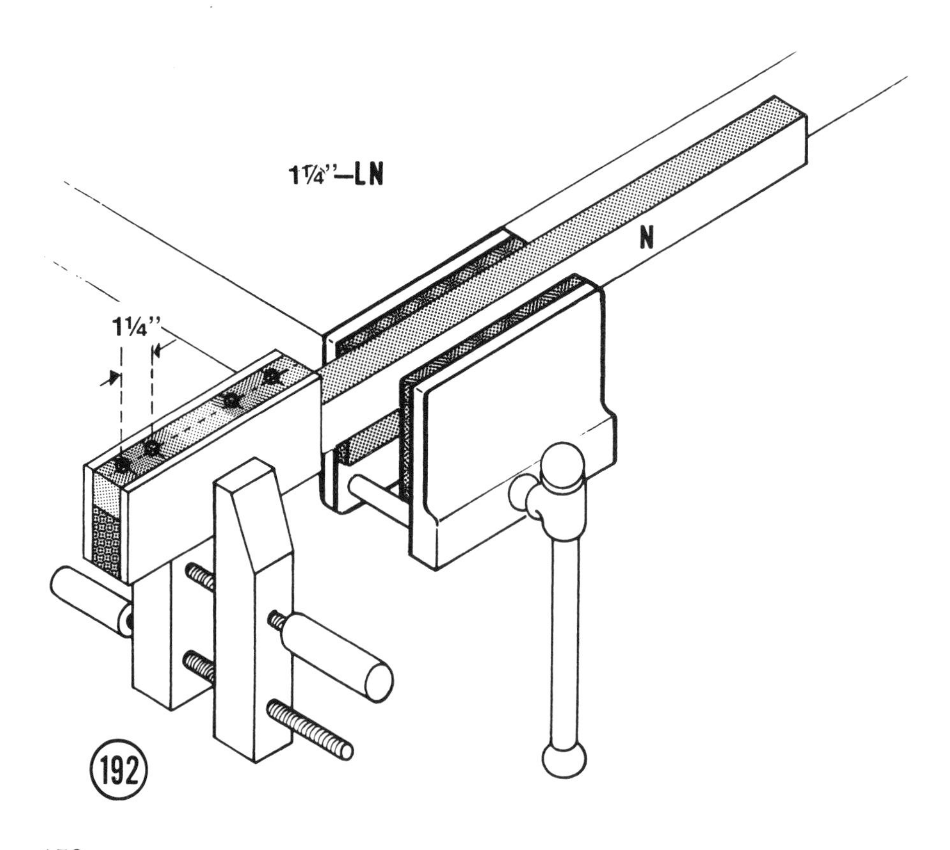

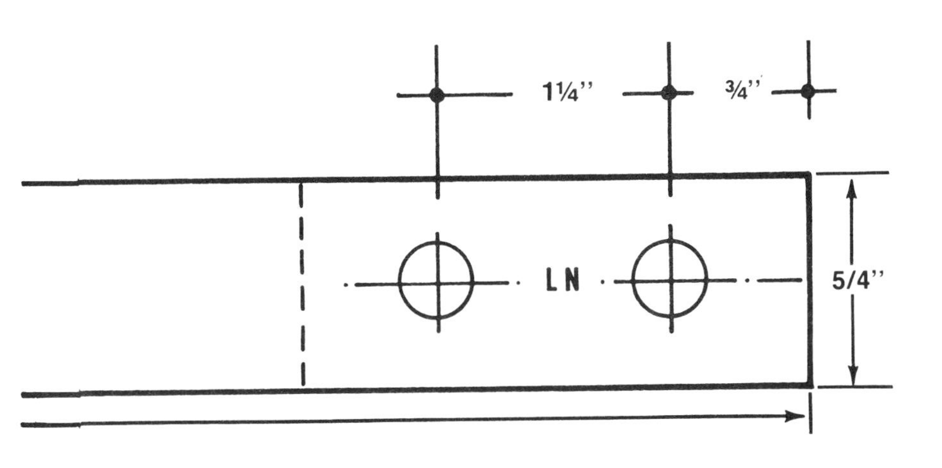
1¼''
¾''
LN
5/4''

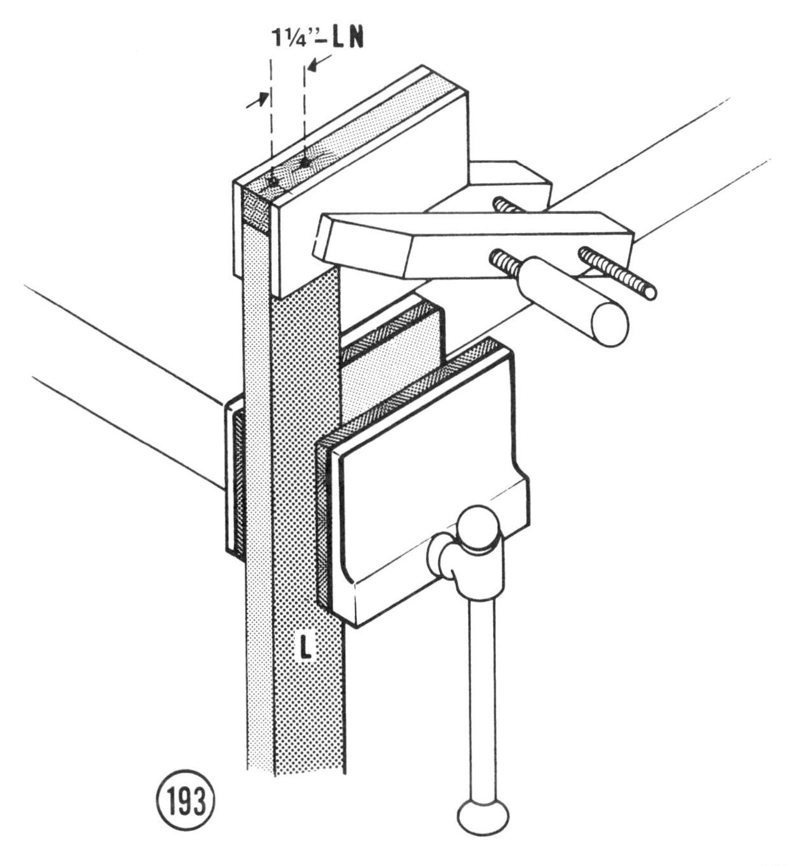
1¼''-LN
L
193

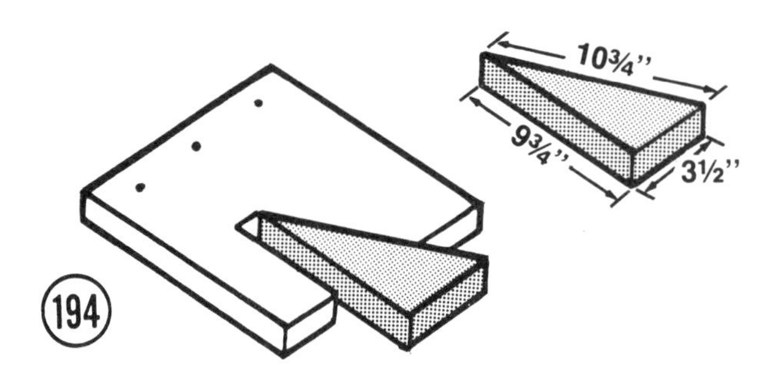

A bench clamp can be made by cutting the base 9 x 14". Saw a wedge 3½ x 9¾ x 10¾". This permits standing frame in position shown, Illus. 194,195.

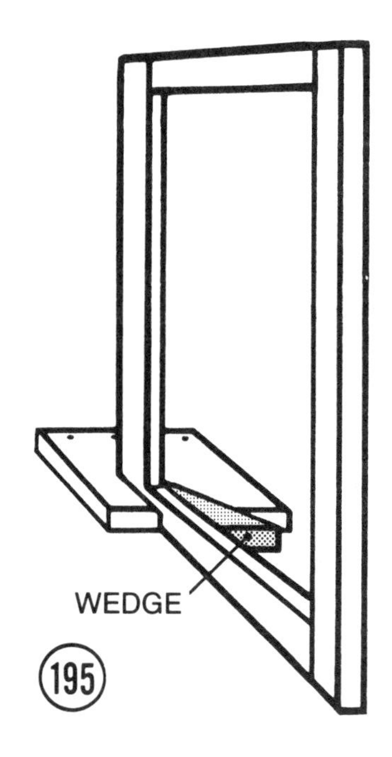

Nailing stops to your workbench, Illus. 196, simplifies driving dowels in position, also squaring up frame.

Place jig over end of L. Drill holes that match those in N. Follow same procedure to drill holes in LO and MO.

Drill ⅜" holes, ¾" deep. Place a piece of tape around end of drill, Illus. 197, at ¾".

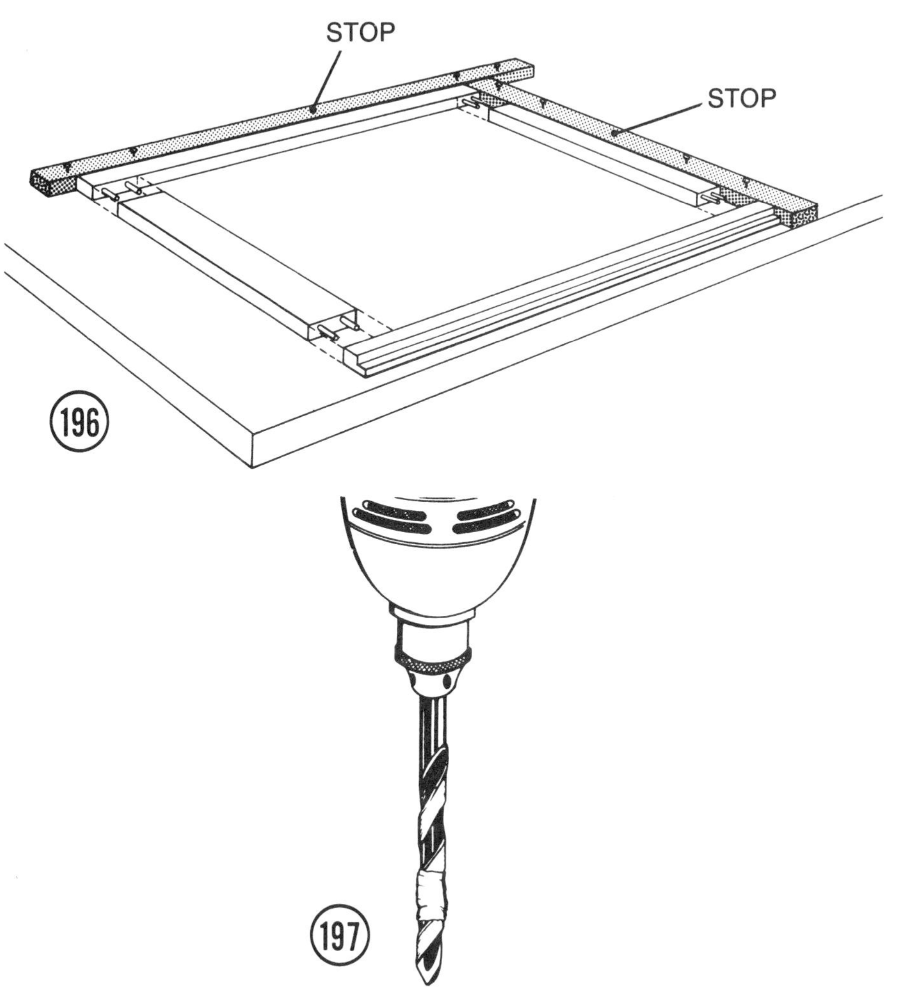

Insert 3/8 x 1 3/8'' dowels dry, no glue. Assemble NLMO without glue to make certain frame is square. When OK, take it apart, apply glue to dowels and assemble frame. Check with square. Hold square with clamps, Illus. 198, until glue sets thoroughly.

198

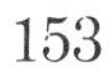

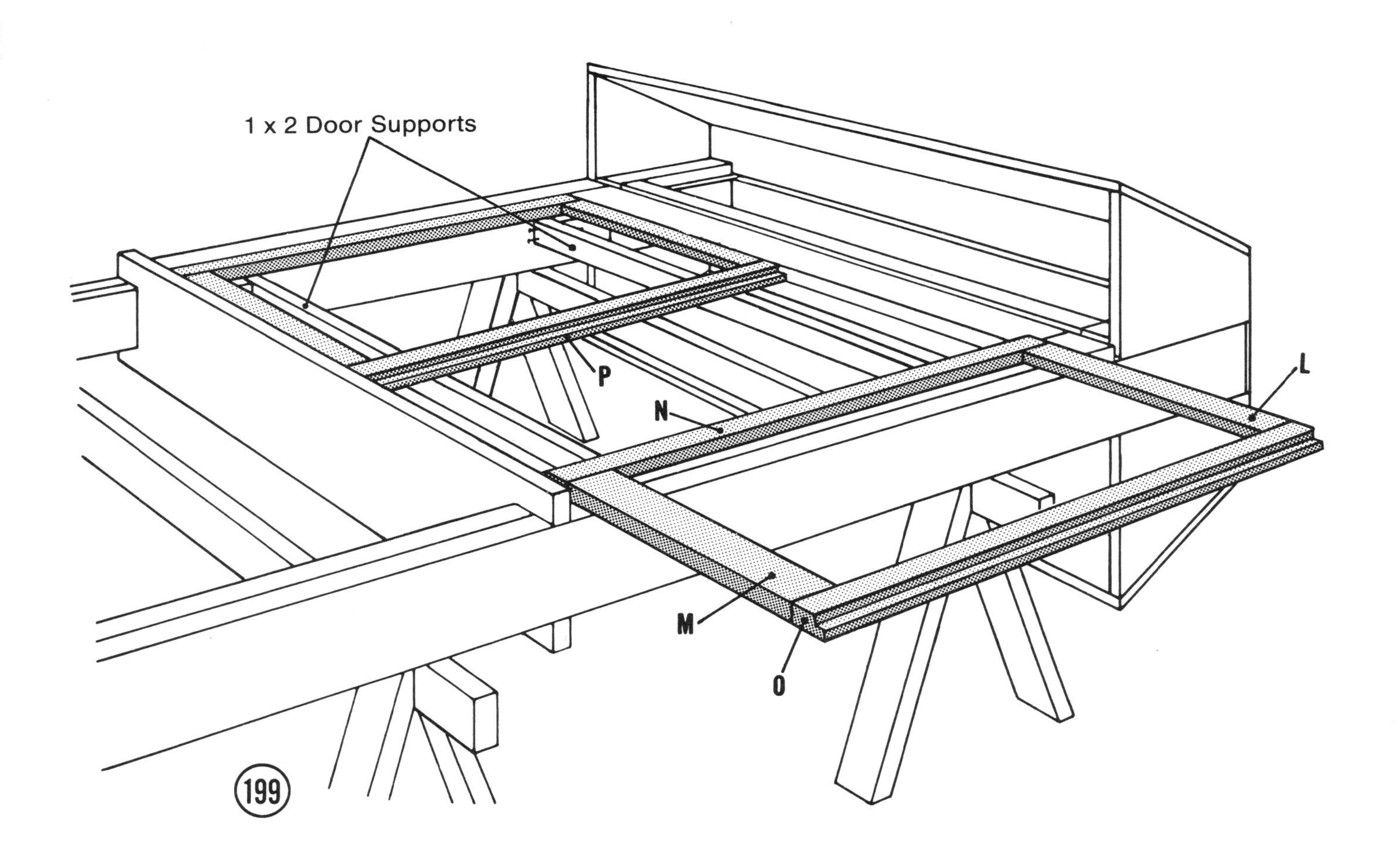
1 x 2 Door Supports
P
N
L
M
O
199

Place assembled frame in opening. Block in position, Illus. 199. After assembling second frame dry, place in position to make certain it fits. Place hinges, Illus. 202, in place. When doors with hinges fit opening, apply glue and dowel frame together. Prior to fastening hinges, paint doors and enclosure inside and out using exterior paint. Apply a prime coat, allow to dry, then sandpaper lightly prior to application of first finishing coat. Sandpaper again before applying second coat.

Cut ¼" acrylic to overall size each door requires, less 3/16" in width and height.

Miter cut ⅜" quarter round to length required. Apply glue and nail quarter round just inside outside edge, Illus. 200. Place acrylic in position and nail inside quarter round in place, Illus. 201. Use 1" brads only, no glue on inside quarter round.

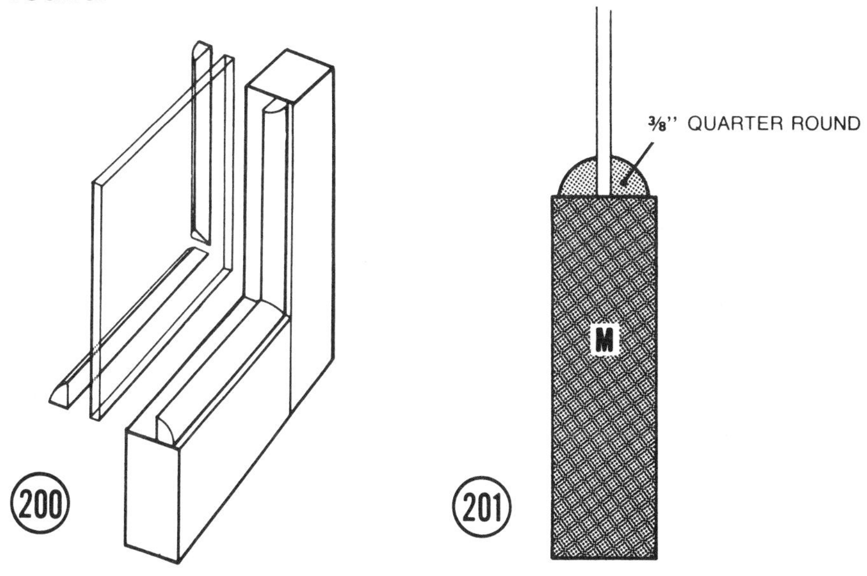

For side without doors, cut one panel of ¼" acrylic to full size of opening, less 3/16" in overall height and width. This allows for expansion. Recess inner quarter round ⅞" from face of E. Apply glue and nail ⅜" quarter round for inner molding. Place acrylic in position. Use 1" brad, no glue, when nailing outer quarter round in position.

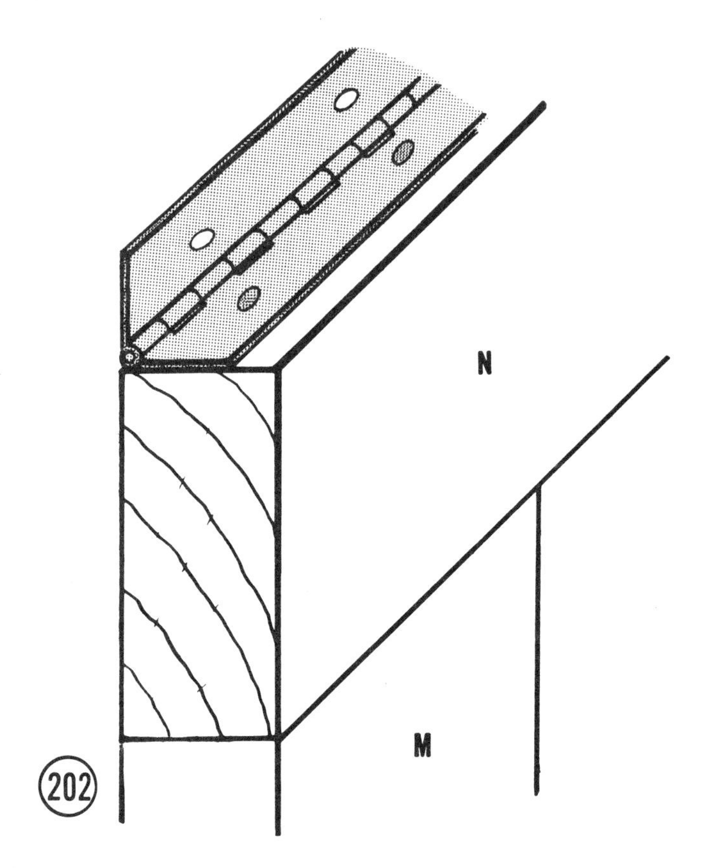

Fasten 1½" continuous hinge to edge of N, Illus. 202, and to edge of E, Illus. 203, with screws hinge manufacturer specifies.

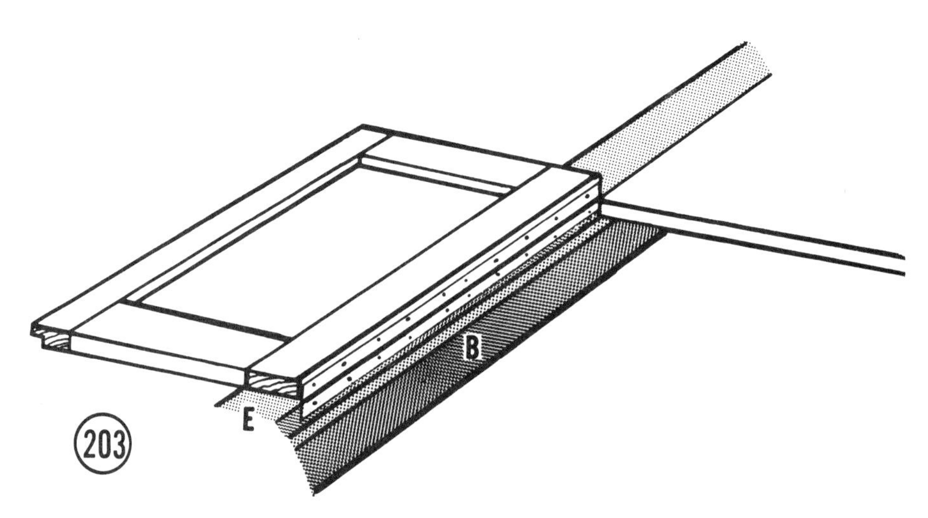

When doors are fitted so they operate freely, fasten 3'' sliding bolts, Illus. 204, at top and bottom, in position shown to left hand door, Illus. 205.

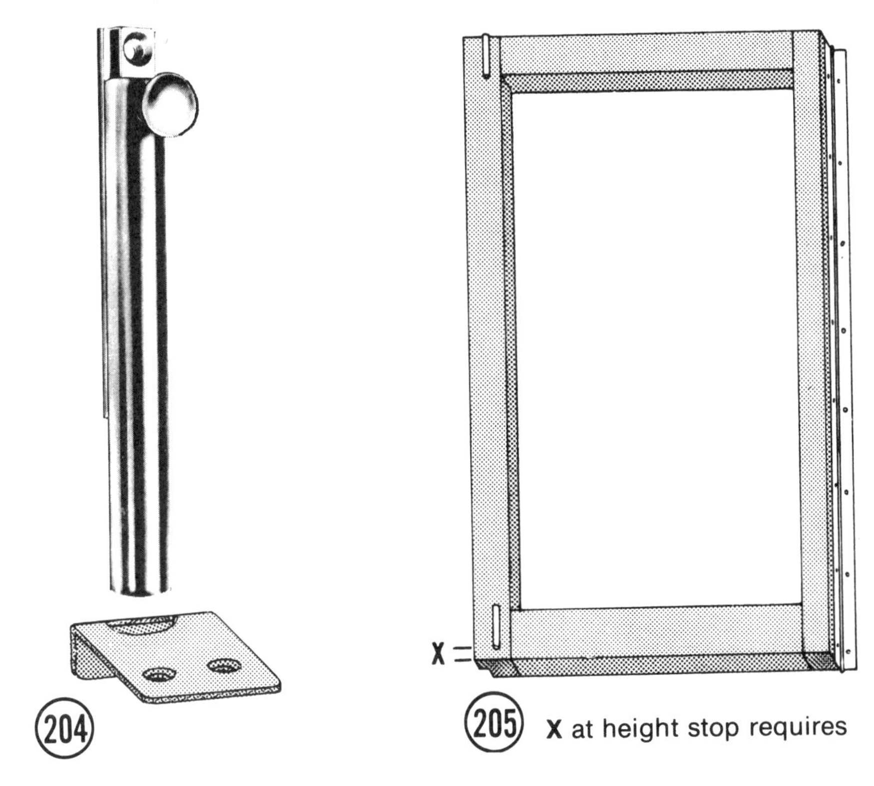

X at height stop requires

Draw outline of strike plate in position required on stop, Illus. 206. Mortise stop thickness plate requires. Chisel hole to receive bolt, Illus. 207. Fasten strike in position, Illus. 208.

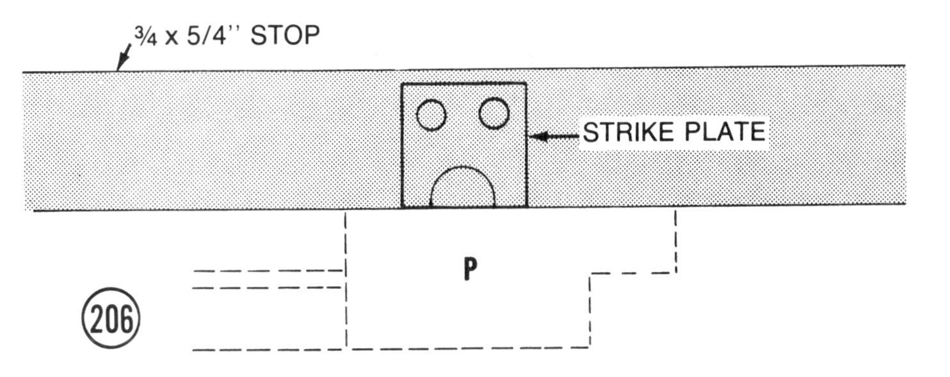

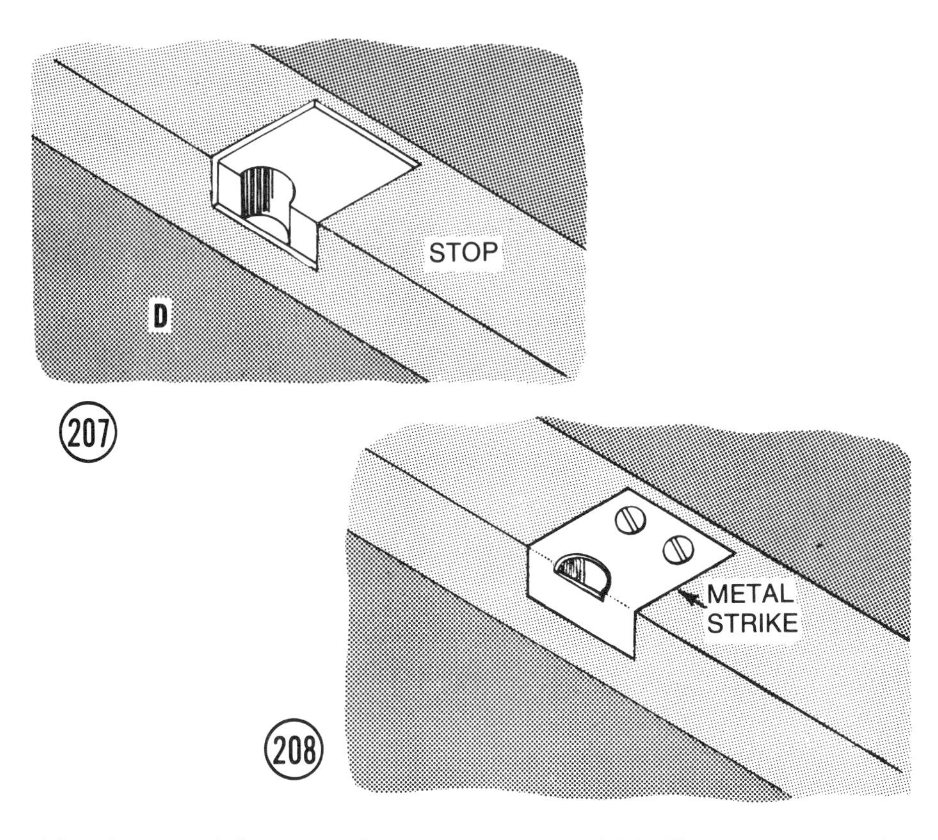

Mortise and fasten plate to stop and K, Illus. 208,209, in position required.

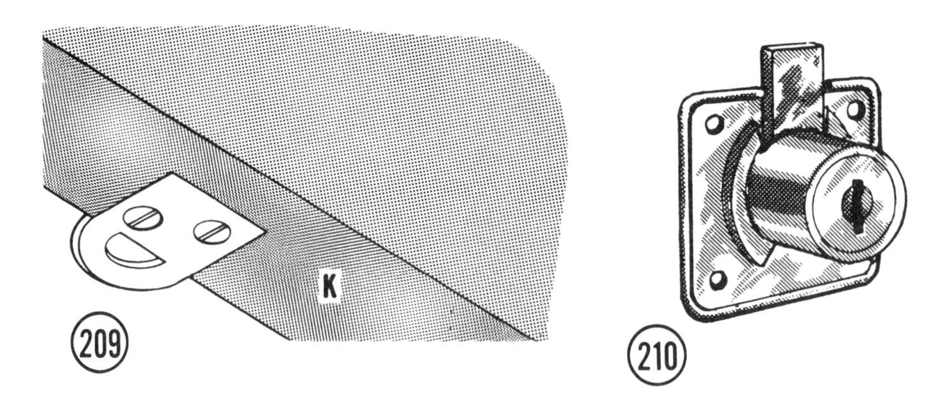

Fasten lock, Illus. 210, to O. Drill hole to size cylinder requires. If necessary, countersink lock following manufacturer's directions. Fasten strike plate in position to P.

Apply wood shingles to canopy, Illus. 211. Allow starter course to project ¾'' over edge of H. Apply a second course flush with edge of starter course. Cut shingles to length required and apply each course to allow a 6'' exposure. Stain shingles.

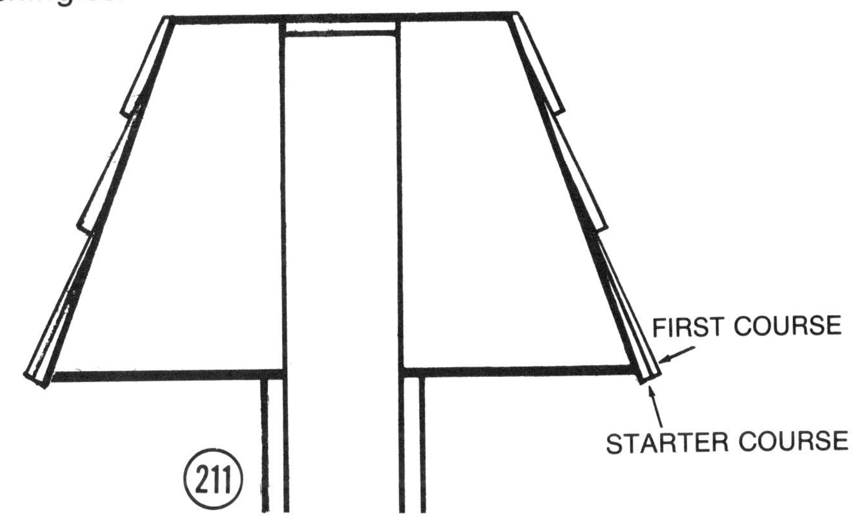

Install a four foot fluorescent fixture to each H in position shown, Illus. 212. Book #694 Electrical Repairs Simplified contains complete details.

Cut a piece of acrylic to width and length needed to slide through slot in EJK.

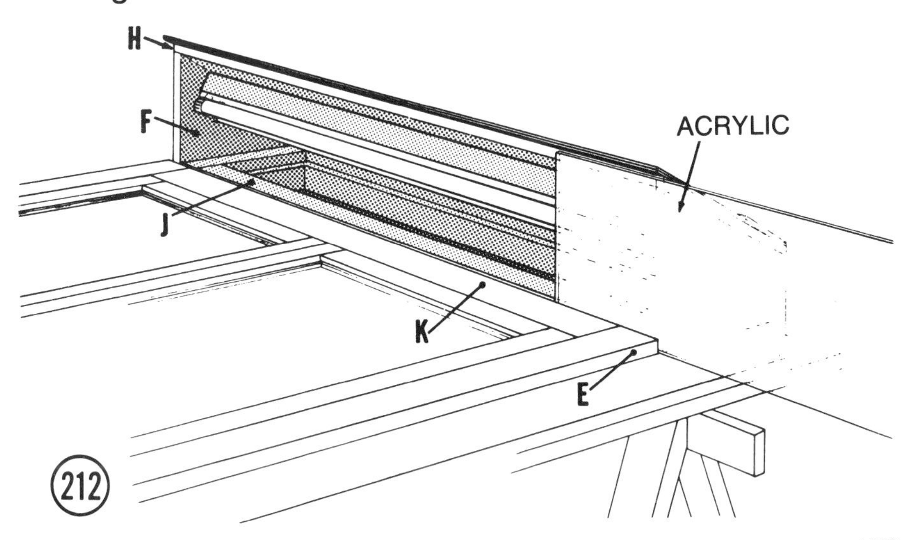

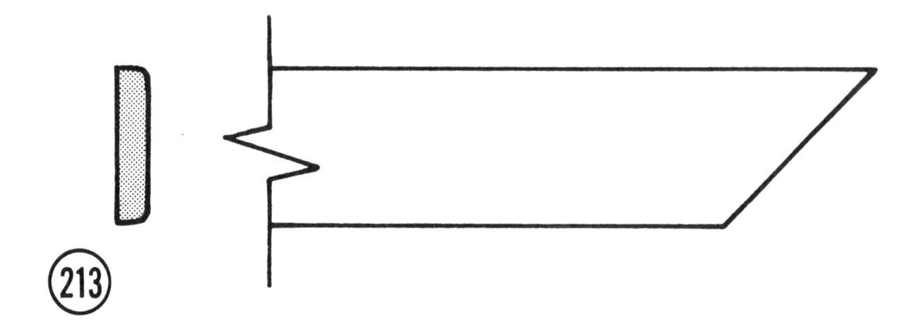

Miter cut ends of ¾" screen molding, Illus. 213. Drill ⅛" holes through molding and acrylic. Fasten molding and acrylic to bottom of F and H with No. 5 roundhead wood screws spaced approximately 6" apart, Illus. 214.

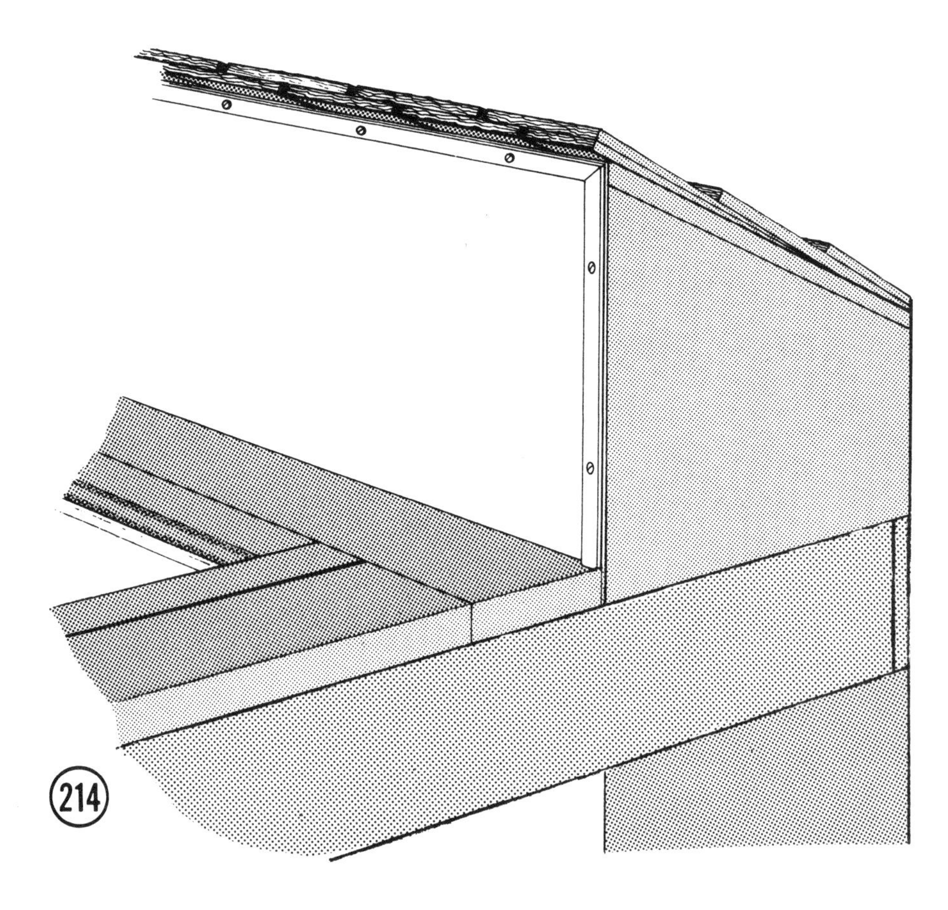

Cut sheet aluminum to overall width of GH and to length of G, plus 2" in width and length, Illus. 215. This allows 1" projection all around. Cut metal 1" in direction indicated at X and Y.

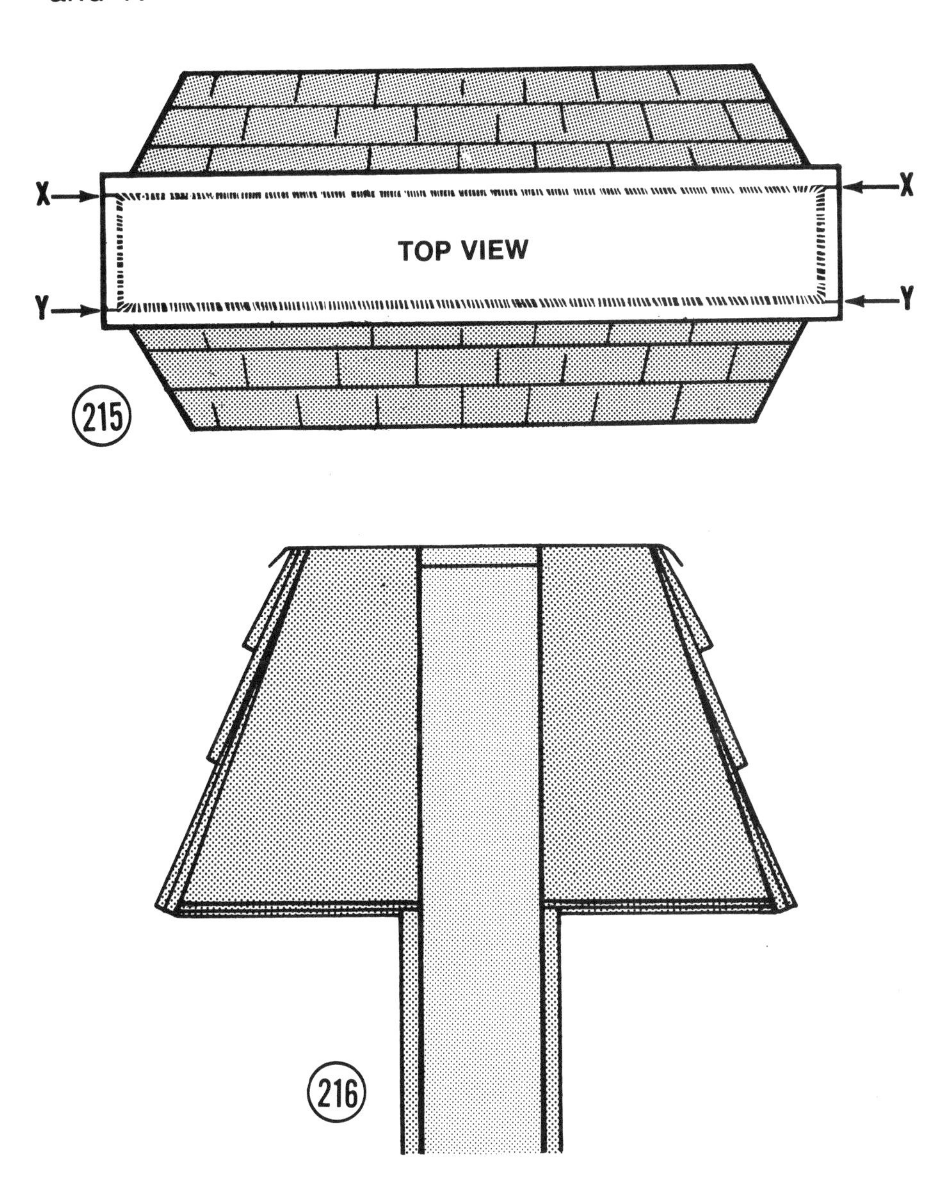

Bend front, back, then ends, Illus. 216. Cut projecting end off tab. Nail in place, Illus. 217,218, using aluminum nails.

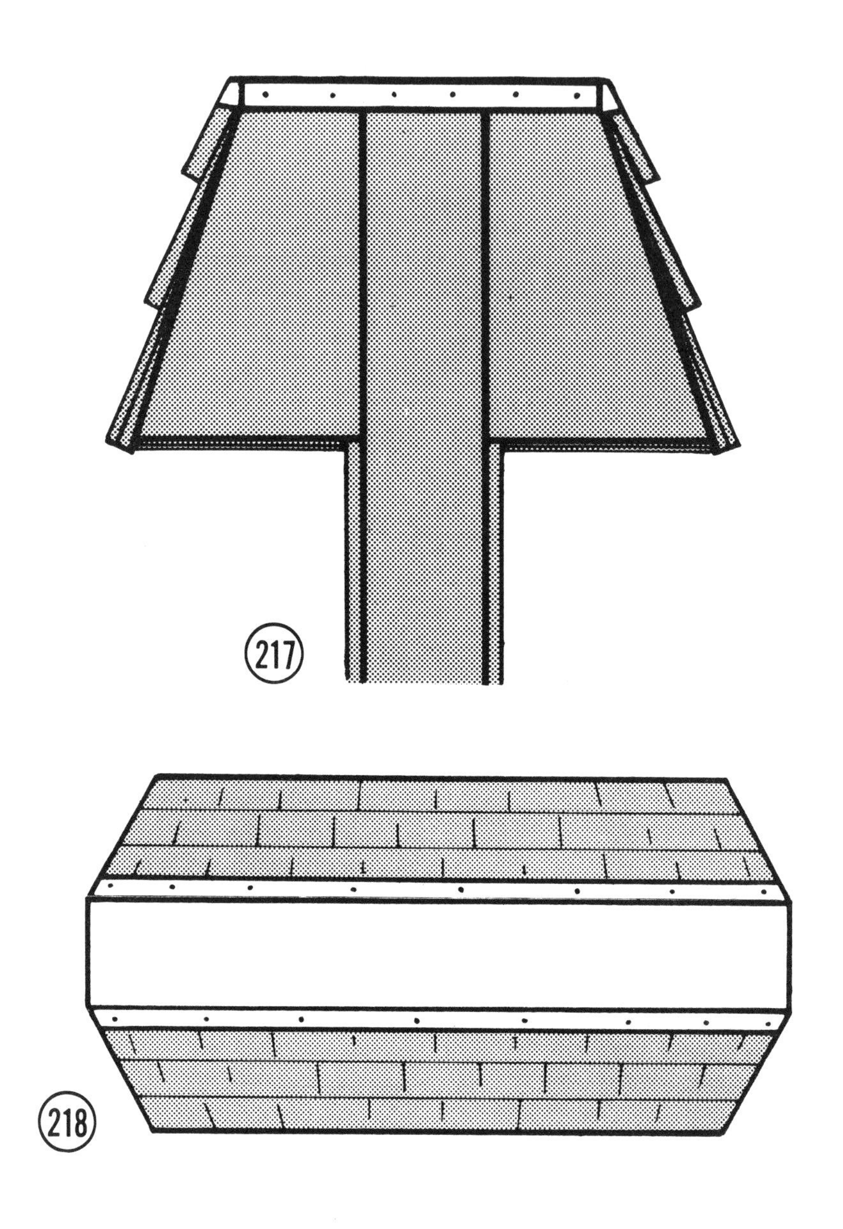

Dig a trench to bury power line to depth local codes require.

With adequate help, place posts in holes and fill area around post with a concrete mix consisting of one part cement, two parts sand, three parts gravel. Brace display with diagonal bracing nailed to stakes until concrete sets.

Shelf standards, Illus. 52, permit positioning shelves at height articles require. For shelves, cut ¼" acrylic by 7" width to length required. To stiffen shelves, follow procedure shown, Illus. 63, 79.

Install shelves, apply nameplate and the enclosure is ready for business, Illus. 219.

A single faced bulletin board type of enclosure can be constructed by following directions offered in Book #607 How to Build Fences, Gates, Outdoor Projects.

TO DISCOURAGE A FORCED ENTRY

As every collector in today's economy soon discovers, a collection can easily double in value in a relatively short time. Regardless of the article, it invariably attracts attention from others collecting the same. While it's difficult not to talk about a time consuming interest in public, every word that describes anything of value is usually heard by those willing to steal anything they can sell. To make a forced entry less easy to accomplish, apply a panel of 3/16 or ¼'' clear acrylic to the inside of a kitchen door, Illus. 220, and to the inside face of first floor windows. To accent the positive, consider etching or painting a design on the more vulnerable areas. The design compounds the positive by showing those outside that breaking glass and reaching in won't work. A second plus feature: acrylic panel creates a dead air space and practically eliminates cold from penetrating both surfaces. It provides an efficient fuel saver.

Apply a 6'' wide piece of acrylic to bottom of door, inside and outside, as a protective kickplate.

Use Easi-Bild Pattern #713, Illus. 221, to trace a suitable decoration on acrylic covering a kitchen door or window.

Cover the full area of a lower sash in a double hung window. Apply a panel to cover the upper half on all windows that do not require opening. Cover only the upper half of the upper window if you want to raise the lower half 6 to 8".

Those interested in starting a part or full time business frequently find factory, store and office building owners, and/or tenants, interested in having all first floor windows vandalproofed.* Schools suffering from vandalism find the application of ¾ x 1" furring strips, Illus. 222, to the outside of windows not frequently opened can lessen breakage considerably. Apply 3/16 or ¼" acrylic to furring.

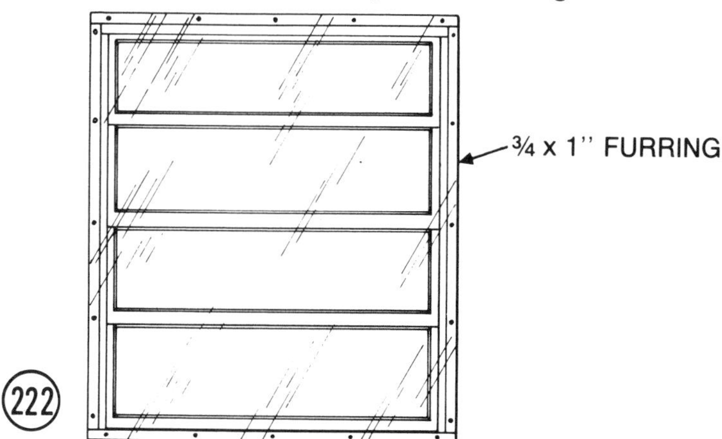

Awning type windows can be protected by cutting and applying furring strips slightly thicker than lipped edge of window, Illus. 223. Using a steel bit, drill holes through steel or aluminum frame.

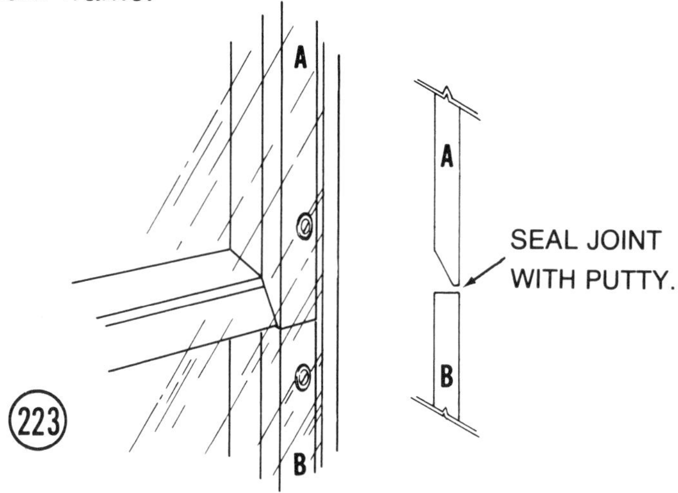

*While no acrylic or vinyl can actually vandalproof a building, the above application tends to make entry far more time consuming. It also keeps out rain when a rock is thrown with sufficient force to break through a 3/16 or ¼" acrylic panel. Make a test. Try breaking a piece of 3/16 or ¼" acrylic with a stone. Show both the stone and the piece of acrylic to a prospective customer.

Countersink heads of sheet metal self tapping screws when fastening furring to frame. Use thickness furring that projects acrylic at least ⅛" from projecting frame. Paint furring with aluminum paint before applying acrylic to aluminum windows.

In areas where vandalism is beyond control, staple #10 or 12 gauge vinyl to furring. A single thickness makes an excellent impact shield. A double thickness is even better. Stretch vinyl to eliminate as much play as possible. Staple vinyl every 6 to 8" to furring all the way around. It's important to stretch vinyl taut. Should an object penetrate the acrylic, the vinyl adds extra protection against breaking the glass. If an object has sufficient force to impact and crack the acrylic and glass, the vinyl provides sufficient protection to keep out rain until a repair can be made.

After stapling vinyl to furring, apply ¼" acrylic with ⅞" No. 7 oval head wood screws and countersunk washers. Drill holes through acrylic using a bit one size larger than shank on screw. This permits acrylic to expand and contract. Fasten acrylic to furring.

When soliciting work at a school, factory, warehouse, professional or business office, etc., memorize this sales message:

> To protect windows against breakage and/or break-ins, we recommend fastening ¾ x 1" furring to the outside face of frame. We then staple #10 vinyl to the frame. 3/16 or ¼" acrylic is screwed to the furring. Any rock or object thrown with sufficient force to break the acrylic would still have to penetrate the vinyl. Even with the acrylic damaged, the vinyl keeps out the elements until repairs can be made.

TO BEND ACRYLIC

Bending acrylic isn't difficult when you use the 36" strip heater, Illus. 4. Handsome articles can be shaped in very little time. Bends of every degree up to a right angle can be made.

An attractive magazine rack, Illus. 224, telephone table, Illus. 225, reading table, Illus. 226, are but a few of the many saleable articles you can shape using a strip heater. Plans for building the above articles are available. Note ordering directions on page 176.

(224)

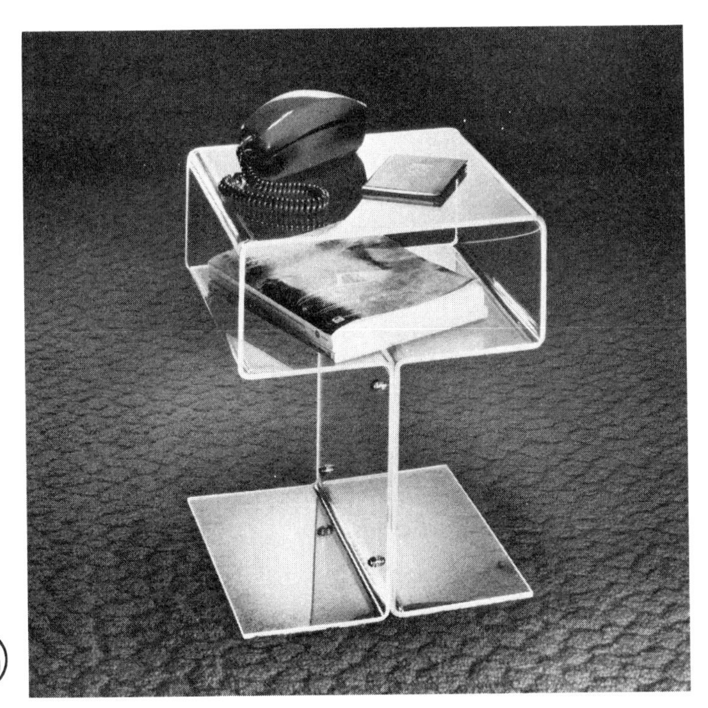

225

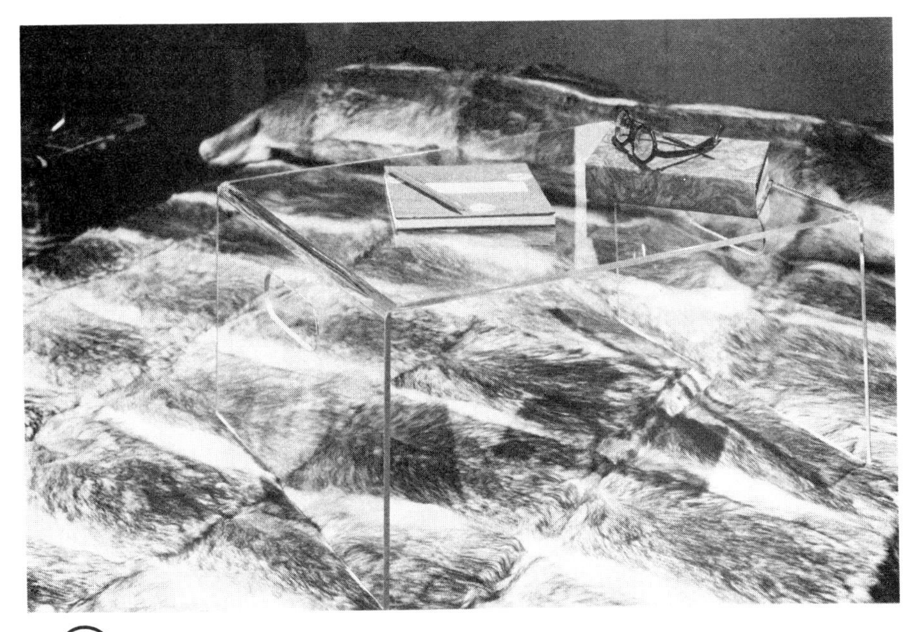

226

The 36'' heating element must be mounted on ½ x 6 x 42'' plywood base A, recessed between two ¼ x 2⅝ x 36'' strips of plywood B, Illus. 227. Those wishing to bend acrylic longer than 36'' should mount two units, end to end, on a ½ x 6 x 72'' plywood base. All other parts are also cut to 72'' length.

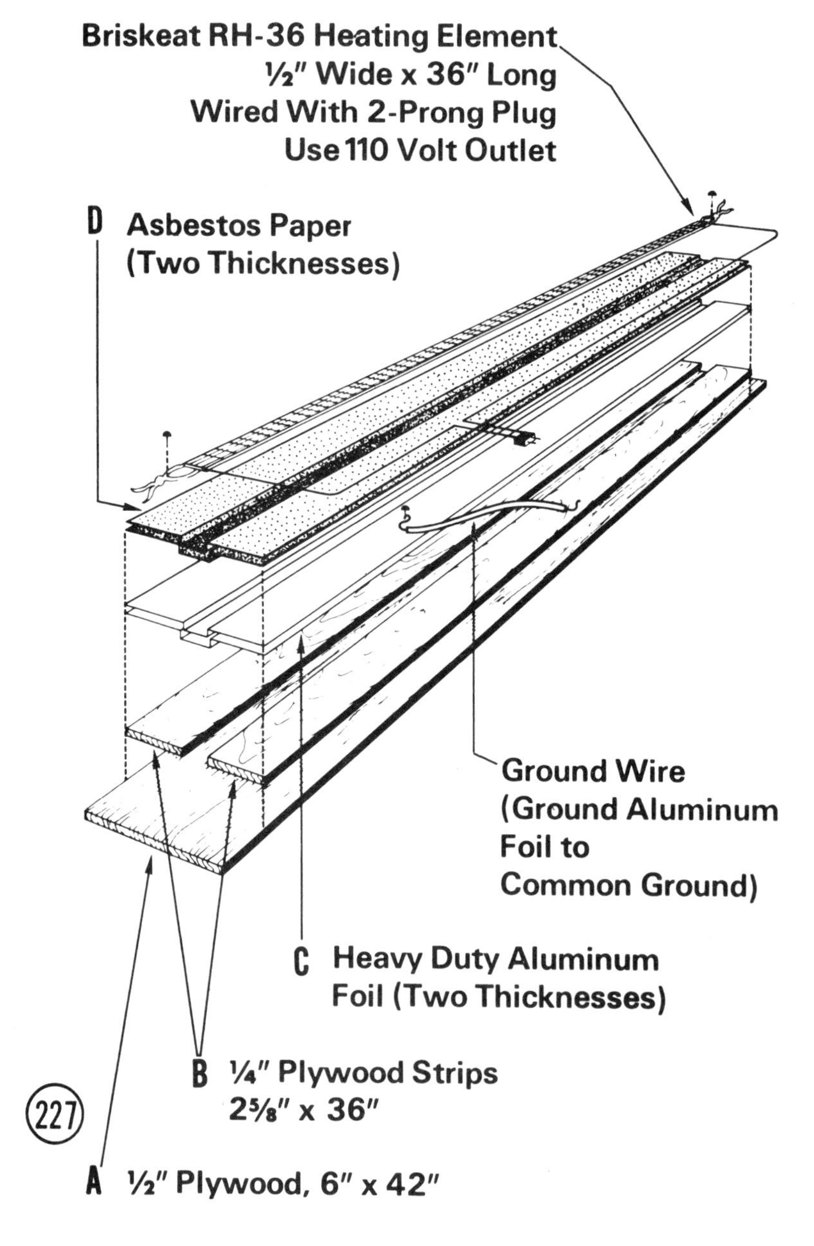

For a 36" strip heater, cut one ½ x 6 x 48" plywood A; two ¼ x 2⅝ x 36" B; two pieces of heavy duty aluminum foil 6 x 36" C; two pieces of asbestos paper 6 x 36" D; one ¼ x ⅝ x 36" strip for E.

Leaving a ¾" wide channel down center, nail B to A with ½" brads.

Place a 6 x 36" strip of aluminum C in place. Press E over C to shape a ¾" wide channel full length. Remove and repeat with a second C. Remove C. Repeat this step using asbestos paper D. To simplify shaping D, dampen center portion before applying pressure with E. Remove D, replace both C.

Drive a ½" No. 5 flathead screw through C in position indicated, Illus. 227. Before tightening screw, strip end of #16 or #18 wire and fasten wire to head of screw. Snug up screw. This screw establishes a connection between foil and ground. Use length wire needed to reach a good ground, i.e., a radiator, water pipe, etc. Apply a clamp to free end of wire when you decide what object clamp will grasp. Or fasten bare end of wire to a screw holding a plate over a wall outlet. Replace both D. Staple along outside edges. Apply adhesive tape to cover edge of asbestos and aluminum to A.

Place heating element in position in channel. Fasten a 1" No. 8 roundhead screw about 1½" from each end of unit, Illus. 228. Tie end strings on unit to screws. With ground wire clamped or screwed to a ground, plug unit into a 110 outlet. Allow to warm up. Remove masking paper. To insure bending where needed, draw a line with a Blaisdell "china marker." Always center line over heater. Allow material to heat thoroughly. It usually takes 5 to 6 minutes for ⅛" material; 12 to 15 minutes for ¼". Exact time depends on voltage available. To get some experience, practice bending using scraps.

Always have a straight edge, i.e., a 2 x 4 or a support equal in length to the bend, Illus. 229. This helps bend to a right angle.

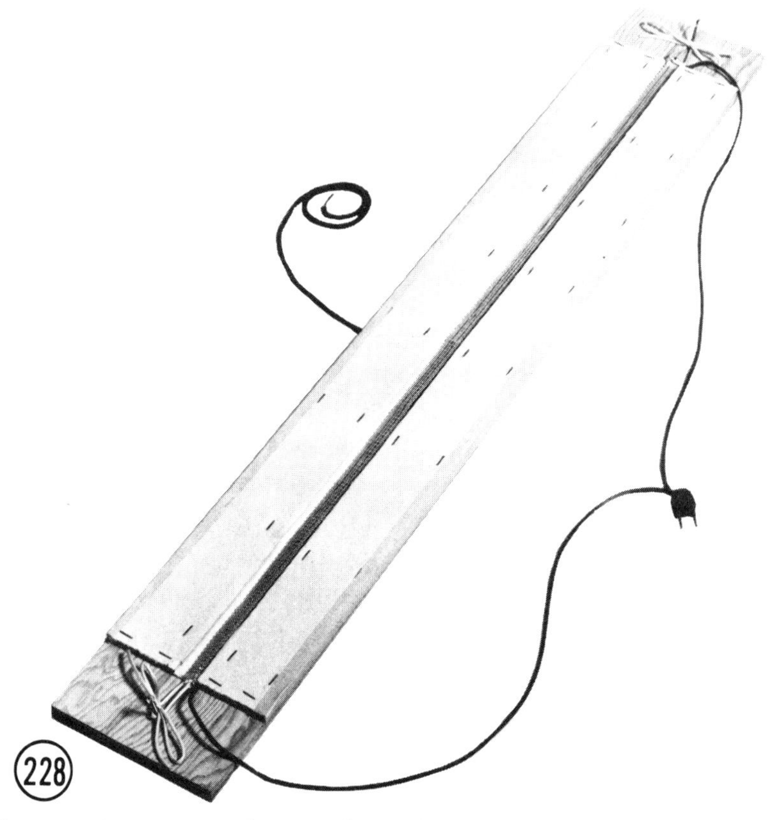

(228)

If you plan on making a long bend to an odd shape, make a wood jig to shape required. If you want to roll the edge, Illus. 229, bend heated area around a curved edge or length of broomstick, clothes pole, pipe, etc. Since heated acrylic cools rapidly, it's essential to have a flat, clean, working surface, and all needed tools as close as possible. Always keep heated face down and bend by applying pressure on left, Illus. 229, when lifing on right.

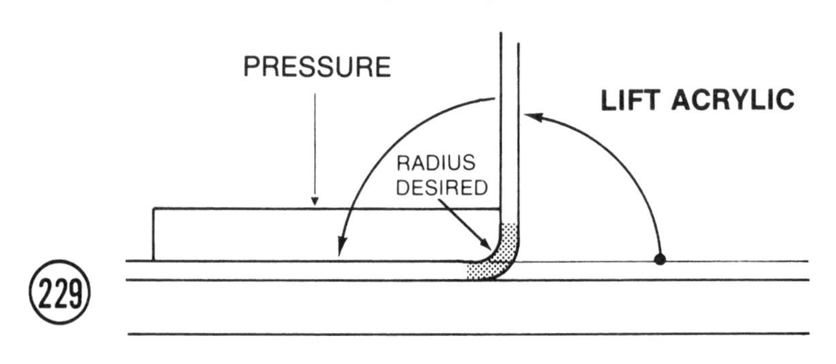

(229)

Always test bending using scrap. Never allow acrylic to touch element. Allow acrylic to heat until it begins to soften along the entire line of bend. Bending material before it is properly heated will cause stress crazing (small fractures). It's important to complete bend before acrylic cools.

While one person can bend a small piece, adequate help is needed to make bends for a larger project. While ⅛" thickness bends easily, 3/16 and ¼" can also be shaped on a strip heater.

CAUTION: Always use a strip heater in a well ventilated area. Disconnect strip heater as quickly as possible after each use. Keep a fire extinguisher handy, just in case.

Read and follow strip heater manufacturer's directions to keep abreast with any recent change in end use.

ETCHACRYLIC

Those who want to etch designs in acrylic should order full size patterns for the Tree of Life, Illus. 155, the Blue Willow and folding room screens, Illus. 156,157. Six other full size tracing patterns are also available. Write to Easi-Bild Directions Simplified, Inc., P.O.Box 215, Briarcliff Manor, NY 10510 for catalog folder illustrating these designs.

❖ ❖ ❖

Directions for building projects of Plexiglas, shown in Illus.5, 224,225,226, and tools described are available from Rohm & Haas, P. O. Box 14619, Philadelphia, PA 19134.

A BUSINESS OF YOUR OWN

If a teenager, retiree or executive seeking release from tension needs something to do, encourage their building one or all the projects in this book. Learning to find a constructive use of free time, doing something today they didn't think they could do yesterday, allows time to resolve many problems. This suggestion is as important to those recuperating from a bout with the bottle or a drug cure, as it is to the teenager searching for a job and finding work they enjoy doing. Building each project provides on the site job experience with only an investment of time and material. It enables each participant to gain confidence without supervision that might dampen their initiative.

A start can be made by building any of the display cases, or a model of each. Show the case, a model or photo to dealers who display collectibles at antique, doll or miniature shows. Many will request a quote on special sizes that complement selected articles.

New business opportunities exist among property owners and tenants living in or close to any area where a burglary, crime or costly act of vandalism has been publicized. To get started, write a letter similar in tone to the one suggested on page 176. Provide the information noted, then have a quantity printed. Place a copy in each mailbox. A week later start phoning each homeowner or business to introduce yourself. Give your name, address and state how long you have lived in the area. Everyone who lives or works near where a crime has been committed needs all the help and information they can get. Even if they don't buy any service or product you offer, each will value your interest and concern. You could be the one person to see, hear or know someone who could help apprehend the culprit.

When a letter or phone call triggers interest, be prepared to estimate a cost. On inspection, base your estimate on thickness of material you recommend. While a homeowner without a collection will be entirely satisfied with ⅛" thickness, those who treasure what they possess will want 3/16 or ¼" on each street level window. Your estimate must include labor plus cost of all material plus whatever markup you want to make. If you buy 4 x 8 sheets, in carton quantities, the savings you effect in bulk purchasing should permit quoting material at twice or more your cost.

An easy way to estimate cost of material is to get a price on carton quantities of ⅛, 3/16 and ¼" 4 x 6' sheets from an acrylic distributor. Then go to one or two retailers and find out what they charge for a single piece cut to size an average window requires. The price they charge per foot establishes a base you can use to price material.

Keep an accurate check of all time needed to cut acrylic to size each window requires, drill holes and make the installation. Check time required to apply to a wood, steel or aluminum frame. Each requires using bits for material specified. You will need ¾ or 1" No. 7 ovalhead screws and countersunk washers, Illus. 223, for wood windows; self tapping screws to apply furring to a steel or aluminum window; 1 x 2 or 5/4 x 2" furring, a roll of #10 or #12 gauge sheet vinyl plus the thickness acrylic customer agrees to purchase.

Drilling holes in a steel or aluminum frame can frequently be a slow, time consuming endeavor. For this reason, continually record the time you spend on each installation so you can more accurately estimate overall time for the next job. As soon as you see potential in doing this kind of work, order acrylic in carton quantities.

While an awning type window in a factory, office building, school or warehouse isn't considered adequate as an exit, a local code may require all windows be operable. Check local zoning before contracting to cover windows on a commercial building.

If a client wants to open a window that requires application of furring strips, apply furring to frame so the window remains operable. In the spring, recommend removing acrylic and vinyl. With the furring intact, acrylic replacement in the fall only takes minutes per window.

(Proposed letter to property owners and tenants in a neighborhood where a burglary occurred.)

Dear

My name is ________________________ and I have lived at ________________________________ for the past _____ years. We recently installed ____" acrylic* to the inside of our first floor windows, and over glass on the inside of our kitchen door. We did this for two reasons: acrylic makes breaking and entering far more difficult and time consuming; acrylic also seals out cold air and helps save a bundle on fuel bills.

We will be glad to quote costs of installing 1/8, 3/16 or 1/4" acrylic to one or as many windows and doors as you desire to cover. This installation will not only make your house warmer, cut heating bills, but also provide more nights of peaceful sleep.

For references please call the following:

(List names of someone in your bank and/or stores, your minister, police chief, or neighbor, school teacher, etc.)

If you prefer to make your own installation, we will be glad to cut all acrylic to exact size you require.

Please feel free to phone for prices and additional information. I can be reached at ________________________ from _____ to _____.

Sincerely,

*Fill in thickness you recommend.

HOW TO THINK METRIC

Government officials concerned with the adoption of the metric system are quick to warn anyone from attempting to make precise conversions. One quickly accepts this advice when they begin to convert yards to meters or vice versa. Place a metric ruler alongside a foot ruler and you get the message fast.

Since a meter equals 1.09361 yards, or 39⅜"+, the decimals can drive you up a creek. The government men suggest accepting a rough, rather than exact equivalent. They recommend considering a meter in the same way you presently use a yard. A kilometer as 0.6 of a mile. A kilogram or kilo as just over two pounds. A liter, a quart, with a small extra swig.

To more fully appreciate why a rough conversion is preferable, note the 6" rule alongside the metric rule. A meter contains 100 centimeters. A centimeter contains 10 millimeters.

As an introduction to the metric system, we used a metric rule to measure standard U.S. building materials. Since a 1 x 2 measures anywhere from ¾ to 25/32 x 1½", which is typical of U.S. lumber sizes, the metric equivalents shown are only approximate.

Consider 1" equal to 2.54 centimeters; 10" = 25.4cm.

To multiply 4¼" into centimeters: 4.25 × 2.54 = 10.795 or 10.8cm.

INCH	MILLIMETER
1"	25.4
15/16	23.8
7/8	22.2
13/16	20.6
3/4	19.0
11/16	17.5
5/8	15.9
9/16	14.3
1/2	12.7
7/16	11.1
3/8	9.5
5/16	7.9
1/4	6.4
3/16	4.8
1/8	3.2
1/16	1.6

INCHES	CENTIMETERS
1	2.54
1/8	2.9
1/4	3.2
3/8	3.5
1/2	3.8
5/8	4.1
3/4	4.4
7/8	4.8
2	5.1
1/8	5.4
1/4	5.7
3/8	6.0
1/2	6.4
5/8	6.7
3/4	7.0
7/8	7.3
3	7.6
1/8	7.9
1/4	8.3
3/8	8.6
1/2	8.9
5/8	9.2
3/4	9.5
7/8	9.8

Inches	Centimeters
4	10.2
1/8	10.5
1/4	10.8
3/8	11.1
1/2	11.4
5/8	11.7
3/4	12.1
7/8	12.4
5	12.7
1/8	13.0
1/4	13.3
3/8	13.7
1/2	14.0
5/8	14.3
3/4	14.6
7/8	14.9
6	15.2
1/8	15.6
1/4	15.9
3/8	16.2
1/2	16.5
5/8	16.8
3/4	17.1
7/8	17.5
7	17.8
1/8	18.1
1/4	18.4
3/8	18.7
1/2	19.1
5/8	19.4
3/4	19.7
7/8	20.0
8	20.3
1/8	20.6
1/4	21.0
3/8	21.3
1/2	21.6
5/8	21.9
3/4	22.2
7/8	22.5
9	22.9
1/8	23.2
1/4	23.5
3/8	23.8
1/2	24.1
5/8	24.4
3/4	24.8
7/8	25.1
10	25.4
1/8	25.7
1/4	26.0
3/8	26.4
1/2	26.7
5/8	27.0
3/4	27.3
7/8	27.6
11	27.9
1/8	28.3
1/4	28.6
3/8	28.9
1/2	29.2
5/8	29.5
3/4	29.8
7/8	30.2
12	30.5
1/8	30.8
1/4	31.1
3/8	31.4
1/2	31.8
5/8	32.1
3/4	32.4
7/8	32.7
14	35.6
16	40.6
20	50.8
30	76.2
40	101.6
50	127.0
60	152.4
70	177.8
80	203.2
90	228.6
100	254.0

FEET = INCHES = CENTIMETERS

FEET	INCHES	CENTIMETERS
1 =	12 =	30.5
2 =	24 =	61.0
3 =	36 =	91.4
4 =	48 =	121.9
5 =	60 =	152.4
6 =	72 =	182.9
7 =	84 =	213.4
8 =	96 =	243.8
9 =	108 =	274.3
10 =	120 =	304.8
11 =	132 =	335.3
12 =	144 =	365.8
13 =	156 =	396.2
14 =	168 =	426.7
15 =	180 =	457.2
16 =	192 =	487.7
17 =	204 =	518.2
18 =	216 =	548.6
19 =	228 =	579.1
20 =	240 =	609.6

INDEX TO MONEY-SAVING REPAIRS, IMPROVEMENTS, PATTERNS AND BOOKS
(Number designates EASI-BILD Pattern or Book)

INDEX TO MONEY-SAVING REPAIRS, IMPROVEMENTS, PATTERNS AND BOOKS

Guides To Good Living

*FULL SIZE PATTERNS INCLUDED

603 — How to Build a Dormer — 82pp. 114 illus.
605*— How to Install Paneling, Build Valances, Cornices, Wall to Wall Storage, Cedar Room, Fireplace Mantel — 146pp. 214 illus.
606 — How to Lay Ceramic Tile — 98pp. 137 illus.
607 — How to Build Fences, Gates, Outdoor Projects—162pp.212 illus.
608 — How to Modernize a Kitchen — 82pp. 118 illus.
609 — How to Build an Addition — 162pp. 211 illus.
611 — How to Build Greenhouses - Sunhouses — 114pp. 110 illus.
612 — How to Build Wall-to-Wall Cabinets, Stereo Installation Simplified — 130pp. 165 illus.
613 — How to Build or Enclose a Porch — 82pp. 112 illus.
615 — How to Modernize a Basement — 98pp. 135 illus.
617 — Concrete Work Simplified — 130pp. 193 illus.
623 — How to Repair,Refinish&Reupholster Furniture—98pp. 138 illus.
630 — How to Build Sportsman's Revolving Storage Cabinet — 98pp. 121 illus.
631 — How to Build Patios & Sundecks — 98pp. 133 illus.
632 — How to Build a Vacation or Retirement House — 194pp. 170 illus.
634 — How to Build Storage Units — 98pp. 145 illus.
649 — How to Build a Garden Tool House, Child's Playhouse — 82pp. 107 illus.
658 — How to Build Kitchen Cabinets, Room Dividers, and Cabinet Furniture — 98pp. 134 illus.
663 — How to Build a Two Car Garage, Lean-To Porch, Cabana — 130pp. 142 illus.
664 — How to Construct Built-In and Sectional Bookcases — 98pp. 137 illus.
665 — How to Modernize an Attic — 82pp. 86 illus.
668 — Bricklaying Simplified — 146pp. 212 illus.
669 — How to Build Birdhouses & Bird Feeders — 66pp. 86 illus.
672*— How to Build Workbenches, Tool Chests — 180pp. 250 illus.
674 — How to Install a Fireplace — 242pp. 354 illus.
675 — Plumbing Repairs Simplified — 194pp. 820 illus.

continued

*** Read * Learn * Save ***

other Easi-Bild® books

677 — How to Build a Home Workshop — 98pp. 133 illus.
679 — How to Build a Stable
& Red Barn Tool House — 178pp. 197 illus.
680 — How to Build a One Car Garage, Carport,
Convert a Garage into a Stable — 146pp. 181 illus.
682 — How to Add an Extra Bathroom — 162pp. 200 illus.
683 — Carpeting Simplified — 146pp. 212 illus.
684 — How to Transform a Garage into Living Space — 130pp. 139 illus.
685 — How to Remodel Buildings — 258pp. 345 illus.
690 — How to Build Bars — 162pp. 195 illus.
694 — Electrical Repairs Simplified,
Dollhouse Wiring — 134p. 218 illus.
695 — How to Install Protective Alarm Devices — 130pp. 146 illus.
696 — Roofing Simplified — 130pp. 168 illus.
697 — Forms, Footings, Foundations, Framing,
Stair Building — 210pp. 308 illus.
751 — How to Build Pet Housing — 178pp. 252 illus.
753 — How to Build Dollhouses & Furniture — 194pp. 316 illus.
754* — How to Build Outdoor Furniture — 130pp. 174 illus.
756 — Scroll Saw Projects — 130pp. 146 illus.
757* — How to Build a Kayak - 14'3", 16'9", 18'0" — 66pp., plus pattern
758 — How to Modernize a Kitchen, Build Cabinets,
Room Dividers — 194pp. 253 illus.
761 — How to Build Colonial Furniture — 258pp. 342 illus.
763* — How to Build a Two Car Garage
with Apartment Above — 194pp. 226 illus.
771* — Toymaking & Children's Furniture Simplified — 194pp. 330 illus.
773 — How to Create Room at the Top — 162pp. 239 illus.
781 — How to Build a Patio, Porch & Sundeck — 146pp. 220 illus.
792 — How to Build Collectors' Display Cases
Dolls, China, Objets d'Art — 194pp. 229 illus.
600 — Complete Catalog — illustrates Patterns and Books
130pp. 300 illus.